# COPYRIGHT IN THE STREET

This book explores how copyright laws are perceived within street art and graffiti subcultures to examine how artists and writers view certain creative aspects of their own practice. Drawing on ethnographic research and fieldwork, the book gives voice to the main actors of these communities and highlights their feelings and opinions towards issues that are increasingly impacting their everyday life and work. It also touches on related and complementary issues, such as the 'gallerisation' and economic exploitation of these forms of art and the curious similarities between the graffiti and advertising worlds. Unique and comprehensive, *Copyright in the Street* brings the 'voice from the street' into the debate over the legal and non-legal protection of street art and graffiti.

Enrico Bonadio is Reader in Law at City, University of London. He teaches, lectures, and advises in the field of intellectual property law. He is editor of *The Cambridge Handbook of Copyright in Street Art and Graffiti* and *Non-Conventional Copyright: Do New and Atypical Works Deserve Protection?* Enrico is also a street and graffiti art aficionado.

Donaukanal, Vienna, May 2022.

# Copyright in the Street

## AN ORAL HISTORY OF CREATIVE PROCESSES IN STREET ART AND GRAFFITI SUBCULTURES

ENRICO BONADIO
City University London

with the research assistance of Carlo Matteo Danusso

CAMBRIDGE
UNIVERSITY PRESS

CAMBRIDGE
UNIVERSITY PRESS

Shaftesbury Road, Cambridge CB2 8EA, United Kingdom

One Liberty Plaza, 20th Floor, New York, NY 10006, USA

477 Williamstown Road, Port Melbourne, VIC 3207, Australia

314–321, 3rd Floor, Plot 3, Splendor Forum, Jasola District Centre, New Delhi – 110025, India

103 Penang Road, #05–06/07, Visioncrest Commercial, Singapore 238467

Cambridge University Press is part of Cambridge University Press & Assessment, a department of the University of Cambridge.

We share the University's mission to contribute to society through the pursuit of education, learning and research at the highest international levels of excellence.

www.cambridge.org
Information on this title: www.cambridge.org/9781009198684

DOI: 10.1017/9781009198653



First published 2023

*A catalogue record for this publication is available from the British Library.*

*Library of Congress Cataloging-in-Publication Data*
NAMES: Bonadio, Enrico, author.
TITLE: Copyright in the street : an oral history of creative processes in street art and graffiti subcultures / Enrico Bonadio.
DESCRIPTION: Cambridge, United Kingdom ; New York, NY : Cambridge University Press, 2023. | Includes bibliographical references and index.
IDENTIFIERS: LCCN 2022050220 (print) | LCCN 2022050221 (ebook) | ISBN 97810091986847 (hardback) | ISBN 9781009198653 (ebook)
SUBJECTS: LCSH: Copyright – Art. | Street art – Law and legislation. | Public art – Law and legislation. | Graffiti.
CLASSIFICATION: LCC K1460 .B66 2023 (print) | LCC K1460 (ebook) | DDC 346.04/82–dc23/eng/20230105
LC record available at https://lccn.loc.gov/2022050220
LC ebook record available at https://lccn.loc.gov/2022050221

ISBN 978-1-009-19868-4 Hardback
ISBN 978-1-009-19863-9 Paperback

*A Mamma e Rui*

# Contents

# Foreword

Most of us think we are familiar with graffiti – lettering on trains or graphic images on walls that follow us as we walk by. But Enrico Bonadio's new book on graffiti and street art opens a door to more complex and nuanced worlds of artists and their communities. The focus is on everyday creators of graffiti and street art. Built from nearly 100 interviews and hundreds of hours of observation, the book is filled with the voices of artists and vivid details of their plein air studios and interactions. Also present in the book is the author, who weaves the artists' accounts of their practices with his voice and reactions as he experiences excitement and awe at the people he meets and art he witnesses being made. This is a special kind of book of scholarship; it is ethnographic and legal. And it is also colourful, funny, and enlightening.

In this short foreword, I could not adequately summarise the book's rich detail, and I would feel neglectful choosing only a few artists on which to focus. I will instead highlight some of the productive tensions around which the book is framed, a kind of stage-setting for the book's unfolding. I will also situate the book within intellectual property scholarship more generally, celebrating its methodological and reformist perspective on the study of copyright and the evolving place of copyright law in the twenty-first century.

In the United States especially, copyright law has struggled with the tension between utilitarian and moral justifications for its existence. Is it a regulation that incentivises the productivity of 'writings' for the purpose of producing 'Science' (qua knowledge) as the U.S. Constitution proposes? Does it also reward authors for their work – not their output but their labour – thereby dignifying their efforts, with a nod towards respecting what Justice Holmes in the infamous *Bleistein* decision from 1903 called 'personality'? When these goals conflict, which prevails? The more we study authors and artists themselves (and especially the artists and authors in this book), and the more we get to know how and why they work, the less meaningful this tension in copyright law becomes. Street art is a form of artistic expression that has existed throughout human civilizations, and until recently was rarely bought and sold in an art market and was largely anonymous. It was for the public and largely transient, part of an ongoing urban conversation that, to many, was as mysterious as it was ubiquitous. To understand the evolution and present instantiation of graffiti and street art as human expression that shapes communities and propels political momentum today is to either discard or profoundly recharacterise the standard story of copyright law's purposes. Utilitarian and moral philosophy are punchlines to the people at the centre of the book. In their place are descriptions of community, skilled practice, and survival in largely inhospitable circumstances.

Lawyers and academics often debate in copyright law the balance between individual rights of ownership and institutional prerogatives of sustainability and growth. Authors create copyrighted works of expression – books, films, paintings, software, music – and transfer some or all rights to an intermediary like a publisher, agent, or gallerist who can more effectively distribute the work to the public for maximum reach and minimal cost. The author receives a royalty or payment in exchange. This standard business arrangement is at the core of many copyright law rules and court decisions justifying their interpretation. Balancing the interests of authors, audiences, and the needs of copyright-holding institutions has been a theme in the evolution of copyright law and copying technology, such as printing technology, copy machines, computers, and online platforms. Shifting alliances and expectations has been especially complicated in the digital age as business structures rapidly change, audiences become used to on-time access, and authors persistently (and not without cause) complain of exploitation and economic precarity. In this book, we get to know the communities of artists who make and display works in public spaces as a first order of creation, largely without institutional intermediaries and digital technology; they exist largely outside the traditional market for art; and their creativity and communities have thrived and diversified over the past four decades of digital disruption. It is a lesson in survival, sustainability, and communitarianism in an era that feels increasingly apocalyptic in terms of wealth accumulation, its unequal distribution, and global democracy deficits. These artists do create and engage institutions to support their art, such as neighbourhoods of abandoned buildings made into galleries or land zoning boards. Eventually, some even directly work with more traditional institutions, such as galleries, museums, and merchandising companies. But the perception of copyright law's predominantly transactional structure is a shadow. They are not living outside capitalism, but they are defying its ideological prerogatives and working around the structures that impede them. One gets the sense reading about the street artists' successes and pleasures that theirs is a deeply meaningful life, and their experiences and perceptions are not idiosyncratic despite the surprises this book contains.

In fact, if one has paid attention to the wave of copyright scholarship over the past two decades, the voices and stories in this book may sound familiar. I and others have written about communities of creators and innovators in terms of the adaptive and insular practices that enable them to keep doing their work despite inhospitable legal rules and business structures. Some communities appear to be discrete subcultures, the way graffiti and street art at first might be perceived: tattoo artists, roller derby athletes, magicians, French chefs, dancers, and comedians.[1] But look further and the studies extend to creators and innovators beyond what might seem niche: photographers, designers, musicians, knitters, and craft beer makers.[2] Some books are devoted to drawing more general principles from the diverse creative communities as a whole[3] and others showcase chapter by chapter singular communities with the cumulative effect of a slow but certain sidelining of formal copyright law for so many contemporary creative practices.[4] Situating the present book within this exploding field of qualitative empirical IP scholarship, we learn that we have so much more to know about IP law's misalignment with everyday practices of creativity and theories of capital accumulation. This misalignment should matter if we think creative practice is something the law should care to promote.

Studies like this book also resituate values from within the creative community at the centre of the investigation. Instead of leading with law – what are the rules and how do the communities follow, bend, or break them – qualitative empirical studies lead with the facts of lived experience and the meanings they are given by their subjects. Grounding one's method in the legal realist tradition of facts first assumes the law needs to care about these facts of the lives it governs to maintain its legitimacy. This method seems particularly apt when studying creative work on the periphery of acceptable art when copyright is supposed to be non-discriminatory and inclusive. Since the turn of last century, questioning who is an 'artist' and what

1 Aaron Perzanowski, 'Tattoos & IP Norms' (2013) 98 *Minnesota Law Review* 511; David Fagundes, 'Talk Derby to Me: Intellectual Property Norms Governing Roller Derby Pseudonyms' (2012) 90 *Texas Law Review* 1093; Jacob Loshin, Secrets Revealed: How Magicians Protect Intellectual Property without Law, *in Law and Magic: A Collection of Essays* (Christine A. Corcos ed., 2008) http://ssrn.com/abstract=1005564; Emmanuelle Fauchart and Eric Von Hippel 'Norms-Based Intellectual Property Systems: The Case of French Chefs' (2008) 19(2) *Organization Science* 187–201; Anthea Kraut, *Choreographing Copyright: Race, Gender, and Intellectual Property in American Dance* (2015); Dotan Oliar and Christopher Sprigman, 'There's No Free Laugh (Anymore): The Emergence of Intellectual Property Norms and the Transformation of Stand-Up Comedy' (2008) 94 *Virginia Law Review* 1787.

2 Jessica Silbey, Eva E. Subotnik, and Peter DiCola, 'Existential Copyright and Professional Photography' (2019) 95 *Notre Dame L. Rev.* 263; Mark McKenna and Jessica Silbey, 'Investigating Design' (forthcoming 2022) 84 *Pittsburgh Law Review* https://scholarship.law.bu.edu/faculty_scholarship/1365; Peter DiCola, 'Money from Music: Survey Evidence on Musicians' Revenue and Lessons about Copyright Incentives' (2013) 55 *Arizona Law Review* 301; Kristy Robertson, No One Would Murder for a Pattern: Crafting IP in On-Line Knitting Communities, in *Putting IP in Its Place: Rights Discourses, Creative Labor, and the Everyday* (OUP 2014) 41–62; Zahr Said, 'Craft Beer and the Rising Tide Effect: An Empirical Study of Sharing and Collaboration among Seattle's Craft Breweries' (2019) 23 *Lewis & Clark L. Rev.* 355.

3 Jessica Silbey, *Against Progress: Intellectual Property and Fundamental Values in the Internet Age* (SUP 2022); Jessica Silbey, *The Eureka Myth: Creators, Innovators, and Everyday Intellectual Property* (SUP 2015).

4 Kate Darling and Aaron Perzanoski, *Creativity without Law: Challenging the Assumptions of Intellectual Property* (NYU Press 2017); Kristy Robertson, Tina Piper, and Laura Murray, *Putting IP in Its Place: Rights Discourses, Creative Labor, and the Everyday* (OUP 2014); Kal Raustiala and Chris Sprigman, *The Knock Off Economy: How Imitation Sparks Innovation* (OUP 2012).

counts as 'art' has been the cause celebre of historians and critics, embracing an expanding tolerance for challenging the status quo. As those on the periphery move to the centre – be it photographers in the 1880s, avant-garde artists in the 1920s, pop artists in the 1960s, graffiti artists in the 1990s and 2000s, or NFT artists today – those who study creative practices and their legal regulation learn how law rarely leads. It is largely an instrument for those in power to maintain it. And thus, reading about the adaptive mechanisms and personal and community values at the centre of these artists' lives – who at times ignore, resist, and reshape the copyright law to work for them, not against them – is a lesson in slow but successful revolution.

What are the values at the centre of the stories this book tells? There are many, but in keeping with some of the literature already cited, they resonate with inclusivity and self-determination on a community level; sustainable relationships that are only marginally structured by dominant market forces; a scepticism of static hierarchy that doesn't obviously support the community's work; attribution and recognition as a practice that indicates belonging rather than authority; and fair resource allocation that supports mutual flourishing. Listed in these general terms are values at the centre of political debates today. The seemingly 'outsider' art community on which this book focuses brings to the fore many of the critically important socio-political issues with which whole nations are struggling in an age of extraordinary creativity and innovation but also of treacherously unstable legal and economic systems.

This is not to say that studying graffiti and street art is going to solve our biggest problems of climate change, housing and food scarcity, health care disparities, and systemic racism and sexism. Wouldn't that be a treat if it could? In this brief foreword, I only suggest the study of creativity and innovation in our revolutionary age of digital technology as an opportunity to rethink the foundational assumptions on which older laws prohibiting copying were built. Where exclusivity and market priorities dominated, the artists at the centre of this book focus on sharing space, mutual recognition, and growing future opportunities. They recycle and renovate, and they think much less frequently in terms of market substitution and competition than does copyright law, traditionally construed. 'Keeping it real' and 'avoid biting' others are only some of the many pragmatic and grounded ways of thinking about their work and place in the art world. (Neither phrase in street art parlance means what you think, but even so, it's good advice!) Studies like this book demonstrate the resiliency and successes of outsider communities who defy odds and champion values many of us share. They make do and some make it big within a legal system biased towards insiders. The book's stories strongly suggest that the communities thrive because expressive experimentation and mutual support are priorities. With some redirection and reform, they could be copyright law priorities as well. This would substantially change our experience of what copyright is for and how it works. That is part of what makes the book interesting and a hopeful account of our creative future. With radical empathy for each other, even those with whom disagreements run strong, the artists in this book demonstrate a purpose of making art under circumstances that make room for those coming along. It is an inspiration to read, not only as someone who studies artists and innovators, but as a person who hopes that our legal systems will eventually be able to better and more systematically reflect what really matters to most of us.

**Jessica Silbey**
**Boston, Massachusetts**

# 1

# Introduction

In 1989 Keith Haring was already a legend. Recognised for being one of the main figures who first bridged the gap between the art world and the urban environment, he rose to prominence during the 1980s and quickly became one of the hottest artists on the scene. He had exhibitions all over the world, including New York, Melbourne, Tokyo, and Rio de Janeiro.

Back then, I was a fourteen-year-old student in high school in the Italian town of Pisa and knew nothing about street art or graffiti writing, and the differences between them. Nevertheless, when my classmates told me that an American guy was painting a wall at the back of a local church in downtown Pisa, I immediately rushed there, unaware of the impact that the awaiting encounter would have on my life. When I arrived, I saw this guy painting with a brush, while DJs were spinning and scratching loud hip hop and break-dancers were performing next to him: our little town in Tuscany immediately got New York–style street cred! And as the artist made each stroke of paint with his brush, I stood there transfixed by the magical play of colours that was taking place in front of my eyes. Again, that day, I had no idea that the guy holding the brush was Keith Haring nor that the piece that he was painting, *Tuttomondo*, would go on to become one of his most famous, and sadly also one of his last, works of art. I, however, was immediately mesmerised by the beauty of it. It was then and there that my passion for art in the street was born.

## BIRTH AND EVOLUTION OF GRAFFITI AND STREET ART

Keith Haring was not a graffiti writer. He used to paint walls and draw his iconic pieces such as the barking dog or the radiant baby on walls and empty billboards in the subway stations in New York. However, he never painted trains nor practiced lettering-based writing, both of which are graffiti's main archetypes.

Modern graffiti writing was born on the East Coast of the US. After the initial marking of names on the walls of Philadelphia and New York in the late 1960s and early 1970s (Cornbread and Cool Earl were amongst the first writers in Philadelphia, and Taki 183 and Julio 204 were the first ones in the Big Apple),[1] a multitude of New York teenagers from different ethnic backgrounds, especially Latinos, further developed the initial wall tagging into an elaborate lettering art form. They called themselves writers, as this was exactly what they did, that is, writing their names on urban surfaces, at the beginning walls and then also subway trains. The term 'graffiti' itself is a symbol of the main characteristic of what would become a new artistic movement. Etymology matters here. The word comes from the Italian word *graffiare* (scratching), which in turn comes from the Greek word *graphein* (writing). And as mentioned, this is what those kids started doing at that time; they repeatedly wrote their names, often followed by the number of the street they were living on. They did so on the back of a society whose rules they refused to follow in an open act of defiance, and left them there for others, especially within their communities, to see and talk about. Stay High 149, Super Kool, Phase 2, and subsequently in the late 1970s and early 1980s Dondi, Blade, Lee Quiñones, Lady Pink, Zephyr, Skeme, Futura 2000, Iz the Wiz, and Seen are just a few examples amongst the many young New Yorkers who came from different boroughs of the city and contributed to building a new urban art style based on the destruction, reconstruction, metamorphosis, and interpretation of the letters of the alphabet.

Graffiti writing in New York continued to develop throughout the 1980s. Yet, after 1989 most writers abandoned the subway system and started to paint again on walls and other surfaces above ground, as the city had won its long war to keep the subway system clean from graffiti – mainly by reinforcing criminal sanctions against writers and making subway yards almost impossible to reach. In the meantime, during the 1980s, the graffiti writing culture expanded to other US cities and to countries around the world. It is also worthwhile to remember that in the US, forms of artistic writing on walls, such as Cholo – consisting of Old English or Gothic typeface which originally constituted the hand style created by the Latino gangs in Los Angeles – had already been practiced before the explosion of graffiti in Philadelphia and New York.[2]

The 1990s was another prolific decade for graffiti art in the US and several other countries. It highlighted a growing divide between graffiti culture (still focused on the re-interpretation of the letters of the alphabet) and the emerging street art movement, which focuses on images rather than letters and was developed by building upon and mixing with established artistic movements, including muralism. After all, art on walls had already been practiced in the US in the 1970s and

[1] The phenomenon was even reported by the *New York Times*, which on 21 July 1972 published an article entitled 'Taki 183 Spawns Pen Pals', writing about Taki's ubiquitous tag spreading all over the city.

[2] For analysis of Cholo and Chicano graffiti cultures see Gusmano Cesaretti, *Street Writers – A Guided Tour of Chicano Graffiti* (Acrobat Books 1975); Jerry Romotsky, *Los Angeles Barrio Calligraphy* (Dawsons Book 1976); François Chastanet and Howard Gribble, *Cholo Writing: Latin Gang Graffiti in Los Angeles* (Dokument Press 2009).

1980s, especially in New York, by fine and multi-disciplinary artists such as John Fekner, John Ahearn, Richard Hambleton, Jenny Holzer, Christy Rupp, Keith Haring, and several others. Art in the street had also been created in Paris since the mid-twentieth century when a French artist, Jacques Villegle, started creating and placing his iconic décollages in the streets. Then, in the 1960s, Daniel Buren started putting up alternative stripes of paper over billboards and advertisements around Paris. Both of them set up a new artistic narrative and had a massive impact on the future of a peculiar French movement. Such a movement was further bolstered in the 1970s by artists such as Zlotykamien as well as Pignon-Ernest, a situationist and a member of Fluxus, the international and interdisciplinary group of artists born in the 1960s that engaged in experimental art performances. Later in the 1980s, French stencil artists such as Blek le Rat, Jef Aerosol, and Miss Tic took this rising art movement to a whole new level. Subsequently, throughout the 1990s, first in the US and then in other countries, techniques other than spraycan paintings were pioneered and experimented with, such as attaching stickers (the infamous *Andre the Giant Has a Posse* sticker, designed and widely disseminated by the US artist Shepard Fairey, is particularly noteworthy) and paste-ups (popularized in the US by Cost and Revs).[3] These techniques, which have been named 'adhesive art',[4] were developed and refined in the subsequent two decades and are still popular today.

As these artistic subcultures continued to develop further in the first two decades of the new century, more and more people outside of these communities have started to appreciate their artistic merit, especially where artworks are produced by individuals who have become iconic stars, like the acclaimed English artist Banksy. Also, it must be remembered that writing on walls and other public surfaces is not a new 'thing' in the history of humanity. It dates back millennia. People have always felt the urge to express themselves in this way, as testified by ancient inscriptions found all over the world, such as those in Lascaux, Pompeii, and Mesopotamia. Indeed, it may be argued that graffiti and street art, in general, are the real traditional art forms. Stik, an English street artist, sitting in his East London studio during our conversation, reiterated this point by saying, 'People have been painting on walls since the beginning of times whereas canvas painting is newer. We're the establishment!'

3 Paste-ups were not pioneered by Cost and Revs, though. In France, for example, the already mentioned Pignon-Ernest became popular for placing in the street artistic wheatpastes infused with politics and poetry and greatly contributed to further widen the scope of early French street art (likewise, Jacques Villegle became famous for his alphabet with symbolic letters and décollage with lacerated posters). And in New York in the late 1970s, Christy Rupp wheatpasted posters in an artistic project entitled Rat Patrol. The posters depicted a rat, and many were pasted close to rubbish cans and sites. As confirmed by Rupp herself during our conversation in a café in Manhattan, her purpose was to highlight the socio-economic and ecological problems of the times.

4 Claudia Walde, *Street Fonts: Graffiti Alphabets from Around the World* (Thames & Hudson 2011).

## DIFFERENCES AND NUANCES

As mentioned, there are differences between graffiti and street art – the former is lettering-based, while the latter is more figurative. The perception of these two art forms in society also differs. Members of the general public and media outlets often consider graffiti lettering (and to a certain extent stickering and paste-up art) as a less valuable and pleasant form of art, if not deplorable visual pollution, while the more socially acceptable street art is often championed and glorified: indeed, street art tours have become a regular feature of many cities, with dedicated street art festivals also being organised in several countries.

Moreover, many writers (but not all) – especially those who paint illegally – express anger against society. Skeme, an influential New York writer from the late 1970s and early 1980s, perfectly highlighted the motives that pushed writers of his generation to leave their mark in the city. He said this to me while sitting in a café in Harlem: 'In one person you could find various reasons as to why he wrote. Some of it was out of, for instance, adolescent, rebellion; a desire to express yourself; the artist in you bursting out'. Rebellion narratives permeate the graffiti subculture, and this has been the case from its very beginning. Unsurprisingly, for a movement that so strictly abhors labels and restrictions, even the term 'graffiti' has been disputed by some early New York writers. Iz the Wiz was reported noting, 'First of all, it's not even called graffiti, it's writing. Graffiti is some social term that was developed (for the culture) somewhere in the 70s,'[5] while Futura 2000 was reported as commenting, 'It's not the word "graffiti" which bothers me, it just doesn't accurately explain the entire picture'.[6] Phase 2, another legendary New York writer, also expressed a negative opinion: 'this word "graffiti" needs to go [...] It means "scribble-scrabble" and does not enhance the value of this cultural art [...] It was made up by the media and accepted by lack of knowledge of (how) complicated, cultural, technical, spiritual, and on and on this art is'.[7] Mico, another writer from the New York scene of the 1970s, has a more race-based and social class–related opinion, saying that 'the term graffiti is a racist, denigrating term that was applied to our culture, a culture invented by the children of the working class, usually people of color: black and Puerto Rican, black and Latinos in the early '70s, not a culture invented by the children of the rich upper classes, because if it were, the media would never have denigrated the new art form with the term "graffiti"; they would have named it a "vanguard pop-art" or something'.[8] The same opinion was expressed by Andre Trenier, a New York muralist, during our conversation in the Bronx: 'I feel it [the word "graffiti"] is a derogatory term'.

5 Stampa Alternativa, *Style: Writing from the Underground* (Nuovi Equilibri 1998) 6.

6 Ed Bartlett, *Lonely Planet Street Art* (Lonely Planet Publishing 2017) 5.

7 D. D. Brewer and M. L. Miller, 'Bombing and Burning: The Social Organization and Values of Hip Hop Graffiti Writers and Implications for Policy' (1990) *Deviant Behavior* 11(4), 360; Ivor L. Miller, *Aerosol Kingdom: Subway Painters of New York City* (University Press of Mississippi 2012) 19.

8 Hugo Martinez, *Graffiti NYC* (Prestel 2006) 54.

Graffiti (and street art) labels are also refused by Lady Pink, an early Ecuadorian American writer (then) and muralist (now), and the first well-known woman practicing graffiti in New York in the late 1970s and 1980s. She said in the interview with me, 'I am a fine artist. Street Art is a new label they are imposing on us. I don't consider myself a street artist'. This is also the position of a British street artist curiously called Copyright (he explained to me in the interview that the choice of that name 'was kind of a joke, a way for me to protect my identity when I was doing artwork outdoors. I liked the duality of the meaning'). He added, 'I never started out calling myself a street artist, always just "an artist". "Street artist" is just a label I've been given by people trying to put me into a bracket in a way to understand what I do'. Similarly, New York artist KR told me: 'I don't want to be defined as a street artist. I have an extensive graffiti background, but I'm not specifically a street artist, it's too narrow. I'm interested in art and creativity'. Likewise, Mosstika (a contemporary artist who creates silhouettes of animals out of moss or grass and attaches them to wooden walls on construction sites) and Andre Trenier confirmed during their interviews with me that they simply consider themselves fine artists. Sitting in a café with me in the Bronx, the latter clarified this point, saying, 'It's all kind of semantics anyway. It is very difficult to draw a line [between street and fine artists]'.

It is also difficult to draw a line between graffiti lettering and street art, and those who practice these forms of art. Although they have developed into two distinct movements, the line distinguishing them is often blurred; many street artists engage in graffiti writing and various writers incorporate figurative elements into their works, and several others do basically both, that is, lettering and figurative street art[9] (moreover, several practitioners of these types of art also create pieces in the studio).[10] Art techniques are also shared. For example, Coco144, an early New York writer,

[9] See also Ronald Kramer, 'Graffiti and Street Art: Creative Practices Amid "Corporatization" and "Corporate Appropriation"', in Enrico Bonadio (ed.), *The Cambridge Handbook of Copyright in Street Art and Graffiti* (Cambridge University Press 2019) 30 (noting that writers and street artists 'often drift across aesthetic styles to the point where it becomes next to impossible to say whether they are a graffiti writer, street artist, both, neither, or something else altogether. For example, is someone like Revs, who is known for his graffiti writing but also for writing diary pages in subway tunnels and the unauthorized installation of sculptures throughout New York, a graffiti writer or street artist?').

[10] It is for this reason that I occasionally use in this volume the terms 'artists' to generally refer to the practitioners of these forms of art. I also sometimes use the words 'mural artist' or 'muralist', especially to refer to street artists engaged in wall painting and not graffiti lettering. This ambiguity of roles was made clear to me when interviewing an informant who both does illegal graffiti in the street and paints canvases in the studio. When he does graffiti he uses his street pseudonym, and when he paints in the studio he uses his real name. He told me: 'they are two different persons. […] As to canvases, I'd have no problem to start a copyright suit, but I'd never commercialise my graffiti'. This double personality angle also emerged in my interview with the Australian artist Damien Mitchell at a café in Brooklyn. When he told me that sometimes he also does graffiti in addition to murals, I asked him about his graffiti name. He answered, '[I]t doesn't matter', making me understand that he did not want to reveal his identity as a writer. It is not uncommon for artists who

explained that in 1972 he started using stencils, a technique typical of modern street artists, because they permitted him to get his name up faster than he normally wrote.[11] Also in light of this, it is understandable why the two terms 'street art' and 'graffiti' are frequently used interchangeably, especially by the media and in popular culture. Furthermore, like writers, street artists are often motivated by anti-establishment sentiments and reject modern consumeristic values and the traditional art world. Alice Pasquini, a street artist based in Rome, said to me: "I come from the academic world, but I developed a strong rejection towards it, I'm more inspired by a wall covered in tags than by a canvas".

However, there are still differences between these artistic movements. While both entail a creative display in a public space and a desire to leave a mark in the city, street art, being focused on images rather than letters, is conceptually geared towards external recognition and decipherment by the general public. It is a kind of art that connects with the masses – a language open to the world. Graffiti, on the other hand, by relying strictly on the reinterpretation of the letters of the alphabet, which often leads to their complete abstraction, has developed into an internal code, which is fully understood only by other writers. In other words, graffiti is a secret and an internal language.[12] Martha Cooper, the co-author of *Subway Art*, the first and most acclaimed book documenting the graffiti art explosion in New York in the 1970s and early 1980s, noted that this artistic subculture is a kind of 'secret society',[13] and that 'recognizing and deciphering graffiti writing is akin to solving a puzzle'.[14] It is by creating their own world that writers can exclude general audiences from understanding their work, therefore 'reinforcing the vitality of their world'.[15] This has been a structural feature of graffiti from the very beginning – as Skeme noted in the famous 1983 documentary movie *Style Wars*: 'I don't care of the fact that they can't read it [...] it's for us'. He said that while confronting his mother, who was worried about her son engaging in these illegal behaviours. Similarly, London writer Zaki commented in an interview with researcher Nancy Macdonald: 'I see tagging

work in both the studio and the street to use two different names, one for the studio and the other for the street. For example, the fine artist Brian Adam Douglas becomes Elbow-Toe when he places art in the street, while the Australian street artist Lister becomes Anthony Lister when his works are shown in a gallery. In this regard, see Alison Young, *Street Art World* (Reaktion Books 2016) 129. It is also interesting to note that in the interview I had with Copyright, the latter expanded on the different approaches he uses when painting in studio and in the street: 'My studio work is very different from my street work. If it's a canvas, I might spend a month working on [it] (coming back and refining), but for a work on the street I might just have a few hours to create. I make it look as strong as possible to be seen on the street, but it is not created to be sold, it doesn't represent the same thing my studio work does'.

11 Roger Gastman (ed.), *Wall Writers* (Gingko Press Incorporated 2015) 150.

12 Cedar Lewisohn, *Street Art: The Graffiti Revolution* (Tate Modern Publishing 2009) 15.

13 Christopher Grimes, 'Photographer Martha Cooper Captured New York at Its Grittiest' (2 October 2020) *FT Magazine*.

14 Martha Cooper, *Tag Town: The Origins of Writing* (Dokument 2009) 53.

15 Anna Waclawek, *Graffiti and Street Art* (Thames & Hudson 2011) 55.

talking to other graffiti writers'.[16] Also, New York artist KR noted in our interview, 'You may write your tag 100,000 times. For graffiti writers, it's easy to understand tags and relate to the style. It's very difficult to explain to people who are not graffiti writers, it's their own language. The style is attached to the individual's history and context within the greater history of graffiti'. Likewise, David Chino, another New York writer, explained to me that 'graffiti excludes people from the conversation, with these complicated letters'.

Complicated? Yes, indeed. What is more complicated to the general public than these indecipherable letters? Street art is instead easier to understand and capable of reaching wider audiences. The repertoire from which street artists take inspiration is far broader than that of writers, which makes street art more lexically and aesthetically open-ended than graffiti. And its openness towards non-insiders and the public, in general, is one of the main reasons behind its larger social acceptance. As Morley, a Los Angeles street artist who specializes in wheatpasting, explained to me in our interview: 'with street art […] it's taking your work and injecting it into the world around you. So instead of asking the audience to travel into the artist's world, it's the artist bringing their work to the audience. For me, this is a much more creatively gratifying experience'.

These differences also sometimes lead to conflicts and vivid clashes between street artists and writers, with the former occasionally looking down on the latter, who may be 'accused' of focusing more on quantity (the desire to 'bomb' the city as much as possible, and therefore to 'get up' and be seen by other writers) rather than artistic quality. A few interviews I had confirmed this tension, with a former writer – and now respected street artist – referring to writers who had tagged around his mural as 'fucking writers'.[17] This feeling is shared by several writers who have given up on illegal graffiti and now only paint legally. For example, Yes 2 – a New York writer active since the 1980s – was reported as saying, 'People generally like when we do a legal production because the areas are so fucked up with tags and scribbles and we come in and make it look nice'.[18] This sentiment of disrespect works both ways, though. Writers' communities are often critical of the openness – and 'mainstreamisation' – of street art. This is what New York artist Resa Piece noted during our interview in Manhattan (I spoke with her while she was painting a legal mural on a business property): 'murals and street art are not as respected in writers' community. They think like "ah you are just doing art stuff"'.

16 Nancy Macdonald, *The Graffiti Subculture: Youth, Masculinity and Identity in London and New York* (Palgrave MacMillan 2001) 203.

17 The negative reputation that graffiti has amongst the general public may also have repercussions for the way artists who practice both street art and graffiti present themselves, especially when it comes to attracting commission opportunities. Gabriel Corti, a US writer and mural artist whom I talked to in a Long Island café, told me during the interview that he prefers 'being called a muralist over a graffiti artist as when I approach companies for work, I tend to sense that "graffiti" as a word turn people off'.

18 Karla Murray, *Broken Windows: Graffiti NYC* (Gingko Press 2009) 181.

## WHAT THIS BOOK IS ABOUT

So, why do we need to learn about the intersection between these art forms and copyright laws? Why is this book titled *Copyright in the Street – An Oral History of Creative Processes in Street Art and Graffiti Subcultures*?

The answer to the first question is rooted in an inherent characteristic of these art forms. They are created and displayed in public spaces. Because of that, and also due to their increasing appeal amongst certain sectors of society, especially young people, they are at risk of being appropriated and exploited for commercial purposes. And indeed, in recent years, there has been a sharp increase in cases where street and graffiti artists have complained about corporations (from sectors as diverse as fashion, food, entertainment, cars, and real estate) appropriating and exploiting their artworks without authorisation, for example, in advertising campaigns or as decorative elements of products. This confirms that these forms of art are vulnerable to exploitation. They are actually more exposed to unauthorised exploitation than works of fine art, precisely because they are placed in the public environment and not in closed galleries or museums. This unjust exploitation has recently pushed several practitioners of these art forms to look at copyright laws as a possible tool to protect the fruits of their creativity.

And indeed copyright-focused legal actions have recently proliferated, as will be mentioned in Chapter 3. There have also been legal disputes focusing on whether graffiti lettering per se could be considered original enough to attract copyright, with judges reaching interesting conclusions in favour of writers and graffiti style in general, as we will see in Chapter 2, where we will also look at the different graffiti styles that have been developed throughout the years, especially in New York.

Complaints have been brought against not only commercial exploitation. There have also been cases against those who destroy murals or other street artworks without following the appropriate legal procedures, as we will see in Chapter 4. In the 2018 case involving the destruction of pieces (legally) located at the world-famous *5Pointz* mural point in New York, a judge awarded a record $6.7 million in damages to twenty-one graffiti and street artists who had sued the owner of the complex.[19] The award was decided under the Visual Artists Rights Act (VARA), the piece of legislation which protects artists' moral rights in the US, including the right to oppose the destruction of their pieces. The site's owner had whitewashed the murals without serving artists with the ninety-day written notice required by VARA. Also, and more importantly, the artworks in question had been considered to have 'recognised stature', which is what is needed to get this form of protection.

Street and graffiti artworks may also suffer from another prejudicial treatment. As we will see in Chapter 4, there have recently been 'surgical' removals of pieces

[19] *Cohen v. G&M Realty* 320 F. Supp. 3d 421, 2018 U.S. Dist. LEXIS 22662; *Castillo v. G&M Realty L.P.*, Nos. 18-498-cv. (L), 18-538-cv (CON), 2020 US App.

originally placed in the street, and they have been relocated to galleries, museums, auction houses, or other indoor venues, often for the purposes of being exhibited, sold, or exploited commercially in other ways – all without the artists' consent. This has happened with several of Banksy's murals. Such a practice is controversial, as these types of artworks are often site specific. Several artists and writers have complained in recent years about these removals.

Who would have imagined such a scenario in the late 1960s and 1970s, when a bunch of kids in Philadelphia and New York started tagging and painting their names on walls and subway trains? Most graffiti pioneers of that era obviously could not care less about asserting copyright on their pieces (predominantly painted illegally on walls or subway trains), or about trying to save them from whitewashing. After all, how could you ask the company that is managing the subway system to preserve a piece you have painted on the external panel of a train? Instead, early writers' focus was on improving their lettering style, competing with their peers, and eventually advancing the artistic subculture.

Coming to the second question, why does this book have that specific title? The title is self-explanatory. This study will make the point that copyright-related narratives have entered these artistic subcultures. As also confirmed by several interviews I conducted, more and more artists and writers – even those who are not very famous and do not have the financial means to afford lawyers – have started looking with increasing interest at copyright to protect their art from both corporate appropriation and destruction or removal. Many of them have entered the professional art market (and thus not only paint in the street but also produce artworks in studios and show them in galleries and museums) and have accepted its rules, which inevitably include copyright laws. After all, few early New York writers also accepted painting and showing canvases in galleries in the old days; and many street artists and writers nowadays embrace merchandising and the sale of products that incorporate their art, such as posters, postcards, bags, and hats. I will expand on this in Chapter 5.

This book will also touch on characterising features of these art forms, including their (often) anti-establishment nature (in Chapter 5) as well as their sharing and appropriation approach (in Chapter 6). It is well known that many street and graffiti artworks aim at conveying anti-establishment messages. Pieces placed in public spaces often oppose war; criticise consumerism and capitalistic values; question the function of modern media; or denounce police brutality and racial discrimination, with the worldwide spike of murals commemorating the murder of George Floyd in Minneapolis in May 2020 epitomising this trend. One may therefore argue that (what are considered by many) pro-establishment legal tools like copyright should be considered antithetical to, and in contradiction with, those values. Also, street artists and writers frequently borrow styles, concepts, and details not only from popular culture and the everyday world but also from fellow colleagues, without engaging in legal complaints or objections. Again, one may note that such characteristic suggests that copyright laws, which usually push the right owners to complain about imitations, are not suitable for governing these art practices.

But the fact that street artists and writers do not bring legal complaints against peers who may imitate them does not necessarily mean that copyright is not fit to regulate these artistic subcultures, as will be seen in Chapter 6. Indeed, many fine artists often decide not to take action against imitators. Moreover, copyright regimes are flexible enough to allow artists to decide whether to enforce some rights and waive others or to waive all of them. Also, in Chapter 5 we will see that many street artists and writers do not see an inherent contradiction between these art forms carrying anti-establishment meanings and their creators' desire to protect them via copyright laws. As will be noted in Chapter 3, some street artists and writers would even take into account the idea of starting legal action to protect pieces created illegally which would expose them to the risk of being identified and criminally prosecuted.

This book also recognises that street art, and to a larger extent graffiti communities, has a developed system of social norms, which regulate the creative processes from within: 'be original', 'don't bite' (biting means 'copying' in graffiti jargon), and 'don't go over' (which requires writers not to destroy or damage the work of other writers) are the most important.[20] These norms do certainly play a role in regulating the behaviour of artists within street and graffiti art scenarios. Yet, they may not be enough, as is also confirmed by the fact that some artists and writers have had to bring legal actions or other complaints against appropriators. Social norms are therefore not sufficient here, but they are just complementary to a set of legal norms – namely, copyright and moral rights – which street artists and writers are increasingly looking at. I will cover these issues in Chapter 6.

## PREVIOUS LITERATURE IN THE AREA, OTHER SOURCES, AND THE ETHNOGRAPHIC ELEMENT OF THIS STUDY

This book has benefited from previous legal and sociological studies on the creative processes within these artistic subcultures. For example, ethnographic research conducted by sociologist Ronald Kramer has demonstrated that since the 1990s, a constantly increasing number of graffiti practitioners have not only created art legally but have also looked for integration within the society at large.[21] These findings are in line with the present study, which aims to show that graffiti and street art can be reconciled with a body of legal norms – copyright and moral rights – widely accepted by the general public.

[20] These norms have been highlighted by Marta Iljadica, *Copyright beyond Law: Regulating Creativity in the Graffiti Subculture* (Bloomsbury 2016).

[21] Ronald Kramer, *The Rise of Legal Graffiti Writing in New York and Beyond* (Palgrave MacMillan 2017), noting at p. 55 that the terminology has also changed. While in the 1970s and 1980s writers used terms such as 'bombing', 'hitting', or 'killing' when referring to their actions, more recently they have increasingly used the – more traditional – verb 'painting'.

Moreover, in 2016 Marta Iljadica published the well-researched book entitled *Copyright beyond Law: Regulating Creativity in the Graffiti Subculture*, which provides a first legal and ethnographic analysis of copyright issues related to these forms of art. This study has certainly been an inspiration for the present book. Yet, while this monograph argues that copyright regimes may be fit to regulate creativity within the street and graffiti subcultures, the book published by Iljadica casts some doubt on whether those regimes can work within these communities.

The existing literature on graffiti and street art has also inspired me. Craig Castleman's *Getting Up: Subway Graffiti in New York*, published by MIT Press in 1984, is the first comprehensive (academic) book to thoroughly describe writers' artistic activity in the New York subway system as it documented their inside stories through interviews the author conducted.[22] Similarly, Jack Stewart in *Graffiti Kings: New York City Mass Transit Art of the 1970s*, published in 2009 by Abrams after his death, narrates the artistic competition amongst early graffiti writers that focused on advancing an emerging form of letter-based subway art. Then Jeff Ferrell in his 1996 book *Crimes of Style: Urban Graffiti and the Politics of Criminality* (Northeastern University Press), draws on his field research to brilliantly analyse the practices of graffiti crews in Denver (Colorado). Gregory Snyder's ethnographic study *Graffiti Lives: Beyond the Tag in New York's Urban Underground*, published in 2009 by NYU Press, is also noteworthy as it shows how writers can turn their artistic passion into adult and socially acceptable careers – from professional muralists and fine artists to graphic designers and tattoo artists, as well as advertising experts and fashion designers. The street art movement has also been covered by Alison Young in her book *Street Art, Public City: Law, Crime and the Urban Imagination*, published by Routledge in 2013, in which she challenges the conventional understandings of culture, law, crime, and art. All of these studies, and several others, have benefited from brilliant ethnographic research and a multitude of targeted interviews with insiders. This book cites some of these interviews.

The inspiration for this book also came from the many photographic books which have documented these forms of art throughout the decades. First and foremost, Martha Cooper and Henry Chalfant's *Subway Art* (Thames & Hudson 1984), considered the Bible of graffiti, documents the explosion of graffiti creativity in the New York subway system in the late 1970s and early 1980s. This was followed by Henry Chalfant and James Prigoff's *Spraycan Art* (Thames & Hudson 1987), which also covers the spread of these forms of art to other cities in the US and around the world. Yet, the very first photographic book on graffiti was produced in 1974 by Norman Mailer and Joan Naar, that is, *The Faith of Graffiti* (Praeger), where Mailer's words on the origins and relevance of graffiti in modern urban culture

[22] An earlier academic account of the 1970s New York graffiti scene was a university thesis published in 1978 by Italian researcher Andrea Nelli, titled *Graffiti a New York*. The book soon disappeared from the shelves, but the publisher Whole Train Press republished it in 2012.

match Naar's photographs of writers' works. More recently, Roger Gastman and Caleb Neelon's book, *History of American Graffiti* (Collins Design 2011), provides a detailed analysis of the development of this culture in several US cities; and Roger Gastman's book *Wall Writers* (Gingko Press Incorporated 2015) explores not only early graffiti's place on the wall but also its place in the culture of the time. Photographic books have also focused on more figurative street art. The first important one was by Allan Schwartzman, *Street Art*, published by Bantam Doubleday Dell in 1985, which documents the ephemeral urban works of artists like Richard Hambleton, Christy Rupp, John Ahearn, Keith Haring, and Jean-Michel Basquiat. More recently, *Graffiti World* by Nicholas Ganz (Thames & Hudson 2004) provides a detailed analysis of the development of this culture in the Americas, Europe, and other parts of the world. The book *Street Art: The Graffiti Revolution* by Cedar Lewisohn, published by Tate Modern Publishing in 2009, is also worth noting – it provides illustrated insights related to these forms of art that are both global in scope and attentive to local scenes. Meanwhile, *Children of the Can: Bristol Graffiti and Street Art* by Felix Brown (Tangent Books 2012) pays homage to the scene of Bristol, one of the UK and Europe's most influential cities for these artistic movements.

Several documentary movies have also been inspirational in writing this book. The most important and iconic ones are *Wild Style*, directed by Charlie Ahearn (1982), and *Style Wars*, directed by Tony Silver and Henry Chalfant (1983), which narrate the artistic lives of New York graffiti writers of the early 1980s. Another interesting film is *Bombin'*, directed by Dick Fontaine (1987), which shows how US graffiti culture made its way across the ocean to the UK in the 1980s. Then *Graffiti Wars*, a Channel 4 documentary produced in 2011, shed further light on the UK scene and highlighted the rising tension between street artists and writers by focusing on the feud between Banksy and Robbo. The many internet blogs dedicated to street art and graffiti, such as Art Crimes (the first webpage devoted to graffiti and street art), with interviews with protagonists within these communities and myriads of photographs capturing their art, have also provided plenty of food for thought.

With that said, academic works, photographic books, movies, and blogs are not enough on their own to create a comprehensive analysis. What gives the present study an 'insider' twist and dimension are the findings of the ethnographic research I have conducted in recent years, which has included participant observation. This is a category of data collection used in qualitative research – and it aims at getting familiar with a group of people and their practices via a deep and protracted involvement with them in their own cultural environment. This is exactly what I did. I had the privilege of befriending several writers and street artists and observing them in action. I saw several of them painting walls and other urban surfaces, also in the context of street art festivals. I talked to them and in most cases gained their trust and respect. I conducted semi-structured interviews with ninety practitioners (both street artists and writers), during a period of five years that preceded the publication of this book. The group of interviewees was quite heterogeneous, including old and young people, male and female, those belonging to different ethnic and social backgrounds, and both established and less famous artists. The interviews took place in various settings and towns, including in New York and London, next to the wall where artists or writers were painting, in cafés or bars, or remotely through internet platforms. I asked participants questions about, for example, whether copyright was the right tool to protect their creativity and if they would be ready to take legal action to stop others from appropriating their works without their consent, even where their pieces had been created illegally – and whether destroying or removing their pieces for the purpose of relocating them to indoor spaces would be so unacceptable that they would possibly try to oppose it via a lawsuit. These artists and writers also explained their feelings when someone publishes photos of their artworks without acknowledging their authorship or in general misattributes their works, and if a legal reaction would be worth it when this occurs. They also expanded on more general issues related to the level of originality of their writing style, and whether relying on the law to protect their art would contradict the values of their subcultures (what I have learnt is that the latter point is not relevant anymore for several artists, especially those who have already entered the mainstream). Direct quotes from these interviews are regularly inserted into the book, as I believe it is crucial to report the participants' points of view in their own words.

Encounters with artists, especially writers, have not always been smooth. After contacting two writers on Instagram and asking if they were available for an interview, one replied, 'Haha … You're a cop … You think I'm gonna give you my email address or show you my face?' And the other wrote, 'Red flag bro. Y'all pigs gotta do better'. Another artist simply (and abruptly) asked for money in exchange for accepting to be interviewed.

I also talked to people who are inside these subcultures but do not place art in the street, including photographers and video-makers of street and graffiti art, owners and managers of galleries specialising in urban art, and collectors of what have been defined as 'street art souvenirs' or 'street art flavoured' studio artworks.[23] Conversations with them have been interesting, allowing me to understand these artistic practices from other complementary perspectives.

More importantly, living for several years in the East London area of Shoreditch, where creativity has literally exploded and developed after the arrival of the new millennium, has certainly increased my curiosity towards these forms of art. Walking through Brick Lane, Red Church Street, Hackney Wick, and other London neighbourhoods full of free-hand graffiti pieces, stencilled images, myriad stickers and paste-ups, street poetry and sculptures, abandoned miniatures, and many other artworks further opened my eyes and broadened my knowledge of these artistic

[23] Jim Carey's interview with Banksy, 'Creative Vandalism' (30 May 2012) *Squall Magazine*.

movements. Moreover, visiting, discovering, and experiencing graffiti-friendly areas around the world – including Stoke Croft in Bristol, Kreuzberg in Berlin, Williamsburg and Bushwick in Brooklyn (New York), Hosier Lane and Fitzroy in Melbourne, Florentin and Nachalat Binyamin in Tel Aviv, and La Candelaria and Puente Aranda in Bogota' – filled me with even more curiosity and a willingness to further study and understand these creative subcultures.

Against this background, the present study will not focus on to what extent street art and graffiti works are regulated by copyright regimes. This has already been done elsewhere,[24] and only a few legal notions, as applied to these artforms, will be given here. Rather, the book will predominantly look at how such laws are perceived within these artistic subcultures, and how artists and writers view certain creative aspects of their own practice. It will give voice to the main actors of these communities and highlight their feelings and opinions towards issues which until recently they have often felt are far from their everyday life and practice. This book, in other words, will bring the 'voice from the street' into the debate over the legal (and non-legal) protection of street art and graffiti. It will also touch on related and complementary issues, such as the 'gallerisation' and economic exploitation of these forms of art (e.g. via merchandising) and the curious similarities between the graffiti and advertising worlds.

[24] See Bonadio (ed.), above fn. 9, and several other works such as Elena Vicente Domingo, *Los Graffiti como Obras Protegibles* (Editorial Reus 2021).

# 2

# Creativity and Originality of Graffiti Lettering

An O can be absolutely anything you know: you can out motion it, you can layer it up, turn it into objects: the possibilities are limitless. It's a very basic structure so you don't have to put that much information there for people to realize what it is: so, a lot of time that's the centerpiece and it saves me from all the other lawful letter around. Thanks God for the O![1]

This quote by Epok, a Bristol writer, perfectly tackles the issue this chapter is going to focus on. Should we consider graffiti lettering original enough? And more specifically, what's the writers' opinion on this issue? The answers to those questions are not only important towards granting an entire artistic movement the dignity it deserves but they also have fundamental legal consequences, as only original works of art are eligible for copyright protection. The chapter will not focus on works of street art, which are often more figurative and therefore raise less doubts about their originality.

## OF LETTERS AND PREJUDICE

Once the superficial veil through which the general public looks at graffiti lettering (especially tags and throw-ups, to which we will come back later) is lifted and we are able to examine and perceive the creative process that drives writers, we can realise that the letters they paint often become works of art. In other words, letters such as the 'O' glorified by Epok are the perfect canvas for writers to unleash their creativity and project onto them their artistic ideas, namely by reinterpreting the alphabet according to their personal style. The letter 'O' and the artistic freedom it gives writers has also come up in my fieldwork. Ozmo, an Italian former writer turned street artist, told me in our interview that the fact that his name had two O's allowed him to be extremely creative by transforming them in funny faces and inserting other figurative elements.

1 Felix Braun, *Children of the Can: Bristol Graffiti and Street Art* (Tangent Books 2012) 125.

Other letters may give writers similar freedom. When proudly saying that his tag was original, New York writer Dave Chino told me during our interview: 'even if I was a bit restricted in freedom, the "C" of CHINO for example had to be a bit standard, with the other letters I could be creative, like the "H" and "I". I wasn't looking at anyone's for inspiration when I devised the letters "H" and "I"'. Likewise, New York (former) graffiti writer Lady Pink has been reported saying that 'nothing is more feminine than "Pink", and the letters appealed to me: the "K" kicks out real nice; the "I" is really cute and you can do it with a heart; and the "P" begins very slight and you can do things before it. It was all about style'.[2]

It is important to provide a reminder about the taxonomy of writers' output, not only colourful and sophisticated pieces, but also tags and 'throw-ups'. Tags are painted or drawn on walls and other urban surfaces and are often executed in condensed calligraphic form. A throw-up consists of a one-colour outline and another layer of full-colour, frequently painted in bubble-style letters. Tags and throw-ups represent the tagger's chosen name and thus are like a personal signature and street logo that glorify one's identity.

I mentioned earlier the general public's 'superficial veil'. As noted in the previous chapter, graffiti are perceived negatively by large sectors of society, as opposed to more elaborate pieces of street art, which are increasingly accepted and appreciated, instead. There is a rooted and widespread misconception that promptly stereotypes graffiti lettering (especially tags and throw-ups) as non-artistic and therefore – one may note – not eligible for copyright protection. For example, Danwill Schwender, a US attorney, is skeptical about considering tags and throw-ups copyrightable. He argues that tags are mere pencil stroke words indicating a name and a place and that throw-ups, although having some stylistic nuances, remain words indicating a name and, as such, they cannot get copyright.[3] Such belief may be reinforced by the assumption that graffiti lettering seems to the untrained eye (i.e. the eye of the general public outside this subculture) easy to execute or somehow a product of mischievousness rather than intelligence or artistic efforts.[4] One may indeed think that these letters are painted or drawn by using similar patterns and just end up being different as to their content, namely the writer's name. Also, the fact that writers sometimes choose specific letters for practical reasons, such as the speed with which they can be written (this has been confirmed to me in several interviews), may be used to highlight their functionality and therefore non-copyrightability.

2 Henry Chalfant and Sacha Jenkins, *Training Days: The Subway Artists Then and Now* (Thames & Hudson 2014) 94.

3 Danwill Schwender, 'Promotion of the Arts: An Argument for Limited Copyright Protection of Illegal Graffiti' (2007–2008) 55 *J Copyright Soc'y USA*, 264–265.

4 Alison Young, *Street Art, Public City: Law, Crime and the Urban Imagination* (Routledge 2013) 23.

## ORIGINALITY OF GRAFFITI LETTERING

But if general assumptions and prejudices are set aside and more knowledge about these subcultures' creative processes is acquired, one cannot help but notice that writers develop and perfect their own lettering style over many years – a style which derives from countless hours of perfecting their craft, even if the final image may appear to the general public less than perfect.[5]

### *Tags and Throw-Ups*

Take tags. They represent the first step in the career of a writer.[6] Indeed, the piece is frequently an extension of the tag (and often the throw-up).[7] The tag is the root of graffiti – and there would be no graffiti piece without the practice of tagging.[8] In other words, graffiti as we know it would not exist without the tag, as tags are the essential component for learning, practicing, and mastering the form of graffiti as 'vandalistic' art.[9] As noted by writer Delta in the 1998 *Kings and Toys* documentary, directed by Michael Power: 'every piece came from tagging, a piece is nothing more than a fat tag with outlines and designs'.

Even tags which at first and unexperienced sight might seem banal, meaningless, and always similar[10] (as opposed to more elaborate piece, i.e. 'the good colourful graffiti')[11] may be considered creative and original instead. As Alison Young noted, '[P]utting up a tag is not mindless. It represents imagination, dedication to an art form, and the willingness to take a risk in a public place to achieve an aesthetic outcome (even if it is one that we don't happen to like)'.[12] It should also be noted that

5 Mark Halsey and Alison Young, 'Our Desires Are Ungovernable: Writing Graffiti in Urban Space' (2006) 10 *Theoretical Criminology* 275, 294.

6 Rob White, 'Graffiti, Crime Prevention & Cultural Space' (2001) 12 *Current Issues in Criminal Justice* 253, 255.

7 See also Ivor L. Miller, *Aerosol Kingdom: Subway Painters of New York City* (2012) University Press of Mississippi, 197.

8 Anna Waclawek, *Graffiti and Street Art* (Thames & Hudson World of Art 2011) 21.

9 Gregory Snyder, 'Long Live the Tag: Representing the Foundations of Graffiti', in Konstantinos Avramidis and Myrto Tsilimpounidi (eds.) and Street Art: Reading, Writing and Representing the City (Routledge 2017) 264.

10 Charlotte Gré, *Street art et droit d'auteur: À qui appartiennent les oeuvres de la rue?* (Editions L' Harmattan 2015) 44–45 (noting that tags constitute a 'repetitive technique', and they are not fruit of 'artistic research').

11 Ronald Kramer, The Rise of Legal Graffiti Writing in New York and Beyond, Palgrave MacMillan 2017, 129 (highlighting 'the impression, at least amongst viewers outside of the graffiti art community, that pieces are somehow more legitimate – that they have a more intrinsic connection to fine art than do tags and throw-ups, which can more readily be stereotyped and dismissed simply as spray-painted scrawls').

12 Young, above fn. 4, 21–23 (pointing out that 'tags may be included in the repertory of street art techniques and a motivation for tagging is to contribute something valid to the conversation with the street and to create something that is in its way as image, an icon and an urban text'); see also Alison Young, *Judging the Image, Art, Value and Law* (Routledge 2004) 51 (noting that 'far from being an undifferentiated mass of scrawl, graffiti writing is a highly nuanced, subtle form of communication with clearly developed styles and a sense of its own history').

the chance of even two tags being exactly the same is close to nil.[13] West One, one of the most prolific writers in New York throughout the 1980s and 1990s, is even more direct and has been reported as saying: 'A tag itself is art, in terms of its meaning, graphically, the whole shit'.[14]

Of course, this is not to say that tags are *always* artistic. There are plenty of tags painted by 'toys' out there that are not stylish and original (in graffiti jargon, toys are unexperienced young writers). Practice, and patience, are needed.[15] Zephyr, the influential New York writer of the 1970s and 1980s, said in an interview with me in a café in Manhattan that when he started painting graffiti, he didn't understand tags and what they meant. It took him a while to understand what a tag truly is. However, the more he observed tags, the more his eyes became trained to actually see them and that is when he realized that every tag is different and is the unique identity of the artist, especially if it is a good one and has some style. This is also what US New York artist and writer Depsone told me during our encounter in a Brooklyn café: '[W]hen I started painting graffiti I didn't really understand tags as much, and I was kind of like "Oh it's a tag, whatever". But the more I did it, the more I understood. I think that your eyes kind of have to be trained to see it. [....] what matters is training your hands over years and years'. Similarly, another of my interviewees, New York writer Hoacs, pointed out: '[I]t's a matter of practice'.

Practice is thus key. Former writer Rubin, now a New York–based studio and street artist, noted in a conversation with me in his studio in Brooklyn that 'a tag takes years of practice. When I see tags, I can see if writers have done their homework, if they've a long history of practice. A tag is not as complex as a mural, but it's definitely a piece of art which requires years of practice'. Christian Acker in his book *Flip the Script: A Guidebook for Aspiring Vandals & Typographers* echoes this: '[T]hese artists/vandals develop their hands via the repetitious writing of these letter forms thousands upon thousands of times, often before even approaching a public space [...] the flow will only come with time'.[16] This point was also stressed by New York writer Easy in our conversation at a café in Brooklyn: 'People put a lot of effort into their tags, their throw-ups, their pieces and their work [...]; if you're going to get into this *art form* [writing], you should perfect your art. Those who don't practice,

[13] Rafael Schacter, 'Graffiti and Street Art as Ornament', in Jeffrey Ian Ross (ed.), *Routledge Handbook of Graffiti and Street Art* (Routledge 2016) 153.

[14] Joe Austin, 'From the City Walls to "Clean Trains": Graffiti in New York City, 1969–1990', in Ross, above fn. 13, 230.

[15] In our conversation in the Bronx, Andre Trenier commented on the non-artistic nature of his first tags. He said, '[T]he stuff I've done in the past, I wouldn't even consider it necessarily art because it was more tagging and more of me developing my art to where it is now. So, it might have been part of a learning process, but I did not look at it as art. But some do, and should. For me it was part of a learning process. [...] And then I practiced that tag day in and day out, until I felt that I had the best variation on writing those forms of letters'.

[16] Christian P. Acker, *Flip the Script: A Guidebook for Aspiring Vandals and Typographers* (Gingko Press 2011) 9.

those who don't try to come up with creative and original works, are condemned to remain toys' (emphasis added). Similarly, Dejer (a former writer who spent seven years painting graffiti in New York) commented in an interview with me: '[T]oys either stop or evolve. When they evolve, they do it quite quickly, let's say a year'.

Tags therefore can show style,[17] and several writers do agree with this. This is the case of Oker (whom I interviewed at a café in Central London) and Mastro (whom I met in Brooklyn). The former told me that 'there is more style in tags than in pieces'; and the latter argued that a tag 'is like a hand style and signature. Everybody has his own signature. Some people take pride in it. You see people who are really trying to be their own "lettersmith" and that are proud of their style. So even a little tag is still an artwork'. Similarly, Andrea Nelli in his university dissertation *Graffiti a New York*, which as mentioned was first published in Italy in 1978 and offers a clear and detailed analysis of the thriving New York writing culture of that era, notes that the writers' signature is simply the 'artwork';[18] and more recently, anthropologist Rafael Schacter has commented that tags can be ornamental as they tattoo the skin of the city.[19] The artistic nature of tags is also stressed by graffiti photographer Martha Cooper, who reminds us, in her book *Tag Town*, that tags are 'the jazz of lettering'.[20] Tags may also reach such an artistic level so as to be able to convey writers' attitude or describe their feelings.[21] Damien Mitchell, the New York–based Australian muralist I met at a Brooklyn café, told me that 'my tag is original because it's a combination of all the things that I've seen around and experiences I've had. Observing the tag, you can see where the writer has been, which places he has visited and got an influence'. One may go as far as claiming, particularly if she is an insider to these communities, that tags (and throw-ups) may be considered as embellishing the environment in which they are painted. This is what many writers think, including Reskew, whom I met and spoke with at a café in Manhattan: '[I]n my opinion, graffiti makes it look better than when it's a blank wall, even if it's simple bubble letter or tags, which most people judge as "scribbles"'.

Having said that, one may note that tags (and throw-ups), especially when created by experienced and talented writers who can display 'can control',[22] should be

17 One of the most famous tags, the Banksy one, is also very unique, 'with the upright back of the capital B missing, the k relying on the n for support, the s with the top shaved off slightly and the final y that looks almost like a hieroglyphic', as noted by Will Ellsworth-Jones, *Banksy: The Man Behind the Wall* (Aurum Press, 2013) 60. On Banksy's writing style see also Ulrich Blanché, *Banksy: Urban Art in a Material World* (Tectum 2016) 56–57.

18 Andrea Nelli, *Graffiti a New York* (Whole Train Press 2012) 11.

19 Schacter, above fn. 13, 144 and 153–154.

20 Martha Cooper, *Tag Town: The Origins of Writing* (Dokument 2009) 9.

21 See also Waclawek, above fn. 8, 14; Lisa Gottlieb, *Graffiti Art Styles: A Classification System and Theoretical Analysis* (McFarland & Co 2009) 43.

22 On the concept of 'can control' see Marta Iljadica, Copyright Beyond Law: Regulating Creativity in the Graffiti Subculture (Bloomsbury 2016) 30 (noting that it is 'the ability to use a spraycan to create clean lines without dripping' and that this is 'the mark of a technically proficient writer').

considered original enough to attract copyright.[23] Some writers actually believe so. They show interest in copyright, as we will see more in depth in the next chapter, for example, by incorporating the copyright symbol © into their tag. Some tags or throw-ups have also been deposited with copyright offices. For instance, before taking legal action in 2016 against the food giant McDonald's for the commercial exploitation of a throw-up painted by the deceased New York writer Dash Snow, the artist's estate filed an application for a federal registration of the artwork (i.e. the throw-up itself) with the US Register of Copyrights.[24]

The artistic nature of tags has also been dealt with by German judges, specifically over the issue of whether a tag can be a copyrighted work.[25] As reminded by Marc Mimler in his analysis of the intersection between copyright and street art and graffiti under German law,[26] in a case before the Court of Munich the debate revolved around the artistic level of a tag's letters. The claimant was a graphic designer (the tag was created in studio, not in the street). The defendants instructed him to design the combination of letters and a number K1K in graffiti style. A first ruling held that the logo was the author's own intellectual creation, and therefore copyrightable.[27] The court clarified that the design of the letters and the number – the curvy x, the elongation of the left line of the k, and the underline which would cross with the letter k – are undoubtedly the claimant's creation – and importantly the fact that the logo was created with a pen rather than spraycan did not modify this finding.[28] A higher court in the same case confirmed this finding by taking into account the unique, innovative, and aesthetic design of the sequence of the letters and numbers in graffiti style.[29]

### *Pieces*

What about intricate and colourful graffiti pieces? Even persons outside the graffiti subculture have started seeing them as art, even if many still do not like them. This point is important because the claim that even an intricate graffiti piece is not creative enough has sometimes been made, also in a copyright dispute. More precisely, in a US case the sunglasses maker Oakley had used a piece painted by US writers

[23] Tomasz Rychlicki, 'Legal Questions about Illegal Art' (2008) 3(6) *Journal of Intellectual Property Law & Practice* 396–397.

[24] See p. 9 of the complaint in *Jade Berreau v. McDonald's Corporation et al.*, 2:16-cv-07394 (Central District of California).

[25] Urheberrechtsschutz für ein Logo in Form eines Graffitis ZUM-RD 204 (LG München) (2015); Urheberrechtsschutz für die grafische Gestaltung eines Schriftzuges ZUM-RD 423 (LG München) (2015).

[26] Marc Mimler, 'Street Art, Graffiti and Copyright: A German Perspective', in Enrico Bonadio (ed.), *The Cambridge Handbook of Copyright in Street Art and Graffiti* (Cambridge University Press 2019) 192–193.

[27] Urheberrechtsschutz für ein Logo in Form eines Graffitis LG München ZUM-RD 204, 205 (2015).

[28] Urheberrechtsschutz für ein Logo in Form eines Graffitis LG München ZUM-RD 204, 205–206 (2015).

[29] Urheberrechtsschutz für ein Logo in Form eines Graffitis OLG München ZUM-RD 190, 190 (2015).

Donald Robbins (aka Keptione) and Noah Daar (aka DJ Rakus) in their advertising campaign.[30] The company tried to make the point that that the artwork did not have the 'modicum of creativity' required under US copyright law[31] and was just generic markings which could not be protected. The case was then settled. One cannot help noting that the argument put forward by Oakley is quite weak. The piece incorporated in their ad was very colourful and elaborate, and leaves no doubt about its originality, also taking into account that the level required by law to attract copyright is low.

The originality of graffiti lettering, especially pieces, is reflected in the terminology used in the literature and specialised circles to actually describe it. When looking at the countless ways such lettering has been defined, we can realise that what we are talking about here is definitely art. Below you will find some definitions of graffiti, which I came across during my research and which – I believe – give an idea of the artistic level this subculture can reach.

- 'twisting the letter forms to create a new language, a new alphabet, a language that most people can't read';[32]
- 'pushing lettering towards complexity and away from legibility';[33]
- 'pushing the aesthetic limits of the alphabet';[34]
- 'reshaping the letters to such a conceptual and artistic state to turn them into a work of art';[35]
- 'transforming the name from a simple verbal expression – a word – into a complex visual expression';[36]
- 'deconstructing the alphabet and creating new one through their stylised letters';[37]
- 'visionary use of the alphabet';[38]
- 'breaking apart and repurposing letters';[39]
- 'letters getting bolder and wilder';[40]
- 'making letter dance';[41]
- 'letters being released from their duties as conventional carriers of meanings and becoming more or less autonomous symbols in a word like string';[42]

[30] *Robbins and others v. Oakley, Inc and others* (2018) Central Californian District Court 2:18-cv-05116.
[31] *Feist Publications, Inc. v. Rural Telephone Service Co.*, 499 U.S. 340 (1991).
[32] Michael Walsh, *Graffito* (North Atlantic Books 1996).
[33] Lee Bofkin, *Concrete Canvas: How Street Art Is Changing the Way Our Cities Look* (Octopus 2014) 294.
[34] Miller, above fn. 7, 5.
[35] Waclawek, above fn. 8, 19.
[36] Gottlieb, above fn. 21, 6.
[37] Waclawek, above fn. 8, 10.
[38] Miller, above fn. 7, 86.
[39] Roger Gastman and Caleb Neelon, *History of American Graffiti* (Collins Design 2011) 302.
[40] Chalfant and Jenkins, above fn. 2, 80 (reporting the words of a writer named Kel).
[41] Chalfant and Jenkins, above fn. 2, 147 (reporting the words of a writer named Spin).
[42] Joe Austin, *Taking the Train: How Graffiti Art Became an Urban Crisis in New York City* (Columbia University Press 2002) 113.

- 'taking the letter beyond its literary functions and into the realm of feelings and images', thus 'ritualizing the alphabet, making it futuristic and primal, forging the letter into a verb';[43]
- 'using color, rhythm, characters, and style to camouflage and abstract the lettering';[44]
- 'by infusing color and rhythmic structure into the Roman lettering, writers manipulate the alphabet to project their names in masterful styles';[45]
- letters being 'smoothly interlocking, aerodynamics forms that seemed ready to sprout wings and fly off the trains. … [letters] moving like the trains they embellished'.[46]

Writers thus play with letters – and often do so *artistically*.[47] As Norman Mailer reminds us in his book *Faith of Graffiti* about the New York early graffiti in the 1970s: 'What a quintessential marriage of cool and style to write your name in giant separate living letter, large as animals, lithe as snakes, mysterious as Arabic and Chinese curls of alphabet'.[48] Moreover, it is interesting to list other words, mostly verbs, that graffiti commentators and experts have used to describe what writers do with letters:

- 'Manipulating', 'changing', 'reconstructing', 'rewriting', 'fusing', 'elongating', 'tweaking', 'fracturing', 'crumbling', 'interacting', 'connecting', 'inter-connecting', 'dissecting', 'stretching', 'bending', 'distorting', 'extending', 'dissolving', 'evolving', 'formulating', 're-formulating', 'inter-twining', 'elaborating', 'reelaborating', 'exaggerating', 'configuring', 'reconfiguring', 'inventing', 'reinventing', 'interpreting', 'reinterpreting', 'experimenting', 'engineering', 'mutating', 'shaping', 'moulding', 'remoulding', 'imagining', 'reimagining', 'recontextualising', 'decontextualizing', 'animating', 'reanimating', 'humanizing', 'individualizing', 'personalizing', 'making the alphabet malleable', 'removing the letter from its common function'.

It is also curious to note a certain 'military' analogy between graffiti lettering and weapons. The style of New York old school writer and artist Rammellzee is relevant here. In his 1979 manifesto entitled *Iconic Treatise on Gothic Futurism*, Rammellzee asserts that letters, when separated from their literary function, are weapons that can be harnessed to battle the oppression imposed by counterfeit linguistic systems. In an early 1980s interview with art critic and researcher Francesca Alinovi, Rammellzee talks about his manifesto and lettering style, arguing that

43 Miller, above fn. 7, 18.
44 Miller, above fn. 7, 72, 79, 86.
45 Miller, above fn. 7, 36.
46 Charlie Ahearn, *Wild Style: The Sampler* (Powerhouse Book 2007) 35.
47 See also Nancy Macdonald, The Graffiti Subculture: Youth, Masculinity and Identity in London and New York (Palgrave MacMillan 2001) 70–71 (noting that style is crucially important part of graffiti: 'The way you write your name, the letters you use, their shape, flow and form, colours you choose, all these things go into making a writer's "style").
48 Norman Mailer – Joan Noar, The Faith. Graffiti (Prayer 1974) 12.

'[i]t's the letters that kill the other letters'.[49] Similarly, Allan Schwartzman in his 1985 book *Street Art* writes about Rammellzee's 'militarized' letters and 'armamental' style, adding that such an artist 'makes elaborately detailed paintings in which the arrows of wild style become rockets and missiles launched toward other tank-form letters'.[50]

Also, pieces painted by graffiti writers often incorporate figurative elements, which obviously make the pieces themselves even more artistic (such practice started from the very beginning in New York, in the 1970s). Pieces indeed are frequently filled with background, including characters or landscapes, which are elements that, in addition to being complementary,[51] support, frame, highlight, and embellish the letters.[52] As has also been noted, the shape of the negative spaces in between the letters can be decorated artistically and is as important as the letters themselves,[53] or even more important.[54]

The artistic nature of graffiti lettering has also been recognised by courts. In *Reece v. Marc Ecko Unlimited*, a 2011 US copyright case over the use of graffiti in a videogame,[55] the judge not only recognised the artistic level of the specific lettering (including a tag), but also noted that Reece's artwork was registered with the US Copyright Office. Even though the judge did not find infringement in light of some differences between the graffiti and the image used in the videogame, she nonetheless made some interesting points. Judge Freeman in particular noted:

> [T]he form of the lettering at issue is arguably central to the artistic expression of particular words. In this unusual context, aspects of the lettering shown in the Reece art [...] such as the degree of abstraction of the letters, the connectivity of the letters, the relative size of the letters, and the two and three dimensional appearance of the letters, may reveal the artist's personal style and strongly influence the 'total concept and feel' of the subject works. [...] although the words 'Dip' and 'Dipism' are not themselves subject to copyright protection, the original manner in which Reece expressed these words is protectible.

49 Francesca Alinovi, *Arte di Frontiera* (Mazzotta 1984) 41.

50 Allan Schwartzman, *Street Art* (Bantam Doubleday Dell 1985) 106.

51 Macdonald, above fn. 47, 167 (noting that characters complement letters, but they are just a 'side issue').

52 Waclawek, above fn. 8, 46.

53 Fred Forsyth (ed.), *Crack and Shine* (FFF London 2009) 68 (also noting that '[f]low is particularly important: how the piece flows, rolls, travels from left to right').

54 Braun, above fn. 1, 163 (reporting the opinion of Bristol writer and artist Inkie).

55 *Reece v. Marc Ecko Unlimited*, 2011 U.S. Dist. Lexis 102199 (2011). Marc Ecko Limited, founded by former writer Marc Ecko, produced a videogame called Getting up. This company was sued in the US for alleged copyright infringement. The videogame indeed included avatars of famous New York writers of the early times such as Cope 2, T-Kid, Futura 2000, and Smith. It narrated the adventures of a graffiti writer in a futuristic city named New Radius, where graffiti has been banned and free speech denied by an oppressive government. The videogame also featured a Black Book Legends section, which includes reproductions of the artworks of real-life writers and suggestions on how to produce graffiti pieces and avoid the police.

These findings do not leave room for interpretation. Graffiti lettering can be as creative and original as traditional fine art. After all, this is what writers themselves believe. When Italian writer KayOne, one of the graffiti pioneers in Italy, was interviewed by a newspaper after obtaining a preliminary injunction in legal proceedings against another artist that had appropriated some of his studio works without permission,[56] he interestingly noted: 'It's a fair and important ruling. Leonetti [the defendant] has no experience of writing culture, otherwise he'd have never done that thing. Originality is the most important value to us'.[57]

## DIFFERENT LETTERING STYLES AND THEIR EVOLUTION

That graffiti can be highly creative is acknowledged by several commentators. Jeff Ferrell brilliantly highlights graffiti's artistic nature and writers' collaborative efforts. In his 1996 book *Crimes of Style* he notes that 'writers keep up a discussion as to the practical and aesthetic progress of the piece. They argue over the accuracy with which the images are being translated from the piecebook to the wall, and ask for help with perspective and scale. [...] They discuss the appropriateness of blending and juxtaposing particular colors, and of adding star-bursts, thick borders, birds, and other stylized conventions'.[58] Similar scenarios had already been highlighted by Craig Castleman in his 1984 book *Getting Up*: 'Many writers also spend a great deal of time sitting in subway stations watching and criticizing the pieces that go by, passing around their sketches, and "autographing" each other's "black books" (hardbound sketch pads that almost all writers carry with them). Many writers put a great deal of care into these autographs, and a writer who does an exceptionally fine drawing in one of them is said to have "burned the book"'.[59]

It is also interesting to expand on the evolution of graffiti from simple handwriting on walls into a fully fledged lettering art. As mentioned in the previous chapter, in Philadelphia and New York in the late 1960s and early 1970s young kids started

56 Milan Court decision of 2 November 2011, *Marco Mantovani, Igor Seghizzi and Stradearts S.r.l. v. Nicola Leonetti*. The legal action was taken together with another Italian writer – Tawa – and the company Stradearts S.r.l., which owns the copyright in the artworks created by the two artists. As mentioned, the pieces the case focused on were not street artworks, but abstract art canvases produced in studio.

57 Chiara Sarra, 'Anche i graffiti possono essere opere d'arte – Un writer milanese vince la causa per plagio', *il Giornale* (3 November 2011), www.ilgiornale.it/news/anche-i-graffiti-possono-essere-opere-darteun-writer.html.

58 Jeff Ferrell, *Crimes of Style: Urban Graffiti and the Politics of Criminality* (Northeastern University Press 1996) 78.

59 Craig Castleman, *Getting Up: Subway Graffiti in New York* (MIT Press 1984) 21. Two famous places where early New York writers used to gather, draw, and exchange their graffiti experiences were the Writers' Corner 188, on the corner of 188th Street and Audubon Avenue (Washington Heights), and the writers' bench at 149th Street Grand Concourse, in the Bronx, on the 2 and 5 IRT lines. At that time such benches and corners represented for writers what is now internet and social media. See also Roger Gastman (ed.), Wall Writers (Gingko Press Incorporated 2015) 100.

spray-painting their names (and often the street number) on walls. The letters were very simple and with no decoration, though. In *Graffiti Kings* Jack Stewart calls this kind of writing 'linear graffiti'.[60] The whole thing then started to evolve. Legendary writer Stay High 149 has been reported noting that 'after 1973, it became bigger and more iconic. You wanted to magnify it to make it more noticeable to the public'.[61] Similarly, writer Jaes was reported as saying, 'In the early stages of graffiti, people used straight letters and did things quickly, basically just tags. Then they progressed to bigger letters and letters with thickness from fat to thin and then bubble letters. After that, writers started adding outlines around the letters and adding dimension to the letters by adding shadows and making them look like they were popping out at you. Then they started putting a slant to the letters so they looked cooler'.[62]

Jag from Washington Heights was one of the first writers to add decoration to linear signature. Unlike fellow writers such as Taki 183 and Julio 204, he opted not to include the street number – instead he started drawing a flower on top of the 'J' and a peace sign on the bottom of the 'G', to make it beautiful and to distinguish its style from others.[63] Additionally, writer SJK 171 first had the idea to add the second colour around his name. He was reported as commenting, 'I just love colors, and I wanted to express the colors on the trains and for people to see it and be happy that they saw this'.[64] Letters' embryonic decoration had also been embraced by early Philadelphia writers of the late 1960s and early 1970s, for example, Cornbread (using the crown), Cool Earl (incorporating a crown and a face), Kool Klepto Kidd (again using the crown), Neptune (incorporating a pitchfork and a planet), Joe Cool (using the crown and the peace sign), and King Smooth (using again the crown).[65]

Thus, in the early stages of graffiti in New York (and Philadelphia) writers painted and drew just straight non-stylish letters with no particular decoration. Then many progressed to bigger letters with different degrees of thickness – and after that they started adding outlines and dimension around them, for example, by inserting shadows and making them look tridimensional.[66] Such an evolution was also facilitated by the invention of different types of caps for spraycans, which allowed for fine lines, broad lines, and different textures, which in turn permitted artists to unleash their creativity further, leading to the creation of new and different styles. The passage from skinny caps to fat caps was particularly important.[67] Throughout the years, the advent of fat caps (which make lines thicker) and the production of differentiated spraycans for writers (and at a later stage for street artists as well) with a variety of

[60] Jack Stewart, *Graffiti Kings: New York City Mass Transit Art of the 1970s* (Abrams 2009) 20.
[61] Roger Gastman and Caleb Neelon, *History of American Graffiti* (Collins Design 2011) 74.
[62] Karla Murray, *Broken Windows: Graffiti NYC* (Gingko Press 2009) 86.
[63] Gastman, above fn. 59, 72, 74.
[64] Gastman, above fn. 59, 122.
[65] Gastman, above fn. 59, 224.
[66] Murray, above fn. 62, 86.
[67] Castleman, above fn. 59, 64.

paint colours available, enhanced cans' effects and had a lasting impact on writing styles, further spurring experimentation and innovation.[68] These tools certainly proved important. Yet, it was also the ingenuity of writers that brought about stylistic changes in graffiti writing. Young writers started adding their creative idea to spray-paint, such as figuring out that nozzles from other household products were also a great tool to add artistic effects to their works.[69]

The high degree of originality graffiti can reach is confirmed by the different styles that have been developed over the years, each of them a reflection of the creative process of the writers who designed and worked on them. This has been the case from the very beginning. An important role in the development of graffiti as a whole, in both New York and Philadelphia, was played by the fact that styles greatly varied from neighbourhood to neighbourhood: the cross-contamination between writers' style across the boroughs,[70] and often the rivalries that played out between them, led to the birth of hybrids that further bolstered and enriched the arsenal available to writers. For example, Philadelphia's writers have been known for writing very high letters,[71] and even within the city different styles developed and spread between the North, West, and South parts of the town.[72] Interesting academic research was conducted in the early 1970s by Dr. Julie Reich Mackey from Philadelphia's Moore College of Art, after she noticed the wall writing that had started to appear in the streets. She analysed and categorised the many writing styles that had already spawned at the time, marking their respective distinctive features. There was the 'Cornbread' tag, a totally plain style that she considered to be the 'classic' one. Another style was 'baroque', as it offered a balance in style and writing design. Then she also noted that there was an even more florid style which employed images such as crowns, more cursive elements, and a visual complexity unknown to the precedent two – a style that she dubbed 'rococo'. And finally there was an almost unreadable style which she labelled 'decadent'.[73]

Philadelphia certainly did play a role in the artistic development of graffiti. Also, writing on urban surfaces was not limited to the East Coast. As mentioned in the previous chapter, Los Angeles has been home to the Cholo graffiti, a lettering style developed by Latino gangs and rooted in Mexican culture, dating back to the 1930s. Over the years, this style has evolved into an art form (e.g. see the iconic skulls painted by Chaz Bojorquez), borrowing from the gothic style as well as Mayan and Aztecan visual arts. But obviously what New York eventually managed to achieve cannot be matched by any other city. New York writers developed over the years a number of styles that differ from one another. Take the Manhattan style,

68 Bofkin, above fn. 33, 181.
69 Gastman, above fn. 59, 23.
70 Cooper, above fn. 20, 71.
71 Stephen Powers, *The Art of Getting Over: Graffiti at the Millennium* (St. Martin's Press 1999) 18.
72 Gastman, above fn. 59, 314–316.
73 On the research carried out by Dr. Julie Reich Mackey see Gastman, above fn. 59, 328.

invented and subsequently brought to New York by Philadelphia writer Topcat, who in turn claims to have learned it from Cornbread. As noted by Christian Acker,[74] around 1971 or 1972 Topcat moved from Philadelphia to 126th Street in Manhattan and brought with him the Gangster style which consisted of blocky square and long letters that stood on little platform alongside tall prints and wickets. By mixing the style of Philadelphia Gangster prints with the New York practice of adding the street number where the writer lived, the Manhattan Style was thus born – which shortly thereafter started to be called the Broadway Elegant style. This style employed loud colours and flames, and drew the outline of its aggressive characters to reinforce the shape of its letters.[75] Several iterations were later developed such as the employment of soft bubble letters (as mentioned), which was greatly appreciated by the art crowd: these letters were rounded and 'puffy', meaning inflated in appearance. The most famous representative of this style was Phase 2 from the Bronx.

The list of the different New York styles is long, and includes:

- Candy cane letters, developed by Hondo 1;
- Polska dot style, started by Super Kool 223;
- 3D letter style, that is, block letters with a three-dimensional appearance, first used by Pistol I, who painted his name in red and white and partially outlined it with a blue band that gave it a 3D appearance;[76]
- Shadow 3D, using whole families of colours and ending up in a three-dimensional effect so realistic that 'it looks like you could pull it right off the train';[77]
- Marshmallow style, pioneered (again) by Super Kool 223 and other writers;[78]
- Brooklyn style, that is, a Pseudo-Celtic style which makes great use of free-flowing letters, embellished with hearts, arrows, swirls,[79] and spirals.[80]

Yet, the most acclaimed and successful style is certainly the Wild Style, whose creation and development is attributed to Bronx writer Tracy 168 and originated in that borough. It was initially known as mechanical lettering, a name frequently still employed today. Wild Style incorporates several different innovations from prior styles, such as twisted, fractured, or crumbled letters; penetrating arrows; bars; and extensions. It requires both a great level of experience and a high degree of artistic skills to be correctly carried out.[81] As a result of the frequent and structural use of interlocking and interconnecting letters, it is difficult to read, especially from outside the subculture.

74 Acker, above fn. 16, 97.
75 Nelli, above fn. 18, 30.
76 Castleman, above fn. 59, 25, 56.
77 Ibidem, above fn. 59, 64.
78 Stewart, above fn. 60, 112.
79 Castleman, above fn. 59, 55.
80 Nelli, above fn. 18, 30.
81 Austin, above fn. 42, 112.

Because of the extremely complex configuration and interconnection of lettering, Wild Style recalls the Celtic interlaces (as the Brooklyn style): the letters are closely intertwined with one another, each of them forming an integral part of the next one, to the extent that it becomes difficult to ascertain where one ends and the other begins.[82] Letters are here interconnected so that each of them forms an integral part of the next, with arrows being an important element and writers being obsessed with the idea of movement and flow. In other words, the letters look like they are moving or even dancing,[83] with some of them looking like they are hitting each other.[84] These features have led this style to gradually become highly abstractive, and have spurred comparisons with established artistic movements such as cubism.[85] Wild Style has also been constantly adapted over the decades, in the US and beyond. A particularly relevant variation is the so-called computer rock style developed by New York writer Kase 2, a form of Wild Style where letters are broken into boxes and scrambled, thus presenting dynamic movement and offering an extremely aesthetically pleasing look.

### *Intersection with Calligraphy and Typography*

We have seen that graffiti writing is an art movement that revolves around the formation and development of letters, a sort of modern hieroglyphics.[86] As such, it inevitably borrows from, and intertwines with, calligraphy and typography.[87] Indeed, as we have just seen, graffiti is all about the artistic use of letters. As Snyder rightly puts it: 'the meaning of words actually meant very little as writers were more interested in the aesthetics of letters'.[88] This is even more evident in *calligraffiti*,[89] an art form practiced both in studio and in the street, which combine calligraphy, typography, and modern graffiti.

The comparison with typefaces and fonts makes sense. Like fonts which enrich language by allowing people to send subtle messages not carried in the text itself, but still capable of influencing it, graffiti letters convey an artistic message which goes beyond the textuality of the tag, throw-up, or piece. US writer Jurne, interviewed

82 Janice Rhan, *Painting without Permission: Hip-Hop Graffiti Subculture* (Praeger 2002) 14.

83 Rhan, above fn. 82, 14.

84 Miller, above fn. 7, 39.

85 Maia Morgan Wells, 'Graffiti, Street Art, and the Evolution of the Art Market', in Ross, above fn. 13, 465. For writers who have focused on extremely abstract graffiti style see Futura 2000, Rammellzee, Blade, Jon One in the old days, and KR more recently, as also noted by Cedar Lewisohn, *Abstract Graffiti* (Merrell 2011) 24, 106, 112.

86 Gregory Snyder, *Graffiti Lives: Beyond the Tag in New York's Urban Underground* (NYU Press 2009) 68.

87 Cedar Lewisohn, *Street Art: The Graffiti Revolution* (Tate Modern Publishing 2009) 21. For a book focusing on the many shapes graffiti letters may take, see Claudine Walde, Street Fonts – Graffiti Alphabets from Around the World (Thames & Hudson: London 2011).

88 Gregory Snyder, 'Graffiti and the Subculture Career', in Ross, above fn. 13, 198.

89 Miller, above fn. 7, 85.

by Rafael Schacter for his book *Ornament and Order: Graffiti, Street Art and the Parergon*, best expresses this by claiming that 'this use of the letterform aimed to eclipse the traditional idea of type as merely functional and return to the calligraphic understanding of its potential power and beauty'.[90] Likewise, US writer and muralist Gabriel Corti explained to me that making lettering unreadable has to do with 'artistic and aesthetic exploration and seeing how far you can twist your lettering, how wild you can make it or if you can intertwine it in a certain way. You can make lettering unreadable by design or color pallet, so if you use a monochromatic pallet, you can really hide lettering. Writers seek to explore how far they can take their lettering'. Gabriel Corti also expanded on how his career started: 'I've always been a fan of lettering as I've a degree in graphic design and I love typography and stuff like that ever since I was a little kid'. Also, he directly linked the originality of his lettering style to his studies in typography: '[these studies] have helped me with the understanding of the basics and certain styles of writing, like your baselines and how far you want to pull up a letter or how down you put it, establishing visual balance like adding quotes on one end and adding stars on the other so it looks more balanced, adding a line to show emphasis and stuff like that'. The importance of studies in typography is stressed by several other writers. Ryze, a writer from Boston cited in the book *History of American Graffiti* by Roger Gastman and Caleb Neelon, reminds us that he 'took classes in Celtic lettering at the Cambridge Center for Adult Education […] specifically to try and do more of that in my letters'.[91]

The encounter between writing cultures and typography also emerges clearly in the *Pichacao* and *Grapixo* practices in Brazil.[92] The former is a lettering style native to São Paulo, with tags being created on walls using buckets of latex paint and three-inch paint rollers – which generates letters of uniform width.[93] The latter is a purely Brazilian writing style based on the concept of multi-coloured pieces and mixed with an angular typographical style.[94] Also, in Argentina the fileteado tango-style lettering has flourished, mixing fileteado fonts (inspired from 'tangueros art') with pure graffiti.[95]

The typography comparison is also useful to highlight once again the artistic element of graffiti lettering, and accordingly its copyrightability. Indeed, typo art is an accepted and appreciated form of art – it is the art of making and decorating letters, which is also exactly what writers do. And, importantly for our analysis, typefaces can attract copyright or other forms of intellectual property protection, at least in some countries like the UK.[96] There is even an international treaty which protects

90 Rafael Schacter, *Ornament and Order: Graffiti, Street Art and the Parergon* (Ashgate 2014) 65.

91 Gastman and Neelon, above fn. 61, 280.

92 On this see Tristan Manco, *Graffiti Brazil* (Thames & Hudson 2005) 10.

93 Gottlieb, above fn. 21, 99.

94 Manco, above fn. 92, 34.

95 Matt Fox-Tucker and Guilherme Zauith, *Textura Dos: Buenos Aires Street Art* (Mark Batty 2010) 13.

96 On this debate see Nicole A. Grant, 'Outlawed Art: Finding a Home for Graffiti in Copyright Law' (2012), 24, http://ssrn.com/abstract=2030514.

the artistic elements of typefaces. It is the Vienna Agreement for the Protection of Typefaces and their International Deposit, signed in 1973 by twelve countries, including the UK, Germany, France, Italy, and the Netherlands (though it never entered into force).[97] It provides that typefaces should be protected by either copyright or industrial design law, or a sui generis right, with such protection being limited to their artistic and aesthetic features, excluding any functional elements – namely, those elements which allow people to actually read the letters. Similarly, letters painted by writers have often strong non-functional and artistic elements, which go beyond serving the neutral function of representing the letters themselves. As has been pointed out, copyright should be made available when the graffiti lettering consists not only of alphanumeric elements, but is also elaborate, personalized, and extravagant enough to be perceived and appreciated as an artistic endeavour rather than just letters of the alphabet.[98] After all, as we have seen, many writers also believe that tags are more than just a sequence of letters. A writer called Drone was reported as noting, 'I try to look at a tag as more of a mark in itself. Not really a combination of individual letters but more like a script'.[99]

## *Readability and Originality*

As mentioned, graffiti art is capable of making the letters unreadable (especially to members of the general public who are outside the subculture) as opposed to forms of street art – for example, memorial murals always include readable words for obvious reasons. With that said, one may say that the more unreadable a graffiti piece is, with interlocked and convoluted letters, the more original and creative it is. This belief is based on the assumption that letters which are deconstructed to the point of no longer serving the function they normally serve (i.e. the ability of being read), and therefore are partially or totally abstract, can unleash all their artistic potential and be considered highly original, including for copyright purposes. On the face of it, this argument may make sense. Yet, this is not what all writers believe.

Indeed, Bogotá writer Drop explained to me during our encounter in the Colombian capital that the level of artistic style and originality of graffiti lettering does not and should not depend on the readability of the letter, but on other factors. He added:

> Some people, once they see graffiti, they jump on the fence of all these wild styles and all these colorful things and they think it looks cool because it is visually stimulating, but to the trained eye it's not flowing or even stylish. Sometimes with

97 See in particular Art. 2(i)(c) of the Vienna Agreement for the Protection of Type Faces and Their International Deposit and Protocol Concerning the Term of Protection, June 12, 1973, Records of the Vienna Diplomatic Conference on the Protection of Typefaces 1973, at 10 (W.I.P.O. 1980).

98 Grant, above fn. 96, 23.

99 Acker, above fn. 16, 163.

> the simple things you can really tell the trajectory of the artist just by how clean and how crisp his lettering is and that is something that you can't fake or copy. You can tell that he has put years into learning and studying his craft and you just can't fake this. That's why I like to look at pieces like this and say, yes, they know how to paint but do they really know their letters, like do they know how to form their letters correctly – not just doing it to make their art look cool and unreadable? I have always had this idea of very straight, very big bold letters in my tags, something that is legible and stylish at the same time.

Serk, another New York writer I talked to, is on the same page: 'my tag SERK is original, I'm using an organic representation, it's legible and original'. Legibility and originality are thus not necessarily mutually exclusive. It is also clear that not all writers want to keep the graffiti language secret and internal, a key aspect of graffiti I mentioned in the previous chapter. By making their letters legible, some writers want to reach wider audiences, beyond the subculture. This was confirmed to me by Kasso, a writer and muralist I interviewed in Trenton, New Jersey: 'Kasso [diminutive form of Picasso] is my tag, it's readable, pretty legible, I want people to know who I am. Before my tag was unreadable, but since they started not crediting me, I started doing it readable. I want people to know exactly who I am when they see my work. I made sure that my name is very legible when you read it because I don't want anybody getting confused with who did what'.[100]

## COMPETITION, MENTORING, AND *BITING*

Graffiti lettering has always been an art form spurred by competition – a fierce one. The graffiti subculture is primarily a meritocracy[101] which respects boldness and dedication[102] and strives for perfection and style. Writers battle, and they do it *artistically*. In her 2001 book *The Graffiti Subculture: Youth, Masculinity and Identity in London and New York*, Nancy Macdonald reminds us that '[s]tyle is [a] centrally important part of graffiti. The way you write your name, the letters you use, their shape, flow and form, colours you choose, all these things go into making a writer's "style". And other writers will judge you, often harshly, on this basis'.[103] Writers must consistently meet a certain standard of quality to avoid being forced to leave, or be booted from, their crews if the quality of their tagging or piecing styles falls below accepted standards.[104] As noted by Martha Cooper and Henry Chalfant in *Subway Art*, writers from the Bronx, Manhattan, and Brooklyn simultaneously

[100] The point that graffiti and street art in general can be creative even where works are produced in a simple and not intricate way also emerged in my interview with New York artist, and former writer, KR. He said, '[S]tyle is a relative concept – having style does not mean being complicated'.

[101] Gregory Snyder, Graffiti and the Subculture Career, in Ross, above fn. 13, 206.

[102] Bofkin, above fn. 33, 262.

[103] Macdonald, above fn. 47, 71.

[104] Gomez, The Writing on Our Walls: Finding Solutions through Distinguishing Graffiti Art from Graffiti Vandalism (1993) *University of Michigan Journal of Law Reform*, 646.

intensified their efforts to keep up competing.[105] Writers themselves confirm that. Lady Pink, cited by Henry Chalfant and Sacha Jenkins in their book *Training Days: The Subway Artists Then and Now*, notes that 'it's dark, your friends are pressuring you, and people who are better are looking at your art and criticising it. It's not the nice critique that the movies get. Kids are very cruel. They laugh at you, point, and call you all kinds of names. They're particularly cruel if you fail, so the pressure to do something worthwhile is immense'.[106]

Writers are aware that they need to compete hard to get up and improve their style. This has always been an environment where artistic exploration and competition are the drivers.[107] The pioneering New York experience epitomises this, having produced a subculture environment where the evolution of style resulted from aesthetic battles in which writers competed for the title of king.[108] New York writer Sonic, cited by Karla Murray in her 2009 book *Broken Windows: Graffiti NYC*, expands on this point: 'Battling is what makes graffiti evolve and go to another level. It's what keeps it going. If there was no competition, then no one would have developed different styles and kept it going further and further'.[109] Similarly, as reported by Devon Brewer and Marc Miller in a seminal 1990 article, Seattle-based writer Stash Five reminds that '[t]he more disciplined and complex your individual style is, the more you have to beat your competition. When your piece is up, another writer is going to do better than you. So your letters are the weapons to kill your competitors' letters'.[110] Competition and constructive rivalries have always existed within the graffiti communities, including after the 1970s and 1980s. Writers often tell each other what can be bettered, and it is this feature which feeds the competitive spirit of the subculture.[111] The *5Pointz* experience in New York is a testament to that. Its mastermind and curator, Meres One, told me in an interview in his Brooklyn house that *5Pointz* was 'a very competitive environment'.

Tough competition inevitably brings with it a desire, and a need, to distinguish one's lettering style from that of others. As mentioned, this has been a feature of the graffiti subculture from the very beginning in New York. In those years, as pointed out earlier in this chapter, writers initially (and gradually) added further elements to the simple linear wall writing, such as stylish arrows, crowns, curves, twists, geometrical or symmetrical elements,[112] and later more sophisticated figurative elements. As New York writer Cliff says in *New York Graffiti Experience*, a 1976 short film

[105] Martha Cooper and Henry Chalfant, Subway Art (Thames & Hudson, 1984) 17.
[106] Chalfant and Jenkins, above fn. 2, 97.
[107] Gomez, above fn. 104, 646.
[108] Miller, above fn. 7, 4.
[109] Murray, above fn. 62, 176.
[110] Devon Brewer and Marc Miller, 'Bombing and Burning: The Social Organization and Values of Hip Hop Graffiti Writers and Implications for Policy' (1990) 11(4) *Deviant Behavior*, 358.
[111] Macdonald, above fn. 47, 70–71.
[112] See also Iljadica, above fn. 22, 150.

directed by Fenton Lawless, '[Y]ou have to be recognized, this is the highest thing'. Researchers have analysed this aspect in depth. Jack Stewart explained that when a new letter style appeared on a New York subway train, writers with that particular letter in their name were prompted to design a variation of it.[113]

Several writers I interviewed confirmed this feature of graffiti. Cey Adams, a former New York writer from the 1970s and 1980s and now a visual artist and graphic designer, told me in his studio in New Jersey that to establish themselves, writers need to have a distinctive style. From the early 1970s, when he first got into graffiti, he was well aware of the idea that it was something unique and very specific and original. He further noted that 'graffiti artists want to be unique and distinct. I wanted my signature to be the same all the time, so that people could distinguish me from somebody else. Unlike any kind of art, the tag is just the way to separate yourself from the other. You want to be recognizable'. Similarly, New York writer Hoacs commented during our conversation that 'to make the piece look different, more stylish, I try different colors, angles, I try to do different things'.

Another peculiar aspect of the graffiti subculture is the older writers' propensity to mentor and take younger writers under their wings. Graffiti communities have constantly produced an apprentice culture which promotes collaboration and creativity.[114] Craig Castleman, writing about New York's early writers, reminds us that 'experienced writers have often one or more young protégés they bring along, and they enjoy the role of teacher and pride themselves when their "students" succeed, and take pleasure in receiving admiration and respect from them'.[115] Likewise, Richard Lachmann comments that young kids to mentor are like 'little brothers' as they show respect, while mentors gain satisfaction, and gratification for their skills, from sharing their own style and all they know about writing.[116] A very 'pedagogical' writer was certainly Kase 2, who contributed extensively to the evolution of graffiti style in New York in the 1970s and 1980s. He had a natural talent for mentorship, having taught and shaped younger writers such as Phade, Nome, Moet, Bern, Sento, and Ease.[117] Some of my interviewees also confirmed this pedagogic side of graffiti (and street art). This is the case for New York writers and artists Reskew, David Chino, and Andre Trenier. Reskew noted during our conversation that he regularly organises and gives youngsters graffiti art tutorials, even via his own YouTube channel, to teach basic lettering techniques and to encourage his students to improve their skills. David Chino pointed out that he "was mentored by an old graffiti writer".

[113] Stewart, above fn. 60, 64.

[114] See also Waclawek, above fn. 8, 26.

[115] Castleman, above fn. 59, 24. On the mentoring process within this subculture, see also Camille Lannert 'The Perpetuation of Graffiti Art Subculture' (2015) 1(5) *Butler Journal of Undergraduate Research*, 55–56.

[116] Richard Lachmann, 'Graffiti as Career and Ideology' (1988) 2(94) *The American Journal of Sociology*, 234.

[117] Alan Ket, *Urban Art Legends* (Lom Art 2015).

There is apprenticeship in this subculture'. And Andre Trenier commented that 'there is a sort of apprenticeship where somebody that is a master takes others under his wings and teaches them style and know the ways of writing'. These words are echoed by Damien Mitchell. He pointed out during our conversation that 'I also teach street art and graffiti techniques, especially to disadvantaged kids. I do that also because graffiti and street art had not been officially taught [in art schools]'. It is also interesting to highlight the academic activity of the Spanish writer Javier Abarca, whom I talked to at the Tag Conference in Amsterdam in 2018, an event which focused on the history and culture of wall tagging. Abarca is a graffiti writer, researcher, and educator – and teaches classes on street art and graffiti.

Finally, it should be mentioned how graffiti communities deal with disputes between writers over imitation of tags, throw-ups, and pieces. As we will see more in depth in Chapter 6, controversies are not rare, and accusations of copying styles and details – what in these communities is defined as *biting* – are not uncommon. Many writers do care about being original and – as we will see more in depth in the next and last chapters of this book – are annoyed when others imitate their works. Ferrell interestingly noted that the phenomenon of *biting* reveals situations where the boundaries of personal and collective style are disputed, and the authenticity and legitimacy of a writer's style turn into a point of contention amongst other writers in the community.[118] As Ferrell further puts it, to accuse a writer of imitating the style of a peer is to complain about the writer's willingness or ability to innovate; and in order to be really original, writers need to develop their own style that is not directly appropriated from other writers' innovation. Also, *biters* are often deemed to be thieves in much the same way as traditional fine artists accuse imitators of copyright infringement[119] (although some writers have a more tolerant opinion on this point, as we will see in the next chapter). This puts pressure on them to make their style more complex, both to improve their reputation within the scene and to discourage other writers from copying.[120] Such features have always been the essence of being a writer, as has also been confirmed by Tracy 168, who was reported as noting that 'when you've got enough balls to waste paint and try something new, that's when you're a writer'.[121]

118 Ferrell, above fn. 58, 85.
119 Ferrell, above fn. 58, 86.
120 Cooper and Chalfant, above fn. 105, 71.
121 Cooper and Chalfant, above fn. 105, 80.

# 3

# Copyright within Street Art and Graffiti Circles

Are street artists and writers interested in copyright? Would they take a copyright-based suit if someone exploits or anyway copies one of their works? The chapter focuses on these issues, highlighting the opinions of several practitioners of these forms of art I met during my ethnographic research.

The point has sometimes been made that most street artists and writers show no interest in copyright and in general in legal remedies as a tool to resolve disputes. After all, this is what the most famous street artist in the world, Banksy, once stated. In the introductory page of his 2005 book *Wall and Piece* he famously wrote that 'copyright is for losers'. He also noted in an interview for *The Sunday Times*: 'I certainly don't see money from the T-shirts, mugs and greeting cards. My lawyer calls me "the most infringed artist alive" and wants me to do something about it. … [but] if you have built a reputation on having a casual attitude towards property ownership, it seems a bit bad-mannered to kick off about copyright law'.[1]

It seems, however, that the days of the mysterious artist's dislike for intellectual property are long gone, as he has recently started taking legal actions (via his organisation, Pest Control) to defend his trademarks.[2] Indeed, he won a case of unauthorised

[1] Eleanor Mills, 'Banksy Stars in the World's "First Street Art's Disaster Movie"' (28 February 2010) *The Sunday Times*.

[2] Banksy is not the only artist within the street art community who enforces rights in brands. Futura 2000 has also brought a legal action in California against clothing and footwear company The North Face (*Leonard McGurr (Futura) v. The North Face Apparel Corp et al.*, US District Court for the Central District of California, No 2:21-cv-00269). In January 2021 the former sued the latter, claiming that the company had appropriated his famous stylized atom, which had routinely appeared in his street and studio artworks, to launch a new line curiously called Future-light. The case was settled in 2022. For other cases where street artists have enforced rights in brands see *Jason Williams et al. v. Roberto Cavalli, S.p.A. et al.* Docket No. 2:14-cv-06659 (C.D. Cal. Aug. 25, 2014), where Reyes claimed that his signature elements had been misappropriated by fashion company Cavalli; *Joseph Tierney v. Moschino S.p.A. et al.* Docket No. 2:15-cv-05900 (C.D. Cal. Aug. 05, 2015), where Rime claimed that fashion company Moschino had falsely used his art pseudonym, trade name, and professional signature on various products; *Michael Wild Style Tracy v. Pow Wow Production*, 302 A.D.2d 211 (N.Y. App. Div. 2003), where Tracy 168, the originator of the Wild Style lettering in New York, unsuccessfully claimed that the filmmakers of the *Wild Style* documentary had infringed his alleged trademark rights over such term. The court found that Tracy 168

merchandising in Italy in 2019[3] and has registered many trademarks incorporating his art (but he recently lost several EU trademarks incorporating some of his famous artworks, namely the 'Flower Thrower',[4] 'Raining Girl',[5] and 'Sonar Rat').[6] In November 2022 he also accused fashion retailer Guess of exploiting his art without authorisation – in fact, he posted a picture of a Central London Guess store showcasing clothes bearing his works, and provocatively invited shoplifters to attack it: 'They've helped themselves to my artwork without asking, how can it be wrong for you to do the same to their clothes?'[7] Moreover, in 2022 Banksy's organisation, Pest Control, updated its website by adding a very eloquent disclaimer: 'Saying "*Banksy wrote* **copyright is for losers** *in his book*" doesn't give you free rein to misrepresent the artist and commit fraud. We checked'.

## 'IT HAPPENS ALL THE TIME!'

What about less famous writers and artists? What emerges from my interviews is that there is a growing interest in copyright as a possible instrument to fight the exploitation of these art forms. Such interest is certainly spurred by episodes of unauthorised appropriation of the artworks, especially for commercial purposes. Writers and artists seem used to such phenomenon, as many of them told me: 'It happens all the time!' Indeed, they often feel that their art is at risk of being appropriated. This emerged in my conversation with William Kasso, for example. He noted that 'artists, you know, we paint predominantly on the street; we're taken advantage of, you know? Especially artists that paint on the street like myself'.

The following are just a few examples of the many appropriation incidents I have been made aware by my informants.

Elle – a female New York street artist I talked to in a café in Brooklyn – told me: 'that has actually happened to me once. Someone made up this name like "Ellegangster", putting these naked women all over with like bunny ears. And it sort of looked like my art. And everyone started texting and tagging me and I was

had failed to prove that he held a valid trademark, that the trademark itself was not generic, and that it was used in connection with products and services. For an analysis of arguments in favour of protecting street and graffiti artworks under trademark law, see Danielle Crinnion, 'Get Your Own Street Cred: An Argument for Trademark Protection for Street Art' (2017) 58 *Boston College Law Review*.

3 *Pest Control Office Ltd v. 24 Ore Cultura S.r.l.*, R.G. 52442/2018, Milan Court's decision of 14 January 2019.

4 *Full Colour Black Limited v. Pest Control Office Limited*, Cancellation No. C 33 843, Cancellation Division of the European Union Intellectual Property Office, decision of 14 September 2020.

5 *Full Colour Black Limited v. Pest Control Office Limited*, Cancellation No. C 39 872, Cancellation Division of the European Union Intellectual Property Office, decision of 18 June 2021.

6 *Full Colour Black Limited v. Pest Control Office Limited*, Cancellation No. C 40 001, Cancellation Division of the European Union Intellectual Property Office, decision of 18 June 2021.

7 Lydia Chantler Hicks, 'Banksy Hits Out at Guess on Regent Street for Using His Artwork "without Permission"', (18 November 2022) *Evening Standard*. On this case see also Enrico Bonadio, Banksy's copyright battle with Guess anonymity shouldn't compromise his legal rights, The Conversation, 25 November 2022.

like "What is this shit"? I still don't know who it was, but it was really annoying. So, I started posting [on social media] that "this is not my work and this is not cool"'. Likewise, Laser 3.14, a Dutch street poet who paints socio-critical messages on temporary surfaces such as construction site hoardings, said to me that 'a big brand used my work on the cover of something. It was a picture taken from the street, manipulated in photoshop and placed on the cover of a dictionary without my permission'.

Artworks placed in the street are also sometimes incorporated into virtual and augmented reality support or in general digital platforms, without authorisation and acknowledgment.[8] Anjl, an artist I met at the Cypher Art Community Centre in the Staten Island borough of New York, found out that two murals she had painted were displayed as 'Points of Interest' in the popular PokemonGo mobile game. She told me: 'I personally never had my work on clothing, but I have a couple of walls painted in Brooklyn and I realized that they were shown on this Pokemon game. It's a game and I think that I'm going to reach out to them about that. [...] They didn't ask for my permission and at least they could have put my name up there or my Instagram instead of just "Graffiti Mural" because that's me and my work'. New York artist Murrz, an illustrator and painter who also places art in the public environment, is aware of similar experiences. She said to me in a conversation we had in a Brooklyn café: 'there's an app called the "graffiti maker app" that is using images from legend graffiti writers and I'm sure that they didn't ask them for permission'.

Writers are also exposed to misappropriation of their works. William Cordero, aka Bill Blast, a New York writer and muralist active from the 1980s, whom I met at a café in Washington Heights (the uppermost part of Manhattan), said to me: 'one time I was walking down Manhattan and I saw someone with jeans with the "Sky's the limit" on the side of the jeans ["Sky's the limit" is one of his most famous murals]. It was like "Wow, who created that and who made it into clothes without letting me know?" Also, you can go down to a museum's gift shop where you have like magnets catalogues postcards and books and your stuff is in and you had no idea that this was being done. So yeah, it's annoying because someone is making money out of it'.

Likewise, Mastro, a New York writer I met in a Brooklyn café, explained to me: '[y]ou get some creative type who owns like a clothing company or a lifestyle brand seeing something really cool, but not knowing how to contact the maker of this cool piece. Or if they contact the maker they go like "Oh we'd like to commission you to do this for us" when they realise that it costs too much, they simply decide to steal it'. Another New York writer, Chino, noted in an interview with me that one of his

8 Enrico Bonadio – Siri-Helen Egeland, 'Street and Graffiti Art between Augmented Reality and Artificial Intelligence: A Copyright Perspective', *University of St. Thomas Law Journal*, Vol. 18, No. 3, 2022.

pieces was used without authorisation by a clothing company, and that he complained by sending letters and starting a lawsuit – which turned out to be the right form of reaction, as 'they admitted they were wrong and apologised'. Chino also experienced an analogous incident with another small clothing company. After he sent them a letter, they immediately stopped using his artwork. A similar story was told to me by London writer Oker, who was disappointed when he found out that two famous painters had included his tag in their canvas without his permission. New York writer Reskew had the same feeling. He told me during our conversation: 'I've seen an artist using an image of my work on paintings he was selling at a Christmas market and that made me upset'. Likewise, New York street and studio artist Lamkat told me in our interview in Brooklyn that 'when someone exploits your artwork and makes money out of it without asking your permission – it hurts'.

These conversations with street artists and writers confirm that these forms of art are vulnerable to unauthorised exploitation – such vulnerability coming from the fact that the artworks are created and placed in the public space, where they can easily be photographed and then digitally reproduced. They also reveal disappointment on the part of those who create these works.[9] Art projects have also revolved around, and voiced criticism about, this phenomenon. It is worthwhile to highlight a project masterminded by Eko, an artist based in the French city of Pau. Such project consisted of placing stickers, posters, and other artworks in the street incorporating the words 'don't copy me', a hilarious protest against the imitation of street art and corporate appropriation.[10]

Hearing about imitation and appropriation from my informants did not come as a big surprise to me. Indeed, there has been in recent years a spike in copyright-based complaints and legal actions brought by writers and street artists, especially in the US against corporations which tried to exploit their art. For example, in 2016 the fiancée of the deceased former New York graffiti writer Dash Snow sued the fast-food giant McDonald's, as the latter had incorporated and reproduced the writer's stylish signature on several of its restaurants' walls.[11] Similar complaints and objections

9 While many artists and writers are annoyed by the unauthorised use of their works, a few of them seem to some extent to like such appropriation, sometimes feeling flattered and thus having mixed feelings. For example, CB23, a sticker artist I met in Brooklyn, made clear that he may also be happy if his work is used, especially if such use gives him visibility: 'it would be ok if a TV show includes my art, honestly I often watch TV shows, and wait for a sticker of mine to come out'. New York writer Reskew has a similar opinion. He noted: 'Yes, I'd be angry [about unauthorised commercial exploitation], and conflictingly pleased to see my work being seen by the masses. But mostly angry'. The same goes for Joel Artista, a muralist whom I met in Brooklyn ('but you know, you also can get a lot of free publicity. I mean, people are going to be sharing your work, especially in today's age of social media, Instagram and all these things. So, people will be basically promoting you every time they post it') and the above mentioned London writer Oker, who also seems to have mixed feelings ('and at the end of the day, it's kind of promotion to a certain extent').

10 Tristan Manco, *Street Logos* (Thames and Hudson 2004), 122–123.

11 *Jade Berreau v. McDonald's Corporation et al.*, 2:16-cv-07394 (Central District of California). Specifically, in 2016 the administrator of the estate of the late artist Dash Snow filed a complaint

were also brought by Ahol,[12] Revok,[13] Reyes Steel, and (again) Revok,[14] as well as Rime,[15] Smash 137,[16] Jeff Soto and Max Gramajo, James Lewis, Daniel Bombardier,[17]

against McDonald's alleging, inter alia, that the restaurant chain had violated Snow's copyright by incorporating his graffiti signature (a throw-up) on some of its restaurants' walls, without authorisation (amongst other grounds). The court dismissed the case due to lack of jurisdiction.

12 *Anasagasti v. American Eagle Outfitters, Inc.*, 1:14-cv-05618 (New York Southern District Court). In 2014 David Asanagasti, a Miami-based artist known as Ahol Sniffs Glue, found out that the fashion retailer giant American Eagle Outfitter had launched an unauthorised worldwide advertising campaign that featured two of his most iconic murals. The artworks appeared not only on the company's website but also on its social media platforms, billboards, advertisements, and in-store displays. Asanagasti sued American Eagle Outfitter for copyright infringement, amongst other grounds, but the case was later settled. See also Enrico Bonadio, Graffiti copyright battles pitch artists against advertisers, The Conversation, 9 August 2014.

13 *H&M Hennes and Mauritz GBC, and H&M Hennes and Mauritz L.P. v. Jason Williams a/k/a Revok*, Case 1:18-cv-01490 (New York Eastern District). The case was filed in early 2018 by H&M following an objection made by the artist's lawyer, Jason Williams, known as Revok. In 2017 the Swedish fashion retailer had launched an advertisement campaign which featured a video taken on an outdoor handball court in Brooklyn. The video incorporated an unauthorised mural painted by the artist. After his lawyer sent H&M a cease-and-desist letter claiming copyright infringement, H&M filed a complaint against Revok seeking a declaratory judgement that the artist did not own a valid copyright over the illegally created artwork. The case was subsequently settled.

14 *Jason Williams et al. v. Roberto Cavalli, S.p.A. et al.*, Docket No. 2:14-cv-06659 (C.D. Cal. Aug 25, 2014). This case was started by US artists Reyes, Steel, and Revok. Jason Williams (Revok), Victor Chapa (Reyes), and Jeffrey Rubin (Steel) had collectively painted a legal mural in the Mission district in San Francisco. In 2014, Italian fashion company Roberto Cavalli S.p.A. launched a so-called Graffiti collection, including products incorporating parts of the artists' mural. Cavalli had also superimposed its own brand in spray-paint over the artwork, as if it were part of the original work. The artists sued Cavalli for copyright infringement, amongst other grounds, but the case was later settled.

15 *Joseph Tierney v. Moschino S.p.A. et al.*, Docket No. 2:15-cv-05900 (C.D. Cal. Aug 05, 2015). In 2015 Joseph Tierney, known as Rime, filed a complaint against fashion house Moschino. He claimed that the latter had used his artwork 'Vandal Eyes' (a mural that he had illegally painted in Detroit back in 2012) as a decorative element of a dress used during a catwalk event. The case was subsequently settled.

16 *Adrian Falkner v. General Motors LLC*, Case 2:18-cv-00549 (C.D. Cal.) In 2014 the artist Adrian Falkner, known as Smash 137, was invited by a Detroit art gallery to paint a mural on the external wall of a parking garage. In 2016 a professional car photographer captured a picture of a Cadillac in front of Falkner's mural and sent it to General Motors' advertising agency, which then used the photo in its social media platform to advertise its cars. In January 2018 Falkner sued General Motors for copyright infringement, amongst other grounds. After the court partially dismissed General Motors' motion for summary judgement, the case was settled.

17 *Mercedes Benz USA LLC v. Jeff Soto and Maxx Gramajo*, Case 2:19-cv-10949-MOB-DRG; *Mercedes Benz USA LLC v. James Lewis*, Case No. 19–10948; *Mercedes Benz USA LLC v. Daniel Bombardier* (all Michigan Eastern District). In 2018 car manufacturer Mercedes unveiled its newest luxury SUV and, as part of its advertisement campaign, obtained a permit from the city of Detroit to photograph the car in several locations throughout the city. Mercedes posted on its social networks six separate pictures that showed in the background authorised murals painted by Mr. Soto, Gramajo, Lewis, and Bombardier. The artists threatened to sue Mercedes for copyright infringement. Subsequently the car maker filed three parallel declaratory judgement actions claiming that it had not violated the artists' copyright, and in particular that the reproduction of art permanently affixed to buildings is exempt from copyright infringement under the the Architectural Works Copyright Protection Act of 1990. The three cases were then consolidated for judicial economy, and later settled.

Keptione and DJ Rakus,[18] and Logan Hicks,[19] against companies that had used their art to decorate or promote products without authorisation.[20] Most of these disputes were settled out of court. This – again – should not be a surprise. As noted by Keo in our conversation in Brooklyn, these corporations often use graffiti and street art, especially in advertising messages, because they feel it appeals to a specific demographic,

[18] *Donald Robbins and Noar Daar v. Oakley Inc.*, Case 2:18-cv-05116-PA-KS (C.D. Cal.). As mentioned in chapter 2, in 2018 Donald Robbins, also known as Keptione, and Noar Dear, also known as DJ Rakus, sued sunglasses manufacturer Oakley for copyright infringement. The two artists alleged that Oakley had used a graffiti piece they painted in San Francisco in 2015 in an ad campaign, product catalogs, and retail stores, even superimposing its own logo over the murals. The court rejected Oakley's motion to dismiss and the case was then settled.

[19] *William Logan Hicks v. Nusret New York LLC, Saltbae NY LLC, Nusret Miami LLC, Nusret Boston LLC, Nusret Dallas LLC, Nusret Gökçe and Does-10* (Southern District of New York). In April 2021 New York artist Logan Hicks filed a lawsuit against companies related to restaurant owner Nusret Gokce alleging copyright infringement of his artwork and seeking more than $5 million in damages. Hicks claims that in 2017 he had agreed, alongside fellow artist Joe Iurato, to create murals depicting Gokce in his iconic salt-sprinkling pose to be installed at his Miami, New York, Dubai, and Doha locations. The artists kept control of the copyright but in 2020 found out that the original artworks had been reproduced and used in other locations and contexts around the world, including menus, wipes, and takeout bags and on the label for Nusret Gokce's line of seasonings. The case was later terminated.

[20] On most of the cases mentioned in this section, see also Aislinn O'Connell, 'The Writing on the Wall: Street Art and Copyright' (2019) 14(7) *Journal of Intellectual Property Law & Practice*. Other suits were brought by street artists in the US, including the following.

(i) *Hayuk v. Sony Music Entertainment et al.*, No. 1:14-cv-06659, S.D.N.Y. Aug. 19, 2014. In 2014 the muralist and studio artist Maya Hayuk, known for the bright colours and overlapping geometric shapes and rays of her pieces, sued singer and songwriter Sara Bareilles, Sony Music Entertainment, and Epic Records for copyright infringement. The artist alleged that pictures of her mural New York Chem Trails had been used without authorisation by the pop star and her advertising team. More specifically, pictures depicting the mural were used to promote Bareilles' new album and subsequent live tour. The case was later settled. Hayuk had previously taken various legal actions against Urban Outfitters and other entities that had appropriated her art.

(ii) *Miller v. Toll Brothers, Inc.*, No. 1:15-cv-00322 (E.D.N.Y. Jan 21, 2015). A real estate developer called Toll Brothers was sued by New York street and studio artist Craig Anthony Miller on grounds of copyright infringement. The former had featured prominently the latter's Elephant Mural in advertisements for luxury condos in Brooklyn. The dispute was later settled.

(iii) *Franco Fasoli et al. v. Voltage Pictures LLC et al.*, No. 2:15-cv-00889 (C.D. Cal. Feb 06, 2015). In 2015 Argentinian street artists Jaz (Franco Fasoli) and Ever (Nicolas Santiago Romero Escalada), together with Canadian artist Other (Derek Shamus Mehaffey), claimed that their mural Castillo had been used in scenes of the film *The Zero Theorem* (2013) and promotional materials for the movie without their authorisation. They started a suit in California, but the case was later settled.

(iv) *Julian Rivera v. Walmart, Ellen Degeneres*. Julian Rivera is a New York street and studio artist. His most famous work consists of a particular line drawing of a heart resembling the word 'love'. In 2019 the artist sued Walmart and US celebrity comedian and talk show host Ellen Degeneres in California for copyright infringement and unfair competition. Degeneres had recently collaborated with Walmart on a clothing line called EV1. The artist claimed that several clothing items displayed a similar version of his original design. Rivera argued that the connection between himself and a corporation like Walmart damaged his reputation and credibility as an artist. The case was ultimately settled at the end of 2019.

particularly young and urban folks. Accordingly – Keo argued – such companies are extremely reluctant to be involved in time-consuming lawsuits that carry the risk of alienating the same demographic they are trying to capture. Legal suits have also been brought in Europe, including in France (by the artists Invader[21] and Combo)[22] and Italy (by the artists Jorit[23] and Alessia Brabow).[24] And all the above mentioned are just the disputes which have attracted media attention – many others may have occurred which have not been made public. Artists' expanding attention in their legal rights is epitomised by what happened in the Brooklyn area of Bushwick in 2022, where film and TV producers had to cover up original street artworks with fake (and authorized) graffiti because they were afraid of being sued by writers for copyright infringement,[25] a behaviour which may soon become the new normal.

## GROWING INTEREST IN COPYRIGHT

As mentioned, an increasing number of street artists and writers show interest in protecting their art via copyright. Some of the US street artists I interviewed have also registered their artworks with the Copyright Office. This is the case of Lady

[21] The French artist Invader is well known for creating and placing in the street ceramic tiles modelled on the pixelated art of the eight-bit video games of the 1970s and 1980s. In 2007 Peugeot organised a showroom in Paris where plexiglass reproductions of the Invader's pieces were displayed. The artist sued both Peugeot and the company responsible for the showroom on grounds of copyright infringement. The defendants argued that they had reproduced the original figures from the videogame, not Invader's artwork. The Court of Paris found that Invader's ceramic tile mosaics were original and therefore protected by copyright but that in the specific case Peugeot had not infringed his copyright, since the reproductions exhibited at the showroom were in plexiglass. The company which managed the showroom was condemned for economic parasitism instead, as it was found that it had unfairly taken advantage of the artist's reputation (Tribunal de grande instance de Paris, Chambre civile 3, 14 November 2007, 06/12982). It is interesting to note that the court held that Invader's tiles were original despite drawing on the famous videogame image. What also gave the mosaic tiles originality – added the court – was the artist's choice of where to glue them. This point raised by the court also emerged in my interview with New Yorker and former writer Dejer, who pointed out that 'the choice of the location is part of the aesthetic effort'.

[22] *Combo v. Association LA FRANCE INSOUMISE et Jean-Luc Melenchon*, Tribunal Judiciaire de Paris, 21 January 2021. On this case see also Chapter 4; Enrico Bonadio and Olivia Jean-Baptiste, 'Can Copyright Stop Politicians from Exploiting Street Art? Combo v Jean-Luc Mélenchon before the Court of Paris' (2022) *NUART Journal*.

[23] Jorit is an Italian street artist based in Naples. In 2018 the beer company Peroni launched a new product called Birra Napoli and promoted it on social media by using Naple's attractions. One of these posts used the San Gennaro mural painted by Jorit in the Forcella area of the city (San Gennaro is the patron saint of Naples). The artist sued Peroni for copyright infringement and asked for 50,000 Euro as compensation for damages.

[24] Brabow is a Roman street artist who in 2019 anonymously placed a wheatpaste near Vittorio Emanuele II bridge in Rome. The piece was a reinterpretation of a painting of Jesus Christ made by German artist Heinrich Hofmann in the nineteenth century. I will come back to this case, which seems to be still pending at the time of writing, in Chapter 4. See also Nicole Winfield, 'Vatican Issues a Street Art Stamp, Ends Gp getting Sued' (25 May 2021) *The Washington Post*.

[25] See the Instagram post by "system-boys" account (Daily graffiti news since 2012) of August 2022.

Pink, Andre Trenier, and Logan Hicks, amongst others. Hicks, for example, said in our interview: 'I register any public works with the US copyright office so that there is no question about the copyright holder of the piece for the future'.

Who would have thought that in the New York of the 1970s, when – as we have seen – most writers could not care less about asserting copyright? Yet Zephyr, the New York writer pioneer, makes an exception.[26] He confirmed in the interview with me that in 1979 he was already aware of, and interested in, copyright and the economic potential of his art. When I asked whether he thought that copyright was suitable for protecting his works, he candidly replied, 'Yes, completely. And I've always felt it'. In fact, he said that he has 'been doing it [relying on copyright] for so long, since 1978/79', and that he was probably one of the first writers in the late 1970s who was paid to paint graffiti.

One may also speculate that some New York writers of the 1970s and 1980s would have shown more interest in copyright had they been more aware of such a legal tool. This is what Stefan Eins, the founder of the Fashion Moda gallery in the South Bronx (which he opened in 1978 and was one of the first galleries to exhibit works by writers), confirmed in a conversation we had at his home in Manhattan: '[t]hey would have been interested in getting protection, but they were not conscious about that component. In retrospect from documentation from thirty or forty years ago, they'd probably have copyrighted it, had they known'. Interest in copyright has instead been more evident since the 1970s within another outdoor artistic movement, that is, muralism. In his co-authored book *Toward a People's Art*, John Weber – a famous muralist – noted that he and his colleagues needed to give permission to whoever wanted to publish photos of their artworks and that 'to enforce this, we began copyrighting our murals in 1972. [...] Copyright gives us legal protection to ensure that correct credits are given and enables us to negotiate with publishers for either contributions towards future murals or for number of complimentary copies for distribution in the community'.[27]

What about the current era? Before looking into some of my interviews with writers and street artists, it is interesting to highlight what French artist Combo, via his lawyer, noted at the end of the unsuccessful case he brought against the 2017 French presidential candidate Jean Luc Mélenchon's and his political party La France Insoumise, that had used his wheatpaste in their campaign.[28] The artist expressed his willingness to change the position of French judges on copyright protection of street art: 'It is a fight which concerns all actors in the world of street art, and which deserves a real reflection: by failing to grant street artists full copyright protection, we

[26] Remember, some of those early writers did accept certain mainstream aspects of the traditional art world, as we will see in Chapter 5.

[27] Eva Sperling Cockcroft, John Pitman Weber, and James Cockcroft, *Toward a People's Art Book: The Contemporary Mural Movement* (University of New Mexico Press 1977) 164.

[28] See above fn. 22.

run the risk of denying art its universal character, which is an unbearable attack on its essence and vocation'. It is a comment which does not leave much room for interpretation and confirms how the street art subculture increasingly sees copyright as a tool to protect its creativity. It is also a comment which resonates with the opinions expressed by several street artists and writers during my conversations with them. For example, New York muralist Royal King Bee told me that 'if you work mainly in the public environment, copyright is important'. And Easy, a prolific and experienced New York writer I met in Brooklyn, has also been quite vocal in this regard:

> I think copyright is very appropriate. Especially with the situation I've been through and I kind of blame myself with this because I wasn't paying attention. There are people out there that are forging my name and making money. They do like fake *Easy* canvases, they're incorporating my tag on shirts. It never occurred to me before because I had never experienced anything like that; I didn't even realize what was going on. They put it [the tag] on canvases; they put it on numerous things, they might put it on toy models, I've seen it on trucks, subway map replicas – things like that.

When I asked Easy whether he had ever thought about taking legal action to stop this, he replied that he had never done that but 'if the fakes are increasing to an astronomical number, then yes, I'd have to take legal action'. Keo has a similar opinion. He told me: 'anger has no place in business. I simply do what needs to be done to defend my copyright and claim damages when possible. To be a successful artist today, you have to accept that legal recourse is simply a part of business, the same as finding a good supplier for paint and canvases. If they are using my piece for profit and selling my style, then I might try some legal cease and desist notice. I need to be compensated'. Keo also expanded on three out-of-court copyright disputes he has found himself in:

> I've had cases and I cannot speak on them (because I'm bound by confidentiality), but one involved a piece that I had done on paper for another kind of usage. My friend published a book and I designed the title of the book in graffiti style. He paid me for a one-time usage. Now another company loved that image so much that they began to print it on shirts. The other one was with a major corporation shooting their commercial in front of a wall that I had painted. [...] You don't ever have to go to trial. You just have to threaten them with a lawsuit and they want to have a meeting and negotiate. [In the meetings with the above companies] I said, "You will discontinue any use of this image," and they agreed to pay me a certain amount of money and in return I signed a non-disclosure agreement to never speak of this incident again. [...] And I've another case right now as we speak. They filmed a promotional for a major liquor company focusing on my artwork. They focused on it and they created digital content (for online sites) selling liquor.

Similarly, Drop, the Colombian writer I met in the graffiti-friendly area of Puente Aranda in Bogotá, told me that he would sue a company if they were using his letters without his consent: 'I've done it; I'm doing it right now. I don't see anything wrong with that and I think you've to do what you think is right. If you need the money and they're profiting of your own work then I think it's only right to do that, man'. The same goes for William Kasso, who pointed out that if a company uses his art without permission, he would 'then file some paperwork, and sue'. Kasso actually informed me that he had already enforced his copyright twice. The first time was in 2005, with the artist relying on copyright not over a mural, but in relation to one of his canvases: 'it was before social media. I sued this clothing company for using my artwork without my consent, for advertising: they used a picture of my canvas. I filed the court case, and won. I got a judgment'. The second time was in 2008: 'I did a wall with 14 other writers, and McDonald's used the mural in a commercial: we got $10,000 as an out-of-court settlement'. Kasso also noted that at the time of the interview he was about to start another copyright action: 'there is this couple who are selling prints of that work we did on that wall in 2008. They charge in the range of $1,800 and $2,500 for each piece. It was a legal wall in North Philadelphia and was commissioned. We already signed off on the legal stuff and are working with a lawyer, we are making this happen'.

Same feelings have been expressed by other artists. In his London studio, street and studio artist (and former writer) Ben Eine, a pioneer in the exploration of contemporary typography art, told me: 'there has to be a way of protecting what I do, so other people can't use it the way they want'. Also, during our conversation, studio and street artist Anjl noted that 'it's important to have copyright laws. I'd like to have my work copyrighted and I think it's something that I've thought about, but maybe haven't pursued in the past'. A similar opinion was expressed by Dutch stencil artist Fake: '[a]s an artist you're a creator and as a creator you wonna have rights and protection. Actually, I'm in the middle of a case, trying to agree an amount for compensation, for copying. It's a corporation which sold a calendar showing one of my murals'. Disdain towards companies which appropriate art has also been expressed by Manchester-based artist Akse. He commented in our interview: 'I'd definitely get annoyed if a corporation commercially exploits my street artwork. Corporations have the financial means to come up with fair agreements with artists, so they have no excuses not to'. Female New York artist Kristy, whom I talked to in Harlem, also believes that copyright is necessary because 'my art is not meant for capital gains and if anyone is going to profit of this, then it should be the people who created the art, came up with the idea, bought the supplies, spent time painting it, went through all the stuff that an artist has to take to create the art. And it's so easy for somebody to just walk by with a camera and snap a picture and then use the image for their own benefit. You should ask permission, you should give recognition and you should give a percentage of the profit'.

A series of other interviews I had unveiled similar opinions. For example, Morley, a Los Angeles artist who practices wheatpasting, said:

> I get angry when people take my work and sell it without my permission. I've had to stop a number of people from making merchandise that I didn't approve of and they are often surprised that I've a problem with it, which is hilarious to me. They often act as though I should be flattered but the bottom line is that they are stealing from me by profiting off my work without my permission. It's very frustrating. Usually, corporations can afford to shrug off a lawsuit, but if you've protected yourself, you have at least a little bit of power and that can be vital in not being taken advantage of.

Likewise, Laser 3.14 noted: 'I don't like it [unauthorized exploitation] and I'll always take steps to stop this'. He also informed me about a big corporation using his work on the cover of a dictionary: 'I had my copyright on it and that brand should have paid me for using my work without permission'. Also, I asked street and studio artist Pablo Power, whom I met in his studio in Brooklyn, whether he would take legal action if someone appropriated his art, and he replied: 'sure, yeah, in any way I would'. A similar answer was given to me by Murrz, who said, 'Yes. If I see my artwork and no one asked me for permission and they're making money out of it, I'd be like "what are you doing?"'

While showing interest in copyright, some artists have also stressed that relying on it may be a difficult thing to do. New York artist Greg Lamarche, for example, told me in his studio in Manhattan:

> I'm not looking to go to court or to sue people. That's really not my thing. Once, when I was younger in the 90s, I saw one of my throw-ups in a TV-show produced by a big media company, but I didn't complain, I just didn't want to spend my energies against a bunch of top lawyers, and also I wanted to preserve my anonymity. [...] How do people know where to start? People taking photos of street art know nothing about it and only see pretty murals and colours. So how do you police something like that? There is a part of me that is very protective of my work but then another part of me that has to be realistic about it. Like if you have murals all around the world, it's going to be impossible to police that and make sure that no one is taking pictures of it. Especially in our world where everyone has a camera and video recorder in their pocket.

Similarly, sticker artist CB23, also from New York, noted in our conversation: 'if imitation happens, if it's clearly my character that has been copied, yes I'd expect protection. I'd like to take action. But it may be difficult, you know, I'd need to call a lawyer, seems difficult to me. In case lawyers are free, I don't need to pay them, I'd go'. A similar opinion was expressed by Canadian artist Roadsworth, who is known for transforming city streets (particularly signs) into works of art. Focusing on a perceived difficulty to prove copyright infringement, he said during our interview, 'I did a piece once where I put a zipper on a line and it was copied on a car advert where it was unzipping the road. A lot of people contacted me saying I should sue them as it was stealing my work, but I never pursued that – it's hard to prove it'.

## COPYRIGHT AWARENESS

What has surprised me during my fieldwork is that several writers and street artists have shown awareness of what copyright is, and some of its technicalities.[29] Spanish former writer and now muralist and multidisciplinary artist Suso, for example, told me that he considers copyright as a basic human right which can be used to fence off attempts by corporations to capitalise on his art. Such awareness also emerged in replies to some of my email and Instagram messages. For instance, in response to a message of mine asking if it was possible to interview him, a writer based in the US convincingly wrote, 'everything I put up is copyright protected'. Another US writer (who also paints figurative artworks) replied, 'Hello Enrico, I'm currently being represented by my attorney, and you'd have to contact him regarding any questions pertaining to copyright and intellectual property. Thank you for your interest'. Similarly, another writer from the US replied to me: 'I don't think I could meet up in person, but you're welcome to ask me anything as long as it doesn't require info on any specific case. I'm pretty aware of this stuff, and when I don't have answers, my lawyer is there to fill in my blanks'. And another writer, based in New York, answered, 'Yes, but I'll need to be sure our conversation/content doesn't affect an ongoing case (which I'm sure you're aware of)'. For the record, I was not aware of that case. Also, during my interview with Italian street artist Alice Pasquini, the artist mentioned that whenever she finds a website that sells prints incorporating her art, she immediately contacts her agent and instructs her to write a cease-and-desist letter. Likewise, French artist Jef Aerosol pointed out during our conversation: 'if I discover that such a thing [a corporation selling products bearing his art] was done without asking me, I call the ADAGP [French copyright collecting society] and they solve the problem'. I also noticed that some artists pay due attention to others' copyrights and avoid the risk of being accused of copying. New York muralist Kristy is one of them. During our conversation in Harlem, she confirmed that before finalising a painting, she checks online by googling keywords to check if there are any similar concepts out there.

Many artists and writers I spoke with have also strongly opposed the (erroneous) argument that by placing artworks in the public environment, they impliedly waive their rights – a point which is sometimes made even by intellectual property insiders.[30] One of them is Morley, who told me that 'too often people think that because the art is placed outside, a kind of gift to the world, it's okay to exploit it: we must

[29] See also Cedar Lewisohn, Street Art: The Graffiti Revolution (Tate Modern Publishing, 2009) 111 (noting that 'most street artists have an inherent understanding of the issues around intellectual property and being ripped off by the advertising industry').

[30] See again the decision of the European Union Intellectual Property Office (EUIPO) of 14 September 2020 in the revocation proceedings for the EU trademark Flower Thrower, owned by Pest Control on behalf of Banksy (above fn. 4). The EUIPO invalidated the trademark because it had been filed in bad faith, but obiter mistakenly noted that 'graffiti is normally placed in public places for all to view and photograph, which might also possibly annul any ownership rights in copyright'.

protect ourselves and our work. I do protect my work through copyright'. Likewise, Andy Council, a Bristol-based mural artist and illustrator; Fake; and Paul Richard (a New York artist known for creating works by pouring paint on streets) confirmed that they do not waive their rights when painting in public. Lady Pink reiterated this point. When I asked her whether she thought that by putting her artwork on the street she waived her right, she promptly replied, '[A]bsolutely no'. The same answer was given by New York street artist Lexi Bella: 'absolutely no. My creations belong to me despite of them being in the public space. Anyone else profiting from them is breaking the law unless they hired me and I signed a contract waiving my rights'. Similarly, when I asked New York mural artist Logan Hicks the same question, he replied, '[O]f course not. Not legally, not professionally, not creatively'. An analogous opinion was expressed by Copyright and Akse. The former replied to my question in this way: '[n]o, not at all. I place artwork on walls and spots that have already been heavily vandalized. It's my very small way of beautifying an area, I choose to put the works publicly so that they would be seen, not so someone else could use them'. And the latter responded, '[N]ot at all, placing my artwork in public places does not mean that I want to waive my copyright. It only means that I take the risk for people to exploit my artwork'. This risk was also highlighted by New York writer Reskew. When I asked him if he waives his rights when painting in public spaces, he replied, 'No, though I understand that I have limited control, often none, over what happens to my work'.[31]

I also encountered several artists and writers who have highlighted the importance of contractualising terms and conditions which suit their interests. Australian artist Damien Mitchell said to me: 'in case of commissioned works, I sign written agreements. For example, for a mural in Massachussets it was written that the work can't be used by the commissioner and myself for commercial and advertising purposes, unless an authorisation is given by myself or them'. Pablo Power is also careful when it comes to contracts and – he told me – personally amends the draft agreements he receives from commissioners to be absolutely sure that they reflect his will with regards to usage limitation ('I try to keep control. Or at least the contract should say, "[I]if you want to take the control for what we agreed on, that's great, if you want to make a billboard in time square, then that's a different story"'). William Kasso is also keen in contractually clarifying that he must be considered the owner of the copyright over his creations: 'most of the times these contracts

[31] Very few artists and writers I interviewed were (mistakenly) convinced instead that the fact that their artworks are placed in the public space leaves them without legal protection. For example, London writer Noir said, '[T]his [use of his artwork by third parties without his authorization] has happened on many occasions and still happens regularly. Unfortunately, there is nothing that can be done about it. It's a public artwork gifted by the artists for no financial gain. [...] if you give your art to the public, then it's no longer yours. You can't claim ownership'. Likewise, New York street and studio artist Stephen Palladino, whom I met at a café in Brooklyn, commented, '[S]ome of my legal murals have been incorporated in music videos. They never asked permission. I thought I could do nothing'.

keep the copyright with me – I'm careful about that'. This is also the case of Keo, Akse (again), Andre Trenier, and Elle. Keo showed knowledge and understanding of copyright contractual issues. He noted that 'my work has appeared on many books and album covers. If you do a book cover you first have the hard copy, then you have the worldwide translation, so my rights usually extend to the US, Canada, and England. Now if you want to do worldwide translations you will have to pay me again. When you want to do the soft cover you'll have to pay me again. So not only is the usage limited but also the amount of time and area in the world'. Akse commented, '[Y]es, when I get commissioned for some artworks, I state in my agreement that copyright remains with myself. There have been instances when this had to be negotiated, but at least clients are made aware of this at the outset of the project'. Trenier also inserts clauses in contracts specifying that he keeps the rights so that 'if I want to make t-shirts with that image I can do that, and if I want to make posters and sell prints I can do that'. And Elle during our conversation in Brooklyn said:

> yes, I'm doing a collaboration with a beer company. The owner of the company is a friend who said: I'm making an *Elle* beer, you need to make the can. So, I was like that's really cool, and we talked and decide to do *Elle* posters which are basically my logo and my thing. So, when we were talking about it, they asked: 'can we buy this for 20 years?' and I replied: 'yes, but you can't buy the usage, because that is my poster and I am going to continue to use it'. So, I had to have a lawyer involved and it was like 'you can borrow for twenty years, but it's not exclusive to you'. Also, I did another collaboration: Ikea [the world's largest furniture retailer] bought the usage rights of a specific image for a year, and then I've full ownership of the imagery afterwards.

Several other artists show awareness of these issues. Roadsworth, for example, often makes sure to include a copyright clause when he signs a contract. He told me in the interview:

> yes, I always make sure these are included. I mean, again, I can't control if people decide to take pictures of my work and post them on social media, but the copyright is usually between me and the entity that hires me, so I make sure that if they want to use my work for other things not included in the contract, then they've to pay me or tell me before they do it. Generally, when I do a commissioned work, there is an included general copyright licence to specifically identify what they can use to promote the product. Copyright is always in there.

Joel Artista, a New York street artist, is on the same page. During our conversation in a Brooklyn café, he commented, 'If I'm going to create a mural, whether it's with a community with kids or just by myself, I always make sure that in that contract I've the copyright, I get to have copyright over my own work. Maybe I can share that copyright with whoever is commissioning the piece. But that shouldn't be at the expense of my copyright. I'm aware that the artist has copyright unless he basically waives that right – unless the artist in a contract says, "I give up my rights". And so, I never want to do that'. The same opinion was expressed by Anjl ('when I do commissioned works, I like to have a written agreement and at least have an understanding of what it is') and Morley ('I do commissions frequently and I try to be as clear as possible that they don't own the licence for the art').

Similarly, mural artist Logan Hicks noted in his interview with me: 'I get contracts or at the very least an email outlining what is covered, duration of time it will be up, copyright held and other things. I never would sign a work for hire agreement that forced to relinquish my copyright over the piece. At no point would I allow a corporation to use my work without permission and use it for commercial gain. I'd make all attempts to protect copyright and claim damages when possible'. Likewise, street artist Lexi Bella is vocal on this issue and fiercely defends her rights as an artist. When I asked during our conversation in a Brooklyn café what she thinks about corporate appropriation and if she would react, she replied:

> Absolutely. It's really exhausting and an ongoing battle to educate other graffiti and street artists about their value. Corporations or developers that are swimming in money love to exploit artists' ignorance and perpetuate the idea that these artists are lucky they are getting 'exposure' and a free wall when in reality these people are manipulating artists into doing work for free that the corporations and developers can then use as a draw to make a profit. We've to demand to get paid and own the rights to our images! Contracts and unity can achieve this. [...] I always send cease-and-desist letters.

Other writers and artists I met showed particular awareness of copyright laws and the control they give over their art. Zephyr, as mentioned, confirmed that he has always kept an extremely tight control over his artworks, thus carefully regulating the uses of his pieces by companies and commissioners. This is so true that he has now, in his own words, 'a reputation for being difficult so people are like "I don't work with Zephyr"'. To give an example of how he operates, when a fashion company asked him if he would be interested in designing some clothes, he replied, '[Y]ou need to tell me usage, parameters, which means exactly how many clothes, how many designs and for how long. Is it for one season, one year or forever? Also, the use has to be limited. Can you use this on an ad? No, you can't. If I design a logo for you, you need to be specific'. Former New York writer Cey Adams has the same attitude. He considers copyright to be extremely useful. He noted in our interview that 'the idea is to turn graffiti writing into something positive that you could benefit from, something that you can have control over. And that goes back to copyright: something that you can control'.

Former writer Rubin, who is now a New York–based street and studio artist, is also keen on keeping control over what he creates. He noted during our conversation:

> I sign written agreements. Some commissioners have asked me to transfer the copyright, but I've always refused. Otherwise, my stuff gets out of control. I want to keep control. They pay me for using the work for a purpose – if they want to use

> it for another purpose then we've to renegotiate. I try to be pretty selective in what I do. I had some requests from glasses and watches' manufacturers. I've collaborated with fashion brands, and some of my murals ended up on some clothes. I do research and ask myself if it feels right for me. I want to keep control on the use of my stuff, [I want this] to be specified in the contract. I don't want my stuff to be used in other ways years later.

But probably the best example of a street artist who wants to keep control over the use of his art is Stik, who is well known for painting humanised stick figures on walls and other urban surfaces. When I met him in his studio in the Shoreditch area of the London capital, he showed me what he calls the 'Rules of Usage' of his character. This is a document which meticulously indicates the conditions for the treatment of his artwork – conditions which anyone he authorises to use his art needs to comply with. The document includes the following rules: (i) the body and face of the figure should always be white; (ii) the background should always be one solid colour; (iii) no images should be overlaid on or be made part of the figure; (iv) no speech bubble should be made part of the image; (v) the figure should not be placed in relative proximity to brand identities or logos of any commercial entity; and (vi) the words 'copyright [followed by the year]' should be added at the bottom of texts including the figure. Stik authorises to use his figures only to selected non-profit organisations which promote causes he believes in. One of these is the UK National Health Service, which Stik supports – it is worthwhile to remember the London demonstration in support of NHS junior doctors in 2015, with people holding Stik *Sleeping Baby* placards and the artist waiving any right to royalties.[32]

That many writers and street artists are aware of copyright aspects surrounding their art also emerges from their increasing use of the © symbol. During my encounter with Keo, the New York writer confirmed that he is well aware of the importance of the copyright symbol: 'All I have to do is to sign the piece at the bottom with a © and that artwork is automatically protected'. The copyright symbol is also often used by Tats Cru, a well-known crew of former writers from the Bronx and now professional muralists. The symbol ©, for example, had been inserted in their 'I love the Bronx' mural which was larer incoporated by carmaker Fiat Chrysler in a TV commercial featuring pop star Jennifer Lopez. The artists did take legal action against the car manufacturer on grounds of copyright infringement, and the case was later settled.[33]

The graffiti literature confirms that the copyright symbol was also used by a few New York writers of the 1970s and 1980s, sometimes as an irreverent self-accreditation

[32] Interest in controlling the use of street artworks also emerged in the interview I had with Athens-based artist Sonke. When I asked him whether he also accepts commissions, and if so, whether in the relevant contracts he also makes sure to specify that he keeps the copyright over the commissioned work. He replied, '[Y]es, my lawyer takes care of such things'.

[33] Don Kaplan, 'Fiat Settles Claim with Bronx Graffiti Artists over J. Lo Ad' (30 November 2011) *New York Post*.

criticising corporate ownership.[34] Indeed, it seems there was a minority of writers in that era who showed interest in this legal tool. This has been confirmed to me by Cey Adams: 'at that time there was no[t] much copyright awareness, even though some writers used the copyright symbol, a kind of warning to other writers not to bite'. As mentioned, the graffiti literature sheds some light. Nancy Macdonald narrates that in the 1970s some writers were encouraged to invent new styles, new letter forms, 'claiming these as their own through the use of a copyright symbol';[35] and Martha Cooper reminds us that several writers of the early times used to embellish their tags with various symbols, including the copyright logo.[36] Also, Henry Chalfant and Sasha Jenkins report writer Spin's own words: 'For a long time, a copyright notice was added, which is clearly very important for legal reasons (seriously, a lot of writers really did this – I think I did too)'.[37] Fab Five Freddy and Lady Pink were amongst them.[38] And Jack Stewart recounts that Tracy 168, the pioneer of Wild Style, started inserting the copyright symbol into his train pieces in the 1970s to try to prevent other writers from *biting*.[39] In 1985 Tracy 168 also registered with the US Copyright Office a design containing a person skating, and this is mentioned in a New York court decision in a case brought by the writer in the 1980s against a company called Skate Key Inc., as the latter had allegedly infringed his copyright by producing and selling various merchandise, including T-shirts, skate bags, flyers, and jackets that incorporated that registered design (and others).[40]

Perhaps, the most striking example of use of the copyright symbol within these creative subcultures is the one associated with the tag SAMO ©, created and popularised by Jean-Michel Basquiat and Al Diaz from the mid-1970s to early 1980s in New York. The two of them would spray-paint and draw the tag in the streets of New York, especially lower Manhattan. During our interview in Brooklyn, Al Diaz told me that Basquiat and he decided to add the © symbol to their tag because 'we wanted to give a message that SAMO was a kind of product that you could buy. That was our purpose. It was our brand'. While such sense of property at that time seemed purely symbolic, more recently Al Diaz has shown a more materialistic and commercial interest in the tag. This happened when he opposed a trademark application filed in 2017 by the Estate of Jean-Michel Baquiat for the sign SAMO with the US Trademark Office.[41] Even before this dispute arose, the Brooklyn-based artist had been quite vocal about his paternity and rights over the tag. He said to me: 'I started to approach, via my lawyer, the Basquiat foundation, to regularize

34 Allan Schwartzman, 'Street Art' (Bantam Doubleday Dell 1985) 31.

35 Nancy Macdonald, The Graffiti Subculture: Youth, Masculinity and Identity in London and New York (Palgrave MacMillan 2001) 82.

36 Martha Cooper, Tag Town: The Origins of Watching (Dokument 2009) 53, 88.

37 Henry Chalfant and Sacha Jenkins, Training Days: The Subway Artists Then and Now (Thames & Hudson 2014) 151.

38 Charlie Ahearn, Wild Style: The Sampler (Powerhouse Book 2007) 22, 95.

39 Jack Stewart, Graffiti Kings: New York City Mass Transit Art of the 1970s (Abrams 2009) 73.

40 Tracy v. Skate Key, Inc., 697 F. Supp. 748 (S.D.N.Y. 1988).

41 See *Albert Diaz v. Administration of the Jean-Michel Basquiat Estate*, USPTO Opposition No. 91241549.

the rights on SAMO and to be able not to have problems in commercially using SAMO. I want to be able to make a living out of that. I have a lawyer working on it. I should try to capitalize on it'.[42]

* * *

It is also worthwhile to stress that awareness of copyright issues amongst street artists and writers sometimes arises or anyway grows stronger later in their career, for example, if and once they have taken up traditional jobs in the creative industry, including graphic design, fashion design, tattoo art, fine art, journalism, guerrilla marketing, or within the graffiti industry, including supply of cans and graffiti magazine production.[43] This point has emerged during my fieldwork, for example, in my interviews with New York wheatpaste artist City Kitty and Good Guy Boris. The former said, '[M]ost artists I know are not concerned about copyright until they start getting commercial success, and become concerned with the possibility of a company using their work for another intention'. And the latter pointed out that 'when I started graffiti I didn't think about copyright. I didn't care about copyright because I wanted to increase my fame and I wanted to get my name out there and I just wanted to entertain people, show them something different and funny, I just wanted to build my name'. Yet, his perception greatly changed throughout his career – he now firmly believes that copyright 'is the only way you can protect your art in modern day'. Similarly, Chris Stain, a former New York writer and now a street and studio artist, said to me that 'the copyright issue didn't surface until many years later when I began showing in galleries and making work for TV and galleries'. Rubin was another writer who did not care about copyright when he started in the 1990s. He told me in his studio in Brooklyn: 'I was nine years old when I started with my tag. Never registered copyright. I've never done it. But now I think it's very important to protect street artworks. I've started becoming more and more aware of it'.

## TOLERATING PRIVATE USES OF THE ART, BUT NOT ITS ECONOMIC EXPLOITATION

Several street artists and writers I interviewed made it clear that while they may often tolerate non-commercial uses of their art by other people, what they strongly disdain and would be ready to oppose is its economic exploitation (we have already

[42] The interest in seeking trademark protection had already emerged in my ethnographic research (see also the trademark cases started by several street artists and writers, mentioned above fn. 2). When interviewing John Fekner, a multidisciplinary artist known in the 1970s and 1980s for creating environmental, social, political, and conceptual works consisting of stenciled words on urban surfaces, he commented that 'somebody has approached me and proposed to sell T-shirts bearing those messages. I'm thinking about protecting them as trademarks'.

[43] On the career path often followed by writers, see Gregory Snyder, Graffiti Lives: Beyond the Tag in the New York's Urban underground (NYU Press 2009).

seen that commercial uses of street art are deeply disliked). In other words, it seems they are interested in just some exclusive rights offered by copyright laws. The following bits of interviews confirm this point.

Depsone, the New York writer and street artist I met in a Brooklyn café, told me: 'I'd definitely want to protect my artwork, specifically, if it's being used to sell something and make profit, for example if it's used for a magazine advertisement or something like that'. Similarly, Andy Council commented in the interview: 'They take a photo of the wall and then they use the pic. I don't mind them sharing it, I certainly don't want them to be prevented from sharing (of course provided that they credit the source, which they could do even if the artwork is not signed), for sure – however, I don't want them to put it on a postcard to be sold. I have an issue there'. The same opinion was expressed by street artists Crisp, Lamkat, Mosstika, and Stik. While Australian artist Crisp noted that 'if you choose to put artworks in the street, it's for public consumption, people can take pics. Of course, if a big corporation uses it, it's another stuff', Lamkat said that whether she approves or not the unauthorised use of her art 'depends on what my work is used for. If it's simply in the background in like a movie where someone is directly making money from my work, I think I should be compensated. But if it's something which contributes to a better cause, I'm okay with not getting paid'. And Mosstika pointed out that she 'would mind if someone takes and uses commercially my public work. I'd be ready to take legal action. But private uses of my work are fine, I don't think I could complain about that'. Similarly, Stik does not mind people using his art on something private such as wedding invitations, or for information purposes, for example, on posters to inform the public of non-profit events, and in general for educational or documentary aims. He also said that a university had contacted him about using one of his artworks and that he was happy that they asked for his permission. But Stik does mind, and strongly complains, when his art is used for commercial gains

Likewise, Canadian street artist Roadsworth commented during our interview:

> If someone copies me without telling me and makes money out of my work, I wouldn't be too happy. I don't have a problem with someone taking a picture of it and putting it on the internet or using it, but it is true that that usage is limited. I wouldn't let it happen with a corporate entity to use my hard work for commercial purposes. I think that's when I draw the line and I don't want people using my work for commercial advertisement. [...]. I'm aware that it's the age of the internet and I've seen people copying my work, but in most cases it's just a regular person who has been inspired or want to imitate the work I've done, which I've no problem with. As long as I'm ok with how they're using, then I'm ok with that.

Similarly, New York writer Serk told me in our conversation in Brooklyn that an 'AP [Associated Press] photographer took a pic of a piece of mine at *5Pointz*. It was very legible, it was available for the press – and this photo enlarged ended up at the Museum of the City of New York. Somebody told me about the photo, I didn't complain. I didn't feel ripped off. I considered it was used in a non-profit context, it was a moment of chance'. Ian Strange and Laser 4.14 expressed analogous opinions. The former pointed out during our conversation: 'I think if someone from the public genuinely took a photo of a piece and posted it on social media, or used it in an exhibition, I think that would be fine as you just get a picture of the mural with no context. But if it was to be turned into a highly commercial item like a T-shirt or a cup, I'd be extremely uncomfortable with that. At this point I'll consider the type of protection at my disposal'. And when I asked Laser 4.14 whether he would rely on copyright to protect his work, he replied, '[W]here possible yes, but it's not always possible in this new internet world. If there's a print made on shirts without my permission, I can do something about it, but it's different when someone takes a photograph and post[s] it in social media'.

Thus, it seems that the calculated economic exploitation of street art and graffiti is what enrages street artists and writers, who may tolerate instead private and non-commercial uses. This is confirmed once again by what New York artist Pablo Power told me during our conversation: 'if you want to see something in the street and take a picture and make one shirt for yourself because you think that it's cool, then I will probably not have a problem with that, but if you make 10 out of them and sell them for 500 or 1,000 dollars, then it's really a problem'.

Some interviews have also highlighted how street artists and writers further distinguish between insignificant (and acceptable) economic uses and serious (and unacceptable) uses by people or corporations. London writer Oker, for instance, told me: 'just recently somebody used one of my images to promote a music album by using a photograph incorporating one of my throw-ups. They chose it, it was premeditated. I did not send a letter. I didn't do that because it wasn't Warner Bros, it was just a small band'. The same goes for Elle and Fake. The former explicitly said that she has a monetary threshold. She would complain only if someone was gaining a lot of money from her art without acknowledging and compensating her. She added that '[i]f someone is making a lot of money of my art and not even try to acknowledging or contribute or give me financial gain, that is where it becomes a line for me'.[44] Similar opinions were expressed by Fake ('I don't go after small companies – my lawyer does basically a costs/benefit analysis. We go after the big fishes, I don't want to spend my time against the small fishes'), Pablo Delgado ('if it's a corporation yes

44 Elle showed disgust towards the unauthorised exploitation of her art. She said, '[W]here I do have problem with this is where large companies with a lot of money, who are going to make a lot of money, are using our art to show how cool and urban they are. When they're taking pictures of your graffiti, I think they should pay the artist. They should either hire an artist or they should find the artist, contact him and make sure it is okay for him to be part of that campaign and then pay him'. On the contrary, as several others I spoke with do, she approves of the taking and sharing of pictures of her pieces. She indeed commented, 'I thought it was very cool the first time I saw my art go up on Brooklyn Street Art Blog. It was really exciting and I was like "it's so cool that someone likes my piece enough to take a picture and post it"'.

[I'd take action], but if someone is individually doing the shirts and selling them in a stall in a market, I wouldn't complain'), and Ian Strange ('I'd explore legal action and talk to lawyers to find out what my chances of success are. It would have to be an extreme case of the person making a lot of money off my work. I'd only do this if the person stealing my work was a big company or director for an advert campaign or someone who has the resources to pay compensation. Some people that sell my work don't make a lot of money, so I wouldn't target them').

## ILLEGAL STREET ART AND GRAFFITI

An issue I have been particularly interested in during my research is whether art which is created in the street illegally, namely without the authorisation of the owner of the surface upon which is placed, can be protected by copyright. In some jurisdictions such as the US, this is still a grey area of the law, with several commentators and even adjudicators reminding us that illegal street and graffiti art should be denied protection, with the consequence that everybody would be able to exploit the unprotected artwork.[45]

I noted elsewhere that it would be unfair to allow persons other than the artist to rely on the illegal nature of a street artwork to freely copy and exploit it for their own commercial purposes.[46] As has interestingly been pointed out by Jamison Davies, '[F]ailing to recognise a copyright in [illegal] graffiti could then have the effect of legitimizing its co-option but not its creation'.[47] This result would also be absurd as it would reward blatant imitations by individuals or corporations that have nothing to do with either the perpetrator of the illegal act (the artist) or the victim (the owner of the property). Such absurdity has also been highlighted by my interviewees. New York writer Reskew, for example, noted that 'if it's illegal to vandalize property, why is it legal for a company to take a picture of that crime and sell it, or use it to boost their own image? Would it be very different if, under law, they used an image of a violent criminal to sell or use it in a glorified manner for advertising purposes?' Similarly, New York artist Paul Richard told me: 'whether an artwork is sanctioned or not, it should not be reproduced without permission'. And Spanish artist Suso said to me: 'Copyright for street artists and writers is fair and necessary. Otherwise, third parties with commercial interests in mind would benefit from their art'. Suso added that he once found that a popular retailer in Spain was selling shirts and cups incorporating his illegally placed art and when his lawyer contacted the manufacturers to ask to stop exploiting his pieces, they threatened to report him with the police for vandalism.

45 See again the decision of the EUIPO's Cancellation Division in the 'Flower Thrower' case, Full Colour Black Limited v Pest Control Office Limited Cancellation No. C33 843 Cancellation Division of the European Union Intellectual Property office, decision of 14 September 2020, 8.

46 Enrico Bonadio, Graffiti, street art and copyright, *SAUC Journal* 2018.

47 Jamison Davies, 'Art Crimes? Theoretical Perspectives on Copyright Protection for Illegally-Created Graffiti Art' (2013) 65 *Me. L. Rev.* 27, 51.

On the other hand, a few of my interviewees were convinced that art created illegally cannot be protected, including Lady Pink, veteran London writer Noir, and Damien Mitchell. While Lady Pink commented that 'it doesn't make any sense. It'd be as if a burglar hurts himself while he's robbing a house and he sues the homeowner. He's committing a crime! You can't profit from that', Noir said, '[M]ost of my artworks are illegally placed, which means no rights'. And Damien Mitchell told me: 'if it's illegal, I'd say: it's part of the graffiti game. I suppose I waive my rights'. Similarly, Keo pointed out that '[w]hen we paint, for instance, a subway train illegally, we don't have any protection under the law. You cannot profit from a crime'. And another high-profile insider of the early New York graffiti scene of the 1970s sarcastically replied to my email asking for an interview: '[y]ou believe a crime can be copywritten?'

These comments are reminiscent of the so-called unclean hands doctrine, an equitable defence in which the defendant claims that the plaintiff should not obtain a remedy and profit when the latter has acted unethically or in bad faith, or has anyway carried out an illegal activity. Such a defence is quite popular in the US amongst defendants accused of appropriating and profiting from street artworks that have been created illegally. This happened in *Joseph Tierney v. Moschino*, the copyright infringement case started by graffiti artist Rime against fashion company Moschino, as the former claimed that his Detroit mural *Vandal Eyes* had been copied onto a Moschino dress which was subsequently worn by the pop star Katy Perry at a glamorous event in 2015.[48] The defence was also raised in 2018 by Swedish fashion retailer H&M when Californian writer Revok complained about its use of imagery and videos that incorporated one of his artworks.[49]

Yet, the many writers and artists I spoke with have an opposite opinion. New York artist Kristy confirmed that hypothetically she would take action to prevent the exploitation of her works, as 'to me the legality of the wall is not that important'. The same goes for New York writers Mastro ('[N]ow they think that it's cool to take from the artist since it's illegal. They would think "well he can't fight us in court". Of course, I'd fight them. They're still taking what someone else created and trying to apply it as their own') and Hoacs ('I'd take action to protect an illegal work. But I'd take that risk only if I can get good money as compensation'). Colombian writer Drop is on the same page: 'I think that would be a brave move, because you have to get rid of the mask. I'm willing to do it, but I don't think many people would do it. I'd do it for sure. I went to jail over graffiti in the States for a few months. So, I'm not really afraid of that and I'm going to stand up for what I think is right, so if I think I'm being legally abused by a company or somebody, then I'd get off the mask, for sure'.

Others of my interviewees would be more cautious, instead. While former New York writer Dejer said, 'In principle, I'd be ready to take legal action, my concern

[48] See above fn. 2 and 15.

[49] See above fn. 13.

would be that they may catch me for all the bombing I've done in the past', Al Diaz confirmed with me that in general he would react against an appropriation of his illegally created art: 'absolutely for the recognition, that's my work, and also for some compensation. Especially for the old works, where there is no risk [of prosecution due to the statute of limitation]'. But when it comes to illegal works created more lately, he said, 'I'd think about taking action for the recent ones, perhaps I'd just have to swallow that and maybe not do anything unfortunately'. Likewise, Lady Pink (again) commented, '[I]t's very difficult to start a legal action for the appropriation of an illegal graffiti work, the risk of being arrested is high, it's not worth'. I obviously agreed with these interviewees on this point. Yet during our conversations I reminded them of the statute of limitation issue, noting (as Al Diaz suggested) that in case the illegal piece had been created several years before (the term length changes from country to country), taking a legal action against someone who exploits that work would carry no risk of criminal prosecution. But, as far as graffiti is concerned, New York writer Hoacs gave little weight to this point, noting that 'a real writer will be a writer forever, so the same piece and name will be painted later and later, over and over again'. Hoacs has a point here, as the fact that graffiti practitioners constantly write the same name across the years and sometimes the decades evidently still keeps the risk of criminal prosecution high if they eventually come out and start a legal action. A judge may indeed compare tags, throw-ups, and pieces painted in the early years and those painted recently, and find them similar – which would make it relatively easy to infer that the same person made all of them.

## LACK OF INTEREST AND DISCOURAGEMENT

Not all those I have talked to have manifested interest in opposing the appropriation of their art by relying on copyright, though. A few of them were actually quite reluctant in this specific regard. Linus Coraggio, a New York artist known for his abstract sculptures and sculptural furniture (which he leaves in the street), is one of them. During our conversation in his studio in Manhattan, he ironically commented, 'I'd like more to be protected from the police rather than copyright!' A lack of enthusiasm towards copyright also was apparent in my interview with City Kitty. He informed me about a website selling pictures of his artworks, but did not seem upset at all about that. Discouragement towards copyright has also emerged in my conversations with other artists. Pablo Power, for example, informed me about an incident happened in the late 1990s when he and his crew made a limited number of shirts to promote their artwork:

> around 1998 we were walking down in the lower east side where they have markets and back then the more kind of junky T-shirts and socks and hats and things like that, whereas now it's fancy down there. And there was somebody selling piles and piles, hundreds of our shirts that we made 50 of. And now there are like 500 that we

> didn't make, and they were selling them for $40 each. We freaked out and talked to guy, but he made them and he didn't know who we are, so we looked like a bunch of crazy kids. There was really nothing we could do; for them it was like 'if you have a problem, we will call the cops', because here we are, some young people walking down the street and they are like a business owner selling clothing. So, what can we say of that, we didn't have proof of anything.

Some artists have also shown lack of enthusiasm because of the costs needed to bring an action in court (we have already seen that the difficulty in accessing lawyers may be an obstacle here). New York artist Bill Blast commented during our conversation that 'I'd fight if I'd deep pockets, if I've the resources. But if you're an artist that barely gets by and are thinking about your next meal, you can't afford a lawyer. So, if you don't have the money, the lawyer doesn't have the time'. Also, Australian artist Crisp clarified in the interview that he does not want to pay lawyers: 'my works have been used to promote products such as shoes, in the background. I've never complained about it. If they're using my artwork and I don't have any money to pay lawyers, I can't be bothered'. Some other artists would instead think about starting a copyright action if they could rely on some form of support to cover the legal costs. This is what Chinese street artist Daleast thinks. He told me during our encounter: '[o]nce, an advertising agency on behalf of a telephone company remade an artwork of mine, with a human figure though. That's terrible, but I didn't do anything, I didn't complain. I'd take legal action if I had the energy to do that. If there is an environment which allows artists to protect their works and support them, I'd do that'. When I asked him what he meant by that, he replied that he was referring to 'a community or group that provides artists with affordable legal assistance'.

That there are street artists and writers who are reluctant to claim copyright to oppose misappropriation of their art is not really surprising. After all, even fine artists and other categories of creators often show such reluctance. In her book *The Eureka Myth: Creators, Innovators, and Everyday Intellectual Property*, Jessica Silbey shows how a wide range of creative people, including painters, sculptors, photographers, web designers, musicians, filmmakers, writers, and software engineers, frequently tolerate copyright infringement.[50]

## COPYRIGHT IS NOT THE TRIGGER FOR THE CREATIVE SPARK

Despite the growing interest in copyright amongst many street artists and writers, almost all of them obviously do not believe that copyright itself has ever played a crucial motivating role. In other words, the availability of copyright is not the trigger which sparks their creativity. This has been so from the very beginning of graffiti. Indeed, early New York writer Skeme confirmed during our conversation in Harlem

[50] Jessica Silbey, *The Eureka Myth: Creators, Innovators, and Everyday Intellectual Property* (Stanford University Press 2014) 45, 82.

that 'monetary gains [which can be maximised by copyright] had absolutely nothing to do with it. Property and ownership were not on our minds (apart from a few). Ninety-nine per cent of the time we were just out to write'. Crisp also highlighted the lack of economic motivations. The reason he puts art in the street – he noted in the interview – is definitely 'not economic. I lose money because of the materials, roller and paints, the spray-paint, the blades used to cut the stencils, the time spent. I put it for free, especially in Colombia where people don't pay anything, as opposed to New York where I've done two walls and I was paid for the materials' cost, travel, and accommodation. The majority of my works are paid by myself: I don't get any money; I lose money'.

Other motivations have always pushed, and still push, writers and street artists. Skeme, for example, pointed out that 'basically, it was just to express yourself and be known'. Similarly, London writer Noir noted in our interview that 'from my personal experience, it has always been about getting my name out there. It has never occurred to me who owns the copyright or right to use my image that I've placed'. And Danish writer Bates commented, 'I never did it to claim copyrights, I did it because I love to be creative and I want people to see my art'. Likewise, Sonke, an artist from Athens, replied to my question, stressing that his motivation is 'my need for a public statement. It [copyright] has not been a trigger yet'.[51]

Artists I spoke with also made clear that their desire to create and place art in the street is pushed by their determination to reach the public. For example, New York artist Paul Richard told me in his studio in Brooklyn: 'I started doing street art to draw attention to my work – the streets have a large audience. Copyright in itself wasn't a trigger for placing art on the streets'. Similarly, Logan Hicks said to me that 'the streets are simply another venue to showcase your work. I think that the job of an artist, after the work is created, is to find a way to share it with as many eyes as possible. The street allows a wide range of people to see the work, allows for unfiltered feedback from the public. The threat of copyright infringement has never been a consideration. If you are paranoid about that, then you'd worry too much about it anytime you display your work'. The same goes for City Kitty ('[M]y artistic development moved from graffiti to street art and my style changed but the motivation has always been to broaden my audience, as well as the pure enjoyment of getting the work on the street. Street art allows me the freedom of expression without worrying about making something that needs to be sold'), Joel Artista ('[W]hat prompted me

[51] I heard an analogous opinion during my encounter with New York writer Serk, who expanded further on the intrinsic motivations which pushed him to start writing, and the effects that this artistic practice had on him: 'I started doing graffiti to provide a voice to who are voiceless, people not necessarily popular. I wanted to have a presence, to be respected, I didn't have a vehicle to carry that message. Practicing graffiti has allowed me to become successful, and be acknowledged as a person and human being. I was kind of nobody, but after graffiti people knew me, and that felt very good, people know that I'm here. People know that I've things to say. It was a kind of validation of being a human being, it was like I'm here, I'm present, you've to listen to me'.

to put murals and art in the street is that it always really appealed to me to have an artwork that was made for the public; that was part of the daily life; that was part of a community; that was not in a gallery or a museum; not kind of hidden away behind walls. And so it was in that spirit that I was first drawn to mural art'), Reskew ('many reasons: a desire to have my work seen by the public and to add artistry to the streets'), Stephen Palladino ('exposure is the motivation, and it's compulsive') and Rubin ('the trigger is expressing myself; passion and willingness to communicate something have pushed me to paint').

Again, that copyright does not motivate street artists and writers to produce artworks does not come as a surprise. Many traditional fine and studio artists are not motivated by copyright, either. It has been argued, for example, that Picasso would still have created his wonderful paintings regardless of whether copyright was available or not.[52] This has again been demonstrated by Jessica Silbey's study, which convincingly claims that intellectual property laws are not decisive when it comes to encouraging people to create. The claim that these laws would constitute a trigger of creativity – Silbey argues – is false, basically a myth.[53] Rebecca Tushnet's research also confirms this point. She notes that desire, not calculation, often drives creativity – and many experiences of creativity simply do not fit into the abstract intellectual property incentive model.[54] And we have just seen that the street art and graffiti subcultures do not make an exception.

Yet, the fact that copyright does not motivate street artists and writers does not mean that the practitioners of these forms of art are not interested at all in this intellectual property right. Actually, as we have seen in this chapter, many street artists and writers do nurture an interest in copyright, especially as a tool to react against the misappropriation of their works. In short, most of them are convinced that copyright does not motivate them to create, but nevertheless it is a legal instrument that they can use to protect their art once it is produced and even more after it is exploited by someone else without their permission, especially for commercial purposes.

52 Simon Stokes, *Art and Copyright* (Bloomsbury 2012) 14.

53 Silbey, above fn. 50, 12, 15.

54 Rebecca Tushnet, 'Economies of Desire: Fair Use and Marketplace Assumptions' (2009) 51 *Wm. & Mary L. Rev.* 513, 516, 522.

# 4

# Feelings about Attribution and Preservation

Copyright laws include provisions aimed at protecting the moral rights of authors and artists, including the attribution and integrity rights.[1] The former gives creators of a work the right to be recognised as authors, and can be enforced against whoever does not acknowledge such authorship, for example, a publisher of a photographic book which fails to give proper credits when including the artwork's picture. The latter allows authors and artists to oppose the distortion, mutilation, or other modifications of the work which is prejudicial to their reputation or honour. In this chapter not only will I mention a few cases where street artists and writers have enforced moral rights – I will also highlight the opinions of many of my interviewees about whether they are interested in enforcing such rights. It should be noted that when my informants expressed interest (or lack of interest) in reacting against behaviours of others which may infringe their moral rights, they did not use the expressions 'I'd be ready to enforce my moral right of attribution' or 'I'd invoke my moral right of integrity'. This is technical terminology which is unknown to most, if not all, of them. They just used generic language such as 'I'd take legal action' or 'I'd react' (or 'I wouldn't').

## 'IT'S MY OWN THING'

There is no doubt that writers and street artists are strongly attached to their own creations. This strong bond can help explain why several of them show interest in the moral right of attribution, and may consider enforcing it should the need arise. Cases where street artists have complained about misattribution of their pieces have already occurred.

For example, in 2007 a group of US street artists and writers (including the famous Bronx muralists Tats Cru) objected to the publication of a photographic book on New York murals entitled *Tattooed Walls* and a related exhibition, because pictures

[1] Moral rights are enshrined in international copyright law. See Article 6-bis of the Berne Convention for the Protection of Literary and Artistic Works of 1886.

of their pieces had been included without authorisation. The artists also complained that many of the artworks pictured in the book were misidentified, misinterpreted, or misattributed. The case was settled out of court.[2] Also, as mentioned in chapter 2, in 2011 Italian graffiti writers Key-One and Tawa took legal action against an individual that had incorporated some of their artworks on his website without acknowledging their authorship. Although the case focused on fine artworks produced in studios, the two artists did take legal action to (also) enforce their moral right of attribution.[3]

I also want to mention a story which involves London-based Chilean artist Osch and helps explain the 'attribution' and 'authorship' sentiment typical of practitioners of these forms of art. During our interview in his studio in East London, Osch informed me about a campaign he had recently launched, the 'not a Banksy' campaign. It all started when a street art piece created by Osch – *Cop a Load* – painted by him in various urban settings in London, Berlin, Malta, Tokyo, and Miami was repeteadly attributed to Banksy throughout the years, and offered for sale via online auctions. Osch obviously dislikes such misattribution – and that is why he started this campaign. He does not want his art to be presented as the work of another artist. In an agreement he signed with a gallery (also) aimed at increasing public awareness of his paternity over the *Cop a Load* artwork, it is even acknowledged that:

> Mr. Schade will paint one last 'Cop a Load' painting in a location to be determined by Mr. Schade exclusively, where this painting will be signed 'Osch' which is Mr. Schade's public artist signature with the addition of the hashtag '#NotaBanksy', [and] this hashtag will then be used in a worldwide media and marketing campaign with a matching website (www.notabanksy.info) to allow Mr. Schade to tell his side of the story providing further details to prove once and for all that he is the original artist of the 'Cop a Load' painting found around the world.

As far as graffiti is concerned, its very essence shows how deep the relationship can be between the tag, the throw-up, and the piece and the writer who creates and places them on urban surfaces. Writers do paint and draw their name because they want to 'get up' and get visibility within the subculture. In this sense, graffiti is a powerful and complex assertion of a personal and self identity,[4] which is different from the one that appears on their birth certificates.[5] Many writers feel a sort of

2 David Gonzalez, 'Walls of Art for Everyone, but Made by Not Just Anyone' (4 June 2007) *New York Times*.

3 Milan Court, decision of 2 November 2011, *Marco Mantovani, Igor Seghizzi and Stradearts S.r.l. v. Nicola Leonetti*.

4 Hugo Martinez, 'Graffiti NYC', Prestel 2006, Introduction by Antonio Zaya and Ken Bensinger; Lisa Gottlieb, 'Graffiti Art Styles: A Classification System and Theoretical analysis' (McFarland & Co 2009) 3; Marta Iljadica, Copyright Beyond Law: Regulating Creativity in the Graffiti Subculture (Bloomsbury 2016) 188 (noting that 'the writing of the word comes to be imbued with the writer's personality').

5 Jessica Pabòn, 'Ways of Being Seen: Gender and the Writing on the Wall', in Jeffrey Ian Ross (ed.), Routledge Handbook of Graffiti and Street Art (Routledge 2016) 78. The 'different identity' issue often emerges in the graffiti literature. For example, the book by Janice Rhan, Painting Without Permission: Hip-Hop Graffiti Subculture (Praeger 2002) 65–66, highlights the opinion of Canadian writer Seaz: 'My parents gave my name. I didn't choose it. This [graffiti] allows me to choose my

spiritual attachment to their work. It is more than just communicating a name – writing is akin to expressing their personality and reflecting a harmonious physical movement.[6] The 'reflection of my personality' element also emerged in some of my interviews with writers. While Bates noted that his artwork is 'a piece of me in a larger scale, it's always mine, I did it with my own hands and mind', Skeme said that 'each piece is like one of your kids'. Similar opinions were expressed by Mastro ('my piece is a reflection of how I'm feeling at the moment') and Reskew ('All my art is my own. There is a relationship that has been developed my whole life that goes into every piece') as well as Noir ('It's always been personal. What I create comes from within').

Street artists show a similar attitude. Bronx muralist Andre Trenier told me: 'my artwork is definitely a reflection of my personality and of my thoughts at any given time. It's a reflection of my ideals and what I hope to pass on to other people. You know, when I read things and it sparks new ideas, they find their way into my artwork. [...] My old tag? It was like a signature from an early age. When I was on the road to be an artist – or even before I thought about it that seriously – my signature meant something to me. It was a sense of who I was. It was a part I projected to the world'. The same goes for London-based artist Pablo Delgado ('I'm creating a reflection of ideas and those are mine. There is always a relation with what is done by you'), Anjl ('I do think that there can be some attachment with what I have created'), New York artist Zimer ('describing my artwork as an extension of myself would be an understatement'), Lamkat ('[Y]ou do put time, energy, passion into it and it's a way of expression. So there is an attachment that you always have to something that you create'), Jef Aerosol ('my art is me, I'm my art'), Andy Council ('[i]t's my own thing'), and Logan Hicks ('[I]f there isn't a personal connection between the work and the artists creating it, they are simply illustrators. If you don't feel a connection, it's hard to justify the time, energy and effort that it takes to make the work you do. That's not to say you can't think of it as a job, or a passion, but the seed of your motivation is the connection you have with the work you make'). Similarly, Bill Blast admitted that '[when a piece gets destroyed] it's like a piece of you gone', while Dutch street artist Fake explained that his art 'is my baby', echoing the father–son metaphor used by Skeme. Such metaphor reappeared in the interview with English artist Copyright: 'artworks, particularly those that I've spent of a lot of time over are like my offsprings, I go back and check on them from time to time, touch them up if

identity. [...] I was able to decide on the person I wanted to be'. Similarly, the book by Felix Braun, Children of the Can: Bristol Graffiti and Street Art (Tangent Books 2012) 310, includes an interview with Bristol writer Turo: 'the tag is me now, people know me as Turo, there's a lot of people that don't even know my real name. The persona I've created is actually me'. This is not limited to writers – several street artists also prefer to be identified with their art name only. For instance, when I first talked to Stik in his studio in East London, I used his real name, just to find out that he was more comfortable with me using the pseudonym Stik.

6 Ivor L. Miller, Aerosol Kingdom: Subway Painters of New York City (University Press Mississippi 2012) 139.

they're showing signs of wear'. And Akse noted that 'there is a physical effort to paint the artwork, which is quite demanding due to the amount of details and accuracy required, but there is also an emotional relationship as well'.

## WHAT ABOUT PICTURES OF ARTWORKS INCLUDED IN PHOTOGRAPHIC BOOKS WITHOUT AUTHORISATION?

The bond between these artists and their artwork is so strong that I was not surprised to learn from several of my interviewees that they would be annoyed if a picture of their piece were included in a photographic book without accurate credits (which would amount to a violation of the moral right of attribution, subject to certain exceptions). This can easily happen as the number of books, especially coffee-table books, containing pictures of graffiti and street artworks has increased significantly in recent times.[7] Yet, not all the artists and writers I talked to expressed anger at this behaviour – this is because the insertion of pictures of their works in books increases their visibility.

New York writer Skeme was quite clear: 'I'd say that [publication of pictures without consent] is shitty'. Bates was also quite vocal: 'at least they should name the artist and give credit where it's due. Also, ask artists if it's okay with them to take a photo first and if they want to be part of the project'. Many street artists had similar opinions. Athens-based Sonke said, '[I]t irritates me'; Andre Trenier noted, 'I wouldn't like that. I'd be offended'. The same goes for Akse and Logan Hicks, who stressed the ease with which publishers could trace the artists. The former pointed out: 'I wouldn't be happy if I'm not acknowledged as the artist. I always sign my artwork so people can find out who did the artwork so anybody who take pictures of my artwork has no excuse for not crediting me. In a way it is a way to protect my artwork'. And the latter commented: 'if it's someone taking a picture of just the mural and featuring it without any attribution, I'd be angry because at that point the focus is just the artwork with no context. Also, nowadays it's incredibly easy to find out the artist through google, street art forums, social media, etc. so there is no excuse for not finding out the artist'. Bill Blast echoed this sentiment: 'it's absolutely annoying, because there should be some recognition out of respect'. And Pablo Delgado highlighted the moral aspect as well: 'it's a matter of ethics'.

Several artists also made clear in our conversations that they would be ready to reach out to the publisher or the author, or react in some way. Damien Mitchell told me that he would 'contact the publisher and ask for a fee and acknowledgment'. The same goes for Fake ('if they don't credit me, I'd react and contact them'), Florence-based sticker artist Clet Abraham ('I'm very interested in the credits for my stuff – I'd

7 Not only photographic books have included pictures of street and graffiti artworks without the artists' and writers' permission. In our interview, Laser 3.14 mentioned that a publisher used his work on the cover of a dictionary: 'it was a picture taken from the street, manipulated in photoshop and placed on the cover of dictionary without my permission. The publisher had to pay me for using my work without my consent'.

complain if a photographic book included a work of mine and misattributed the authorship'), Lexi Bella ('yes, I'd get angry and I'd take action to remedy this'), and Paul Richard ('[I]f a book contained photos of my work, I'd ask for a credit. If the photos were responsible, in part, for the success of a profitable book, I might ask for a credit and possibly a payment, depending on the circumstances').[8] English artist Andy Council had a direct experience: 'it happened to me, it was annoying. A book included a mural of mine and others without acknowledging me. Somebody else gave me the book. I tried to email the guy'.

Not all artists expressed anger at this behaviour or manifested a willingness to react, though. For example, US wheatpaste artist Morley said to me: 'if a book or a website or a fan shares something I've done and isn't profiting from it, it doesn't really bother me'. Also, New York–based artist Rubin told me: 'once they did a book and didn't ask permission to include a work of mine. I just asked for a copy of the book. If it's a big publisher, I'd probably inform them they have used my work without permission. I wouldn't start a legal action, though'. Greg Lamarche has a similar opinion. While he noted that it is important and often easy to acknowledge artists' authorship because 'everyone has an email or website and people aren't that hard to find', he added: 'my first thought wouldn't be a legal action. My first action would be to reach out and say: hey, this information is wrong or you should have reached out or this needs to be corrected. And I guess if that was met with some sort of negativity, then the least amount of time I spend in court the better. Going to court is like a bad thing for me. Same as an hospital, if I can stay away, I do'.

Other artists I spoke with made clear they would have no confrontational reaction, or even be happy, because of the increased visibility the unauthorised publication would give them. New York artist Resa Piece, for example, told me: 'I feel like I'd have mixed feelings. A part of me would be: "oh look I'm in a book", but another part would be like: "wait, he should have asked my permission before using my artwork". So I guess it goes both ways'. Likewise, City Kitty said to me that 'while it's important to acknowledge and credit the artist as much as the photographer or author, it's always nice to have people share and enjoy my artwork'. And Crisp pointed out: 'I put artworks in the street for people to enjoy, so if you use a picture of my piece in your book, it's fine, I'm happy about that!' US artists Gabriel Corti and Zimer agree. The former noted, 'I'd be like cool, I got into a book, that's awesome', and the latter said, 'I'd prefer to be credited, but I'd definitely be happy because my art would have been spread to many new people'.[9]

8 Being credited is therefore very important for Paul Richard. He clarified during the interview: 'copyright law also allows me to be compensated for my work if my art is used commercially. If a company wants to reproduce my art, it needs my consent and should compensate me. Compensation could be as simple as crediting me'.

9 Even New York artist Paul Richard, who – as we have just seen – would be ready to react against the unauthorised publication of pictures of his art in a book, would still tend to see it positively. He said to me: 'I might see it as an opportunity'.

Some writers I talked to are on the same page, including Crane DPC, Dejer, and Cept. Crane DPC noted, '[I]t's all exposure I guess'. Dejer explained that while he has mixed feelings in this regard, 'I'd be happy because my piece would be seen more, and you know, exposure is the most important thing for writers. But I'd also feel angry because they have done it without my permission'. And US writer Cept pointed out that 'a publisher of a book which includes picture of my piece? I don't find a problem. I put it up in the public environment, so no much problem. It seems more an appreciation than appropriation. I'd be more excited than angry, they spread my art. I get some form of recognition in the graffiti community'. Moreover, New York writer Keo made a distinction between legal and illegal graffiti: 'if it was an illegal graffiti piece and someone captured in a photograph and published it, I'm happy and proud because I didn't do it with an expectation of compensation. I simply did it to be visible and have the maximum impact. Now if they buff that train, it's gone forever, but if somebody managed to capture and publish the photo with the piece to the world, it lives on and I get more exposure'. Keo also gave me an example of how the insertion of pictures of graffiti in iconic books such as *Subway Art*, even where there is no authorisation by the artist, can be beneficial to writers and artists in terms of visibility and commercial opportunities. He said, '[T]ake the first photographic books on graffiti, that spread this art form [*Subway Art*]. It included pieces made by writers who were teenagers. They were very happy to be in a book and didn't sign any legal release, but they became famous'.[10]

Some other artists also highlighted how difficult it may be for publishers to find both the creator of the piece and the photographer. English artist Copyright said to me that 'if it's in [an] art book, then the intent is to show off the works the photographer has found, it's sometimes difficult to credit every artist if you've just stumbled across a piece and it's unsigned'. Similarly, New York artist Chris Stain noted that 'there's a good chance the photographer has no idea who made the piece'. I also experienced myself such a complicated situation while I was working on a short photographic book focusing on copyright protection of street and graffiti art, titled *Protecting Art in the Street – A Guide to Copyright in Street Art and Graffiti*.[11] It took quite a long time for both myself and the publisher to gather all information on (and the consent of) both the artists and photographers. In that

[10] Keo added that 'from that exposure you could aim at some money down the line. Many never had that opportunity. Many are dead, on drugs and in prison. But a few have been able to capitalize because they have been able to say, "See, I am in *Subway Art* and I'm an old school legend of New York, now you are going to fly me to Italy for me to do an exhibition. Or Coca Cola is gonna hire me for an advertising campaign". So, some of the other artists who were great and active at the time didn't make it to the book, and the rest of the world doesn't know who they are'.

[11] Enrico Bonadio, *Protecting Art in the Street – A Guide to Copyright in Street Art and Graffiti* (Dokument Press 2020).

book I obviously explained that the moral right of attribution can be enforced by street artists and writers against whoever uses their works without properly mentioning their authorship; and that there are exceptions to this rule, for example, when a publisher is not able to find out the identity of the person who created an artwork. I also made clear that, in order to use the picture of the work without attribution, the publisher and the author of the book would need to establish that the search for the artist and/or photographer has been reasonable or diligent; and in that case courts would not be able to find an infringement of the moral right of attribution. I added that that very book – *Protecting Art in the Street – A Guide to Copyright in Street Art and Graffiti* – also contains a few pictures of artworks whose author has remained unknown, exactly because the publisher and I had not been able to find the artists and/or the photographers, even after diligent searches had been conducted.

Thus, gathering all information regarding artists and pieces (and authorisations) may be time-consuming but necessary for completing that sort of book. I also realised during the research for the present volume that a few artists seemed not to bother at all about this issue, because they (mistakenly) believe that including pictures of their pieces in books or other publications would not be against copyright or moral rights, as their art is placed in the public space or created illegally. Australian artist Crisp, for example, told me: 'I don't have major problems if they don't ask for my permission or credit me, it's in public'. And London writer Noir explained to me that 'this has happened many times and still happens regularly. Unfortunately, there's nothing that can be done about it. It's a public artwork gifted by the artists for no financial reasons'. Moreover, New York writer Reskew told me that he would get angry, but 'if the work was not legal, of course I could not get credit, though I find it ironic that someone can make money out of someone else crime'. This latter opinion is reminiscent of what Lady Pink, Noir, Damien Mitchell, and Keo told me during our interviews in relation to copyright claims over illegally created piece (as mentioned in the previous chapter).

## UNWELCOME ASSOCIATIONS WITH AND PREJUDICE AGAINST THE ARTIST'S REPUTATION AND HONOUR

We have seen that artists can also claim the moral right of integrity, which allows them to oppose prejudicial treatments of their art. In certain jurisdictions this right can be enforced to object to not only modifications and mutilations of the artwork but also mere uses of pieces which are considered unacceptable by the artist. This is the case of Canadian copyright law, which clarifies that the moral right of integrity is infringed if the work is 'used in association with a product, service, cause or institution' and such use prejudices the author's reputation or honour.[12]

12 Sections 28(1) and 28(2) of Canadian Copyright Act.

Cases where street artists have claimed the violation of their moral right of integrity due to unwelcome associations have recently occurred, for example, in the suit started in Italy in 2021 by Alessia Brabow against the Vatican City.[13] The latter had used a wheatpaste placed by the former on a wall in Rome to design a new stamp which was then sold to the public, in particular, collectors. Brabow's piece reinterpreted a painting by the nineteenth-century German artist Hoffmann depicting Jesus Christ, by superimposing the anatomic image of a heart and adding the message *Just use it*. The artist argued that associating her piece with the Catholic Church irremediably distorts and alters the message she wanted to convey to the public: indeed, what she meant to do was denounce certain excesses of any religious faiths and urge viewers to adopt a more critical and reflective stance towards dogmatic truths. The case seems to be still pending at the time of writing.

A similar action was brought in France by artist Combo in a case then decided in January 2021.[14] In March 2016, Combo created and placed a large wheatpaste on the wall of the Gustave Flaubert College in Paris depicting a representation of Marianne, the national personification of the French Republic. The artwork was incorporated in several videos supporting the 2017 presidential race of Jean-Luc Mélenchon, the French far left politician who is currently leader of La France Insoumise political party and a member of the National Assembly. The artist was annoyed by the fact that a politician had exploited his art for political gains and claimed that such use of his piece was contrary to the message of equality and openness originally conveyed. The Court of Paris did not agree. It found no offense that could have been prejudicial to Combo's reputation. In order to strengthen this point, the court noted that the imagery of birds (used in one of the disputed videos which incorporated Combo's piece) evoked the very spirit of freedom the artist wanted to highlight.

Several artists and writers I interviewed also confirmed they would be angry at unfavourable associations of their art and are in principle interested in enforcing the moral right of integrity. Specifically, they manifested a clear disapproval of certain juxtapositions of their works with messages they considered objectionable, especially if profit oriented and related to consumerism.[15] One of these artists is Alice Pasquini, who informed me about an unpleasant incident. Years ago she was contacted by a friend asking if she had spray-painted a mural for a musical video made

[13] See above Chapter 3, fn. 24.

[14] See above Chapter 3, fn. 22.

[15] For cases where street artists and writers have voiced disapproval towards associations of their works with consumerism see the US legal actions mentioned in Chapter 3, fns. 11–19. I will come back to these unwelcome associations and legal suits in Chapter 5 when making the point that artists and writers may be anti-establishment and at the same time bring copyright cases against corporations which exploit their art.

by two Italian mainstream rappers whom she dislikes. The artwork had not only been incorporated into the video – animation was also added, for example, snot and tears going down from the faces of the two persons represented in the artwork, who happened to be Alice's sister and cousin. She was annoyed, as she does not want to be associated with such 'banal mainstream artists', and wrote a Facebook post where she confirmed that. She added in our interview: 'I mean, if Bono Vox [U2 leader] shoots a video and uses my mural in it, it's ok. If it's Fedez and J-Ax [the two rappers in question], I really get pissed off'. Alice Pasquini did not take legal action. Yet, it is rather clear that the artist considers her association with mainstream and banal rappers as prejudicial to her reputation and honour. This is due to the fact that – as the artist confirmed in our conversation – she values a certain artistic and underground musical scene. She also noted that if one of her artworks were to be displayed in a video made by Save the Children, she would accept it. If instead it were used by a big pharmaceutical company or a corporation to sell something she does not agree with, it would be a completely different issue and she would consider taking legal action.

Australian artist Ian Strange has a similar opinion. He confirmed with me that sometimes he had to turn down commissions from certain companies 'because it's a loss of reputation when you work with these big commercial giants'. He added that he may accept working with a few companies 'but not McDonald's or those companies'. He clarified that it would depend on 'whether it's in line with the things I do ethically and in line with the things I believe in. As an artist, I need to think of my own values and my own ethos and the authenticity that comes with that. That's why I don't associate myself with certain brands as it will ruin my reputation in the eyes of people who support my work and the value they've for my work'.

The same feeling was expressed by others I interviewed. London artist Ben Eine told me during our interview in his London studio: 'I'm happy in some circumstances for my art to be used to promote something I believe in, if it's for a good cause. I've spent thirty years working hard to get where I'm now, so why should anyone take all my hard work and effort and use it to promote, for example, their new cars? What if they use my art to promote child prostitution? My name will be associated with it and it ruins my credibility'. Also, New York artist Lamkat told me that 'it would totally depend on what brand and what use they wanted it for. Like if it was to represent something that I'm very against, I wouldn't take part in it. For example, there is no way I'd participate if it was for cigarettes'. Likewise, Italian artist Giacomo 'Run' Bufarini said to me (while painting a huge mural on a church's wall in South London) that the decision to take legal action would depend on who uses his art. If it is the little café in East London, he clarified, that would not be a major problem. If it is a car manufacturer instead, that is when he would think about a legal action. Similar opinions were expressed by Crisp: 'I wouldn't like my work to be associated with a brand, for example McDonald's. I don't have problems if it's a community project';[16] and by US writer Cept: 'I feel raged when corporations appropriate artworks, especially when they are not connected with the culture. There are some corporations (skating, street fashion) I'd be ok with – it would come from an entity that would be more respectful, not like Coca-Cola, Pepsi, or CNN'.

A series of artists and writers also stressed their sensitivity towards animals' safety and rights, and noted their opposition to uses of their art which disrespect animals. New York artist Christy Rupp is one of them. During our encounter at a café in Manhattan she told me that if PETA (People for the Ethical Treatment of Animals, an animal rights organization) used her work on a shirt, she would have 'less of a problem' than if a commercial entity would, for instance, if the latter sells a shirt that depicts a rat with its head cut off. She confirmed that her message would be distorted. New York artist Enx is also vocal about animal rights, and would be upset if her artworks are used in a way which harms animal dignity. During our conversation at the Brooklyn Central Library she told me: 'I'd be very upset if someone used one of my wolves for profit and didn't even mention the extreme violent situations wolves are facing. Using any animals image and not defending them or trying to help raise awareness is straight up wrong'.[17] Moreover, New York graffiti pioneer Zephyr commented, 'I'm a vegetarian, so if they use my work for a meat company, then I'm like "ugh this is bad", and I'll have to be aggressive to make sure that they remove it and maybe also make a statement saying we're sorry we used that because he doesn't want to be associated with the meat industry'.

[16] As we have seen, McDonald's is disliked by many street artists and writers. When in 2017 various murals in the Bushwick area of Brooklyn were incorporated without consent in an advertisement by the fast food company, several artists manifested their disgust. One of them, Lmnopi, wrote in a Facebook post that 'McDonald's just teamed up with the Gentrifying Bushwick Collective to exploit street art in Brooklyn to sell Burgers in Netherlands. This will not stand. They did not get my permission to use my work in their psuedo doc and the mural is NOT part of the Bushwick Collective. PERIOD' (The Bushwick Collective is a mural art organization that is very active in the Brooklyn borough of New York). See the Vandalog blogpost of 12 March 2017 at https://blog.vandalog.com/category/art-news. This statement also clearly shows the lack of respect some artists have towards street art insiders who happen to endorse mainstream brands.

[17] In the interview Enx further noted that 'all the time in advertising, even other artists will use animal imagery for selfish gain and not mention the horrible situations every animal is facing. Animals are not here to help humans sell products, or as icons for political parties or to express human conditions. The copyright should go to the animal itself. The payment to the animal should take form as animal activism or financial compensation or donation to that animal cause. This is the sad fact: not one animal exists without a cause'. Enx thus curiously advocates for giving copyright to animals. This is reminiscent of the famous monkey selfie case. In that dispute the animal rights organisation PETA had taken legal action against wildlife photographer Slater, claiming that it was enforcing the copyright on behalf of the monkey, which – the organisation argued – should have been considered the author of the famous selfie. The court disagreed, noting that while animals had constitutional standing, they lacked statutory standing to claim copyright infringement. See *Naruto v. Slater*, 2018 U.S. App. LEXIS 10129 (9th Cir. Cal., Apr. 23, 2018).

Political or demeaning associations are also often unwelcome by street artists and writers (see again the Combo case in France, mentioned earlier). Understandably, they often feel uncomfortable about uses of their art to promote ideas and messages which they may not like or do not want to endorse. Artist John Fekner, who as mentioned acquired notoriety through the late 1970s and early 1980s by stenciling phrases on carefully chosen outdoor locations in New York, was clear in our interview in Queens: 'if someone were to use one of my messages to contribute to the well-being of humanity or mother nature, that would be good karma. However, if Donald Trump or someone similar, co-opted the messages, then that would be a cease-and-desist issue'. Being associated with scandalous contexts is not appreciated, either. Former writer Good Guy Boris told me during our conversation in Athens: 'I've a company that works in collaboration with artists who work in the street, to exploit their art. In the contracts they agree on how their art is to be used, total commission, etcetera, so that they're protected, it specifies that his artwork won't be put on things like sex toys or something that he doesn't want his artwork on'.

## ATTITUDES TOWARDS DESTRUCTION

Laws protecting the moral right of integrity in most jurisdictions do not explicitly clarify that such a right also allows artists to prevent the destruction of their pieces. Some courts, however, have recognised that this right exists, for example, in India.[18] Surprisingly, many civil law jurisdictions that have traditionally fiercely protected moral rights have not incorporated an explicit statutory right opposing the destruction of artworks – but the case law in some of these countries such as France and the Netherlands has clarified that artists can sometimes enforce this right to prevent destruction in certain circumstances. Copyright law in the UK does not provide such a right either, and no British court has ever explicitly dealt with this issue.[19]

A country where the right of visual artists to object to the destruction of their creations is expressly provided by the law is the US. As mentioned in Chapter 1, in the landmark *5Pointz* case twenty-one artists managed to obtain multimillion dollar compensation for the illegal destruction of their works by the property owner. The case attracted wide media attention and can be considered revolutionary. Practitioners of types of art that in the past have been considered by wide sectors of society as having minor artistic value have been given a kind of legal protection which was originally designed with traditional fine artists in mind. In other words,

[18] *Sehgal v. Union of India* [2005] FSR 39 (stressing the 'urgent need to interpret Section 57 of the [Indian] Copyright Act 1957 in its wider amplitude to include destruction of a work of art, being the extreme form of mutilation, since by reducing the volume of the author's creative corpus it affects his reputation prejudicially as being actionable under said section' (para 56)).

[19] For an analysis of how different jurisdictions of common and civil law protect artworks against destruction, see Enrico Bonadio, 'Copyright Protection of Street Art and Graffiti under UK Law (2017)' 2 Intellectual Property Quarterly, 202–203.

what this case confirms is that the gap between street and graffiti art on the one hand and fine art on the other is narrowing – which may contribute to changing the perception that many members of the general public still have of these unconventional forms of creativity (although differences between fine and street/graffiti art obviously still remain).

Due to this seminal case, artists within these communities may now be more inclined to try to save their works by relying on moral rights laws, if they so wish. Specifically, the huge sum of damages awarded in *5Pointz* may convince artists to take legal action against property owners when their pieces are threatened with destruction. I do not share other commentators' fears that after this decision property owners – especially in the US – will now be more reluctant to allow graffiti and other murals to be painted on their walls. If property owners respect the procedures required by law (which was not the case in *5Pointz* because the property owner served no notice to the artists), they are likely to avoid liability. Indeed, this notice requirement is arguably not a very cumbersome burden.

Not only may this historic decision by the District Court of New York contribute to changing the general public's attitude vis-á-vis street art and graffiti, it also shows an evolution of these forms of art, which can no longer be considered as intrinsically ephemeral. This is so even though there are still a relatively large number of street artists and writers who accept the temporary nature of their creative outputs. It should also be noted that some forms of street art are less transient than other and often end up lasting for long periods of time. Take the mosaic tiles and sculptures applied on walls and other surfaces by artists such as Invader (from France) and Cityzen Kane (from England). These pieces often benefit from a long life span, as they are attached to walls with extra-strong glues or sometimes even cement.[20]

Not just property owners often destroy street and graffiti art. *Buffing*, as this phenomenon is known in graffiti jargon, is also carried out by local councils in their struggle to keep neighbourhoods 'clean'. Moreover, street artworks are often attacked by writers who vandalise them with tags. London writer 10Foot, for example, is well known for going over many murals painted by Banksy in England. 'Beefs' between writers and street artists which end up in the erasure or mutilation of murals are not uncommon. In New York the vandalising acts of a street artist (or a collective of artists) named Splasher were notorious in 2006 and 2007, with several works of other street artists like Faile being attacked.[21] Furthermore, as mentioned in Chapter 1, a street artist told me in an interview that one of his murals was vandalised by a writer. The expression he used when referring to the perpetrator of this act explains the sometimes-tense relationship between the two subcultures: 'fucking writers'. A more moderate opinion was

[20] Magda Danysz, From Style Writing to Art: A Street Art Anthology (Drago 2011) 311; see also Gavin, *Street Renegades: New Underground Art* (London: Laurence King Publishing Ltd, 2007) 56 (reporting Invader's opinion: 'the material I use (tiles and cement) are made to be permanent').

[21] Rafael Schacter, Ornament and Order: Graffiti, Street Art and the Parergon (Ashgate 2014) 124.

expressed by New York writer Reskew during our conversation at a Manhattan café: 'when taggers vandalize it [my piece], that feels like a personal attack and is upsetting in its own way, though sometimes it's out of sheer ignorance of a very young artist'.

No doubt street art and graffiti are vulnerable 'to the give and take of the street'.[22] And this is also true of other forms of public art. As has been noted, muralism and public art in general 'differs from art media in that the large scale and public visibility automatically elicit public response'.[23] The art which is produced in the public environment thus becomes part of a broader community life, which inevitably puts creators in a more vulnerable position than if they were creating gallery art (with some artists taking legal actions to try to preserve their pieces).[24]

It is exactly because of their vulnerability that many street artworks are often protected, frequently through special glasses, by both owners of walls and local councils.

[22] Jeff Ferrell, Crimes of Style: Urban Graffiti and the Politics of Criminality (Northeastern University Press 1996) 197.

[23] Eva Sperling Cockcroft, John Pitman Weber, and James Cockcroft, Toward a People's Art: The Contemporary Mural Movement (University of New Mexico Press 1977) 94.

[24] Ibidem. There have also been cases where mural artists and other practitioners of public art have taken legal action, often relying on the moral right of integrity. The following US cases, most of which settled out of court, are noteworthy.

(i) In 1986 the artist Jesus Campusano painted a mural on a building in San Francisco, being assisted by three painters and his partner. After the building's owner covered it in 1998, his partner and children sued under VARA in the California Northern District Court. They claimed the owner had not notified them about the intention to cover the mural. The case was then settled for $200,000. See the University of Missouri–St. Louis handout from 'The Artist as Entrepreneur' lessons, published at www.umsl.edu/continuinged/artist/artist-lesson-VARA-ho2.htm (last accessed 5 May 2022).

(ii) In *Hanrahan v. Ramirez* (No. 2:97-CV-7470, 1998) a group of young artists had painted a mural carrying an anti-drug message on the side of a liquor store with the authorisation of the property owner. After the store owner whitewashed half of the mural three years later, the artists took legal action. The court held in 1998 that the piece had recognised stature because it had won a national prize, received the local community's support, and had been displayed in a government building as a photograph. The judge awarded the artists £48,000 as compensation and ordered the restoration of the mural.

(iii) In 2006 the mural Edward Ruscha, painted by Kent Twitchell over the course of nine years in Los Angeles, was painted over with no preliminary notice being given to the artist. The latter sued the US government, which owned the building, and eleven other defendants for damages under VARA in the California Central District Court. Almost two years later the case settled for $1.1 million. The case was *Kent Twitchell v. West Coast General Corp et al.*, 06-cv-04857 (C.A.C.D. 2006).

(iv) Another case where the recognised stature requirement has been debated was *Henderson v. Ziman* (No 2:14-cv-03042-SJO-AS, E.D. Cal. Apr. 21, 2014). In April 2014, the artist Victor Henderson started a legal action under VARA over the destruction of the mural *Brooks Avenue Painting*, which he had co-created in 1969. Henderson claimed that his artwork had major historical significance. While Henderson seemed to have strong evidence showing that his mural was of recognised stature, the artist voluntarily abandoned the case.

(v) Muralist Dan Fontes painted an artwork on the side of an Oakland building in 1987. In 2015 he filed a suit in the California Northern District Court against the owners of the building after the tenant had whitewashed the mural without notifying the artist as required by VARA, and asked damages for $400,000. The case was *Fontes v. Autocom Networks, Inc.*, C 15–02044 CRB (N.D. Cal. 2015), and was later settled.

The artwork *Tuttomondo* painted by Keith Haring in Pisa (which I mentioned at the beginning of this book) is also protected by a high glass wall, in addition to having been listed by the Italian Ministry of Culture as an 'artistic-historical artwork of particular importance'.[25] One may also note that only murals by famous street artists such as Haring and Banksy are protected – which could be deemed discriminatory and hypocritical.[26] Why should just well-known artists be given such a chance? This occurred, for example, when the deputy leader of a council in the English coastal town of Hastings decided to preserve Banksy's *Tesco Sandcastles* piece by covering it with perspex glass and noted, 'I know that we have a zero tolerance policy on graffiti, and that is absolutely right. However, we have to be flexible so on this occasion I have agreed that Banksy can be an exception to our rule and can stay'.[27] Such hypocrisy may understandably produce jealousy within the subculture and provoke vandalism. In Melbourne, Banksy's piece *Little Driver* was protected by plexiglass by the city after an application to protect it was approved. Yet, the piece was subsequently vandalised by unknown people pouring silver paint behind the glass.[28] Resentment amongst writers also surfaced in my interview with Noir: 'councils have double standards where they buff the artwork and then employ street artists to paint the exact wall at a cost to the taxpayer'.

Indeed, it should be noted that the presence of street art often increases the value of properties on which is is placed. In this regard, what the owner of a house upon

(vi) In 2016 Katherine Craig sued the real estate developer Princeton Enterprises after the latter had allegedly threatened to destroy her watercolor work named *The Illuminated Mural*. The artist had entered into an agreement with the previous owner, specifying that the artwork would remain on the building for at least 10 years. The case was later settled with an agreement that allowed the artwork to remain. On this case see Kirk Phinho, 'Colorful 9-Story Mural to Stay on Milwaukee Junction Building under Court Settlement' (13 April 2017) *Crain's Detroit Business*.

(vii) In 2017 mural artist Monte Thrasher sued several individuals and corporate defendants in the Central District of California, claiming that they had painted over his *Six Heads* mural, without the artist's permission, and substituted it with another mural. *Thrasher v. Siegel*, No. 2:17-cv-03047 (C.D. Cal. April 24, 2017). The case was not settled, nor was there a decision on the merits. The defendant Siegel filed for bankruptcy in 2019 and the Court decided to close the case.

25 Decreto 335/2013. The mural was inserted in the list of 'beni tutelati'.

26 But for an example of preservation efforts directed towards works created by less famous artists, see what happened in Minneapolis in the wake of the George Floyd's murder. Two grassroots organisations, Save the Boards and Memorialize the Movement, joined forces with the aim of collecting and conserving the many outdoor plywood artworks that had been painted to commemorate Floyd. On this project see Heather Shirey and David Todd Lawrence, 'Creating a Global Archive of Covid 19 Street Art' (2021) 3(1) *NUART Journal*, 10–15.

27 See Will Ellsworth-James, Banksy: The Man Behind the Wall (Aurum Press 2013) 101. The council of the Islington borough in London also showed interest in preserving Banksy's street artworks. According to *The Times*, a listing of Banksy's artworks was given to the council's head of environment to avoid his pieces having to be painted over. See Jeffrey Ian Ross, 'London Calling: Contemporary Graffiti and Street Art in the UK's Capital', in Jeffrey Ian Ross (ed.), Routledge Handbook of Graffiti and Street Art (Routledge 2016) 278.

28 Alison Young, Street Art, Public City: Law, Crime and the Urban Imagination (Routledge 2013) 142, 148.

which Banksy painted an artwork did is quite telling. He actually put the art piece up for sale and included the house as a part of the deal: 'a mural with a house attached'.[29] Lessons should also be learned from the gentrification processes experienced by many American and European towns. These processes have partially been fuelled by the explosion of creativity brought by street art,[30] which has helped to revamp and give added value to formerly neglected areas.

As we have seen, only street artworks of a certain importance, but not graffiti pieces, have sometimes been preserved.[31] This is probably due to the fact that many members of the general public still consider graffiti writing a lesser form of art, if not just visual pollution, as mentioned in Chapter 1. But it seems this perception is gradually changing, as has also indirectly been confirmed by the decision in the *5Pointz* case. In that dispute, not only street artists but also writers joined *5Pointz* curator Meres One in the legal action against the property owner who had illegally whitewashed their pieces. Also, restoration of graffiti, especially if painted by well-known writers, could soon become (more) accepted. There are early signs of this happening already. In 2021 Italian writer and studio artist Keyone started a campaign to raise funds needed to complete the restoration of two pieces painted in 1984 by New York writers Phase 2 and Delta 2 in a little village called Quattordio in the north-western part of Italy. The project was started in 2017 also with the support of the local council.

But what do street artists and writers think about the possible destruction of their works? Are they interested in attempting to oppose such a fate, possibly by starting a suit? I posed these and other questions during my interviews, after explaining to my informants that the moral right of integrity may be successfully relied on in some circumstances to object to destruction of their art, especially in countries such as the US. The types of answers I got varied significantly, ranging from total disapproval of, and willingness to oppose, destruction via a legal action on one end of the spectrum, to acceptance of and even praise for the erasure of the artwork, on the other.

29 Ian Edwards, 'Banksy's Graffiti: A Not-So-Simple Case of Criminal Damage?' (2009) 73 *The Journal of Criminal Law* 345, 351; Steve Wright, *Home Sweet Home: Banksy's Bristol* (Tangent Books 2008) 35.

30 While street art is often considered to be a symptom of 'urban regeneration', graffiti (which is less appreciated by the general public) is frequently regarded as a sign of 'urban degeneration'. See Susan Hansen, '"Pleasure Stolen from the Poor": Community Discourse on the "Theft" of a Banksy' (2016) 12(3) *Crime, Media, Culture*, 290.

31 It has also been suggested that a Banksy piece placed on a building would make the latter deserve a Grade II listing, which under UK law is reserved for buildings of special interest, warranting 'every effort being made to preserve them'. See John Webster, 'Should the Work of Banksy be Listed?' (2011) 4 *J.P.L.* 374, 380 (drawing an interesting comparison between Banksy's artworks and the famous Abbey Road Zebra Crossing in north-west London, which was featured on the last studio LP by the Beatles and which has become an iconic symbol of the band and a destination for the fans; the crossing was given Grade II listing by English Heritage due to its national cultural value and status). Actually, when Banksy painted a mural in the English town of Cheltenham (close to the UK Government Communications Headquarters) on the side of a Grade II listed building (and after the local council heard about the possible sale of the artwork), the council retrospectively added the mural to the listing. Yet, the piece eventually got destroyed. See also Will Ellsworth-Jones, *Banksy: The Man behind the Wall*, 2nd rev. ed. (Frances Lincoln 2021) 76.

What has emerged from the research is that when it comes to big projects which require long preparation and actual work, artists are annoyed if their pieces are destroyed shortly after their creation. New York artist Bill Blast, for instance, told me that if one spends a lot of time on anything and it gets destroyed, it is inevitable that he wants to fight to prevent it. Another New York artist, Depsone, is of the same opinion. He noted during our conversation: 'I think it would depend. For example, how much time did I put into it?' Likewise, Italian artist Giacomo 'Run' Bufarini said to me: 'You're asking if I get annoyed if someone destroys my art? Well, it depends on many things, for example, on the dimension and size of the mural. I mean, if it's a huge stuff, like sixteen metres high, if it's taken me weeks of work, and also the quality of the paint is good, well in these cases I do care about its preservation. If it lasts twenty years or as long as possible, I'd be happy. I mean, it's not an intervention on a bus shelter or telephone box!' A similar opinion was expressed by Rubin, Akse, and Ozmo. While Rubin noted that 'sometimes I go and fix murals I've done, that need to be repaired. Because I want my stuff to look good, if it's a big mural I have spent time on, I go and repair it', Akse commented that 'the destruction of my street artwork hurts me as an artist and as a man as I spend a lot of time and energy to produce something for other people to enjoy for free and at my own expenses. It doesn't only affect me but also other people who enjoy my artwork'. And when I asked Ozmo if he cares about the conservation of his murals, he replied, 'I'm currently involved in an urban regeneration project in the Loreto area of Milan, now named NoLo (North of Loreto). I've painted a mural, and proposed that it remains there for at least five or even ten years. I mean, I invest time and money in these works. Obviously, I want them to remain. Sometimes, when I get commissions, I try to insert a clause in the written agreement, specifying that the mural should remain for a few years'. Writer Bates expressed a similar feeling,[32] noting, 'Yes, I'd like to spread my artwork around and hopefully it could stay up'.

But who better than Meres One, the artist who founded and curated *5Pointz* for many years and successfully led the collective legal action after the whitewashing of 2013, could explain the reason street artists are increasingly willing to fight against the destruction of their pieces? Sitting on a sofa in his Brooklyn house, he told me: 'you wanna see your piece last as long as possible. There is no comparison between the real piece on the wall and the photograph. What about the scale? What about the wall's texture? Look at my three-dimensional murals. This effect is given by the original piece, not by the photograph. [...] Pictures are just not enough'. These words were echoed by Marie Flageul, longtime spokeswoman and advocate for *5Pointz*. She commented during our interview in Brooklyn that 'the original

32 The need to take into account the time the artwork has stayed has also been highlighted by Anjl. I asked her if while she accepts that street art is ephemeral, she would nevertheless try to save her piece. She replied, 'Absolutely. Because if you think about things that have been around for maybe 20 or 30 years, those are considered untouchable by those who understand and respect the rules of street art and graffiti'.

piece is the artist's business card, especially in gentrified areas. By placing the work in the street, an artist positions herself. Take the *Mona Lisa* by Leonardo da Vinci, for example – if you look at the original painting in the Louvre, her eyes follow you. This doesn't happen with a picture'.[33]

Many other street artists and writers I spoke with share the same feelings. New York writer Mastro was very clear: 'of course I'm going to fight it [to prevent destruction]. Why would I not? If an idiot is removing your artwork, then you're going to have a conflict and you're going to fight to keep what you have put up'. Similarly, Bronx-based muralist Royal King Bee said, '[I]f I had the legal means and it would work in my favour, definitely [I would try to fight destruction]'. Likewise, Sonke said, '[I]t [destruction] bothers me a lot. Yes absolutely [I would try to prevent it]'. Many others expressed similar opinions. Amongst them, it is interesting to highlight the feelings expressed by US artist Elle. When I asked her if she would feel upset by the destruction of their pieces, she replied:

> Yeah definitely. I started out with wheatpasting and the reason I got into graffiti was because sometimes I spent a week on a piece, put it up and found that it was gone the next day. It was so annoying that I spent so much time hand painting these pieces and they'd be buffed or torn down that night or the next day. So I wanted to move into spray-painting because of the longevity of it, and it's more permanent. That was my motivation. Of course, nothing on the street stays for too long. It's part of the talent if you find a spot where you think that it's going to stay and it actually stays for a while. You're good if you can make it stay for a while.[34]

Other writers and artists made clear they would oppose the destruction of their works subject to certain conditions. Skeme noted that 'as you get older and you become

33 Even some New York writers of the 1970s did have bad feelings when their pieces were erased or vandalised by other writers. One of them is Breezer, whose interview appears in the book *Training Days* by Henry Chalfant and Sacha Jenkins, Training Days: The Subway Artists Then and Now (Thames & Hudson 2014) 38: 'it's not nice to spend a couple of hours doing a car and then see it crossed out or have a throw-up all over it'. Lady Pink had a similar opinion: 'What was the point in spending all night doing something big and beautiful if it was going to end up getting dissed?' ibidem, 190.

Yet, the majority of New York writers of that era undoubtedly did not bother too much about their pieces going. For example, Skeme told me: '[a]t that time I never painted any mural that had any reasonable expectation of permanency. Once you painted on that train, the next day it was painted over. You knew that when you painted on the train, it was going to be gone the following day. If you had asked me thirty years ago, I had no expectations of permanency or "ownership"'. See also Greg Lamarche's opinion infra in this section. Coming to the current times, while it is true that many graffiti practitioners still share the same opinion as Skeme, it should also be noted that writers sometimes choose locations which cannot be easily attacked by other writers or erased by property owners, thus showing some hope that their piece, tag, or throw-up will stay as long as possible. See in this regards Felix Braun, Children of the Can: Bristol Graffiti and Street Art (Tangent Book 2012) 117 (reporting the words of Bristol writer Dot Com: 'I like rooftops because they stay there for years, and people don't usually take them out').

34 Another of my interviewees, New York studio and street artist Stephen Palladino, seems to be keen to preserve some of his pieces. While Palladino admits that 'destruction is a bit upsetting, but expected' (therefore he is in agreement with several other artists I spoke with; see *infra*), he pointed out that 'for big commissions, you try to write that they let you know when it is destroyed' so that he can try to save it.

exposed to different things, like copyright, you start to form an opinion. It [starting a legal fight to prevent destruction] would depend on a couple of things: the type of permission that I got; and if any payment and contract are involved'. London-based artist Pablo Delgado is of a similar opinion. He pointed out that he would start a suit to object to the destruction of his work 'only if the piece was a commission and the owner of the property is not there to defend it'.[35] Likewise, English artist Mobstr, known for painting typographic messages full of sarcasm and irony on walls and billboards, commented that taking legal action to oppose destruction 'depends on the history and context of the piece. For a random street art piece I painted without permission, no'. New York artists Lexi Bella and Depsone instead seemed to focus on their attachment to the artwork. The former said, '[P]ossibly I'd take action if the piece was that important to me. But not all of my work is that important'. And the latter opined that 'it'd depend on [...] what does the work mean to me. You know, there are so many things that go into it, so I can't give an answer to that without having a direct experience, you know? [...] if I know in my mind that this (piece) is going to run for a while and then it disappears the next week, then I'm a little bummed'.[36]

Other artists I talked to were interested in how long the artwork has stayed, and would be upset and/or consider starting a legal action (or try in some other way to preserve the piece) if there are plans to get rid of their work prematurely. Lamkat, for example, told me that 'it depends on how long it was up for. If I did the work one day and it was gone the next, of course I'd be sad, but one year or ten years, it would be different'. Andre Trenier is on the same page, as he commented in our conversation: '[n]ot generally, but maybe if I feel like I'm somehow being deceived or lied to. If the owner told me it's going to stay for this amount of time and then decides before that to paint it over, I might be offended. It would have to be a very specific situation'.[37] Andy Council has a similar opinion, and also highlights the role of the local community. He said, 'Whitewashing? I'd be sad, I put efforts in doing the mural also talking to communities and local areas – the mural is the

Palladino also noted that he was commissioned to do a mural in Los Angeles, and the agreement he negotiated and signed contained provisions which not only secured his copyright ownership but also included a notice obligation requiring the property owner to allow Palladino to get back the mural back if he wanted.

[35] However, in the interview Pablo Delgado clarified that in all other circumstances 'normally I wouldn't object on the removal. You're at the mercy of decisions from others when your art is placed somewhere that isn't yours'.

[36] Depsone would also ponder who destroys the art. He pointed out: 'you know, if it was the city doing this, I feel that it would be something that I'd like to take a stand against and make a point, because in that case they are not dealing with the person who commissioned me or the building owner. But if it was the building owner or the person who commissioned the work, it would be hard to say, "Why are you removing it?" That stuff just happens so often that I couldn't take the time to fight it. But if the city does that, it would be worth trying to protect my artwork'.

[37] Trenier expanded on such a hypothetical situation: '[l]et's say that I painted a storefront gate and the business was going out of business and I wanted that piece and therefore say, "Hey I will pay to remove it," and the owner says, "No, we're whitewashing it or destroy[ing] it", then I might try to take legal action'.

result of a work which also involves the local community. If I had the legal means, I'd try to prevent it. Of course, if more time has passed, my anger would decrease. If it's removed in few weeks, the anger would be higher, if after years, a bit less'. The importance of taking into account the opinion and wishes of local communities was also highlighted by William Kasso in our interview. He said to me: 'if the building where the Gandhi mural I painted is on changed owners, and they decided to paint over it, then they'll honestly not have to deal with me, they'll have to deal with the community, because the city has gotten attached to it. So, they wouldn't even have to worry about me, you know? I mean, Gandhi's grandson came out to see it. To me, that's a landmark. They want to choose to take down a landmark for selfish reasons, they got to deal with the repercussions of the city at large'.

Some artists I interviewed confirmed they would be upset if their piece were destroyed, but at the same time were sceptical about, or not interested in, complaining. Former writer Dejer noted that he would be sad if his piece just disappeared, but it would be more acceptable for him if it were whitewashed rather than gone over by other writers.[38] A similar feeling was expressed by writer Reskew: 'I accept that this is what will happen at some point or other, but it does still upset me'. Also, Claw Money, a New York writer turned fashion designer, told me in our interview: 'I'd be sad if my mural got whitewashed, but I wouldn't try to take legal action – it's part of the game. They pay me for my murals, I don't care what they are fucking gonna do after'. Logan Hicks, City Kitty, and Crisp are of the same opinion. While Hicks said, 'I'm never happy to see a piece go, but any artists that puts up something in the streets and expects immortality for that piece is foolish',[39] City Kitty commented that 'this is a risk you take when you choose to put art on the street. If the idea of dealing with this upsets an artist, they need to find a different outlet'. And Crisp echoed: 'Whitewashing? I don't like this, but it's something that I accept, it's part of the street art scene. It happened to me. If you worry about that, you should not do art in the street. I did a big mural in Bogotá in October 2016, I loved it. And then a couple of months ago I realised they painted over it – you can't be bothered too much about that'. Likewise, Stephen Palladino commented that 'it is upsetting but expected'. Akse has a similar view, and noted in our interview:

> it always bothers me when one of my pieces gets painted over or defaced even if it was meant to be temporary, but I accept it. If the piece lasts for a few weeks or months,

[38] Preference for the total cancellation of a mural was also highlighted by Gabriel Corti during our encounter. He first pointed out that he would be annoyed and offended if his work was removed or tampered with in a disrespectful manner. He then discussed what the term 'disrespectful' means in his opinion: he believes that whitewashing a mural would not be disrespectful because 'it's understandable that they could do so. However, if they paint over the work partially, this could be seen as disrespectful'.

[39] Even Don Rimx, who as mentioned in certain circumstances may consider taking legal action, admitted during our conversation that 'I know the mural will only live for a certain amount of time so I can't really do anything to avoid that. It's not my property, so you have to respect it if they want to do it [destroy the artwork]'.

> that's ok, but if it's defaced after a few days it really annoys me. As I said before, you get emotionally attached to your piece and you also feel for the public who cannot enjoy your artwork anymore. But there is nothing I can do to stop it and after a few years you go over it. It [legal action] never crossed my mind, although I've been offered to protect my first Heisenberg fan art tribute with sheets when it was defaced.

Thus, Akse seems convinced that the law cannot help him prevent the erasure of his art ('there is nothing I can do to stop it'). I heard a similar opinion from US writer Cept, who noted in our interview: 'I'd be upset about it, but it's part of the game. Nothing is permanent. I may try to talk to the property owner but there is little to do about it'. New York street artist Paul Richard has the same view: 'I'm not always bothered if my art disappears. I can't think of a circumstance where I'd have a legal right to prevent the destruction or removal of my art when I paint directly on someone's property without permission. Vandalism is damaging property that's not yours. Technically, some of what I do is vandalism'. Many other street artists and writers do accept the destruction of their works, something which – they believe – is inevitable and should not be opposed. Street and fine artist Cycle, whom I spoke with in his studio in Astoria, Queens (New York), even criticised the legal suit started by *5Pointz* artists and writers. He simply said to me: 'I don't understand it'. Also, New York writer Hoacs noted that 'it's a possibility we need to accept. Sometimes it lasts one day, a month. What are you going to do? Get over it and move on'. Keo was even clearer: 'sooner or later all artworks will go. [...] It's only art and graffiti. If I had the power to fight injustice, how about we fight the police from shooting unarmed babies in the street first. Fuck my artwork'. And writer and muralist William Kasso said to me: '[n]o, I wouldn't even waste my time [trying to oppose destruction]. If they take it down, I'll paint it again somewhere else'. Similarly, Dutch stencil artist Fake noted in the interview that 'if a wall I painted is whitewashed, it's possible that I paint another mural in the same spot'. And Greg Lamarche told me: 'I grew up writing on the subways where you do something and it's gone or cleaned the next day. So from an early age I understood that stuff doesn't last and that's one of the things that keep[s] you competitive since you've [got] to keep going out and getting your name up. So if something gets painted you have already gone into the situation knowing that this may not last. I'm very used to this idea and I've embraced it'.

The following artists and writers I talked to are on the same page. While Enx noted 'I accept it, it's all part of the game. These are first-world problems anyway – this is what I remind myself', Chris Stain confirmed that he is not bothered at all by the erasure of his pieces, as 'everything is temporary'. Similar opinions have been expressed by Damien Mitchell ('I'd accept it. It's part of the game'), Gabriel Corti ('the artwork is not going to last forever – this is part of the game'), Resa Piece ('I accept that this is the nature of street art and it's okay because I'm always painting and if I lose one wall I get another one, so it's not a big deal'), Joel Artista ('[I]t's always sad to see it go, especially if it's a piece I really like; but I accept it and it's something that you know ahead of time. If you choose street art and graffiti and these types of things, it's supposed to be ephemeral'), Murrz ('in an emotional sense it hurts when people paint over my shit, but it's fine because that's how it is'), Lexi Bella ('[T]his is part of the transience of life and this art thing we do. Change is part of life and we have to accept when we put something out there it may be gone tomorrow, in 5 years, 30 years, or be there for 20,000 years'),[40] Easy ('[Y]es, I'd respect it. It's his property. When you do a wall like that, you got to go into that mindset that there's a possibility that he might change his mind and whitewash the wall, it happens all the time'), Oker ('I accept it'), Jef Aerosol ('[I]t's the rule. I don't like to see perspex protections on street pieces – it's totally stupid'), Stik ('I accept it – it's a risk. Putting an artwork in the street means that it's both very powerful and vulnerable. If it's destroyed, then it's destroyed'), Pablo Delgado ('I know the pieces will suffer extinction with time, weather, or people – it's part of it, and I love the process of degradation that the pieces experience'), and Copyright ('it's fine, it's like a baker that bakes a cake knowing it will be eaten at some point'). Daleast echoed these sentiments: '[t]hat's the life of this kind of public art. It happens all the time. It's like a gift to the public space. I accept it – they can do whatever they want. Most of the time they keep it for a long time, but anything can happen'. And Rubin pointed out in our conversation that while he is sad when his mural goes, the ephemerality and vulnerability of these forms of art is 'why I started studio works, canvases or woods'. Similarly, another New York artist, Zimer, told me that 'any writer will be ready for their work to disappear, it's just the nature of the game. In any case these walls are not meant to last a lifetime. On average they will chip to pieces in [a] matter of years. That's why I invest a lot of energy into canvases. History has shown that great canvases will actually outlast empires, while history's best urban art murals are already disappearing. I'd rather use legal means if I were being unfairly censored or being taken advantage of financially'.[41]

In our interview Zimer also expressed the opinion that giving artists the right to oppose the destruction of their murals would be unfair to the property owner, as it would make it difficult for them to redevelop their own sites. This point is reminiscent of what the District Court of New York highlighted in the US case *Ron English et al. v. BFC & R. 11th Street*.[42] This dispute involved a group of related artworks installed in a community garden. A redevelopment of the site was planned that would entail moving the sculptures but leaving the murals intact, although the new construction would obstruct the view of the murals. The artists claimed under VARA that the work

40 But as we have seen *supra*, Lexi Bella may decide to sue the entity that destroys her mural if it is important to her.

41 It is because of such vulnerability that in the early 1980s art patrons like Samuel Esses encouraged writers like Zephyr and Futura to also paint canvases in studio, as he felt that it was important to preserve graffiti works 'which at the time existed only in an ephemeral zone'. See Zephyr's official website at http://zephyrgraffiti.com/the-graffiti-1980-studio/. A scene within the 1983 movie *Style Wars* also shows some writers' growing interest in permanent canvases. Writer Daze is filmed saying that 'the life span of an average [graffiti] piece today only last few months – this [canvases] is something that could last a lifetime' (minute 49.50). On the transition from walls and trains to canvases and in general indoor surfaces, see infra Chapter 5.

42 *Ron English v. BFC & R East 11th St. LLC*, No. 97 Civ. 7446, 1997 WL 746444 (S.D.N.Y. Dec. 3, 1997).

was conceived as a unified environmental work and that therefore removing the sculptures would destroy the whole work. The court found that VARA was inapplicable as the works had been illegally created – and held that protecting these illegal pieces 'could effectively freeze redevelopments of vacant lots by placing artwork there without permission. Such a construction of the statute would be constitutionally troubling, would defy rationality and cannot be what Congress intended in passing VARA'.

Zimer has not been the only artist who seems to agree on this point. Roadsworth, Kristy, Good Guy Boris, Gaia, and Elle are on the same page. While Roadsworth told me: 'I guess that's his right to destroy it if it's done illegally on his property because you did it without permission', Kristy commented that 'you know that the weather could destroy it [the mural]; you know that that building could be painted over tomorrow; and you know that there is a lot of different things that could happen to it because it is not protected in a gallery. Every time I've painted a mural on a wall outside, I go into it knowing that it's ephemeral and not permanent, that I don't own that wall'. And Good Guy Boris said, '[I]f you've done something on someone's property without permission you can't claim "no destruction" – it goes too far. You can't say to people: you can't take this building down because this is my artwork'. Elle – who as mentioned moved to spray-painting because of its longevity – was also keen to look at the entire picture from the perspective of the property owner, especially where the work is not authorised. She pointed out: 'with illegal graffiti it's difficult. I don't think I'd pursue that because how would you go about? [...] I'd never sue a landlord for destroying the artwork that I put up illegally on his building. People may be scared to let artists paint on their walls because of the legal actions. So, it becomes almost this prohibiting act instead of encouraging art'.[43]

What these interviewees meant is that artists should often accept the fact that placing their works on other people's properties may risk losing control over them, especially if they do that illegally. This makes sense. Property owners may, for example, be obliged on safety grounds to remove a wall or other surfaces where artworks are placed. Indeed, artists' attempts to prevent the destruction of their artworks have sometimes been rejected by courts on such grounds. This occurred, for instance, in the case of a monument (a sculpture made from old wooden blocks) placed in the Paul Mistral Park in the French town of Grenoble, which was deemed a threat to public safety because of the deterioration of the material.[44] Similarly, security staff at the Royal College of Art in London destroyed a student's artwork on safety grounds. The piece consisted of a (non-structurally sound) stairway installed between the college's building and a nearby fish and chips shop.[45]

43 But as I noted earlier in the chapter, property owners who do comply with the rules while destroying the piece do not have to fear any negative legal consequences.

44 Trib. Adm. de Grenoble, 18 February 1976, in Revue trimestrielle de droit comparé, 1977, 120 et ff.

45 Tania Cheng-Davies, 'Honour in UK Copyright Law Is Not "A Trim Reckoning": Its Impact on the Integrity Right and the Destruction of Works of Art' (2016) 16(2) *Oxford Journal of Legal Studies*, 295.

A few artists I encountered have even expressed interest in and happiness at their pieces being erased. French artist Jef Aerosol, for example, noted that 'interventions in the public space are bound to disappear, which is precisely what makes them interesting'. Los Angeles wheatpaste artist Morley has a similar opinion. He told me: 'I create my art with paper and paste, so I've embraced the temporary nature of my work. If I wanted it to last forever, I'd use materials that had more longevity. Also, the primary place that I post my work is on temporary surfaces, like boarded up buildings and construction walls. Those spots will always be temporary. I find that I'd rather create art that is not meant to last forever'. Similarly, City Kitty, who also practices wheatpasting, said to me during our conversation at a Manhattan café:

> once I put it on the street it might be the last time I see it. [...] I like the ephemeral nature of street art. Placing a piece of art on the street gives it a different context and allows it to take on its own journey which is different from a piece in a gallery or a home. The ephemeral nature of street art also allows me to build and maintain relationships with a place over a period of time. As one piece deteriorates or is buffed off the street, I can create a new piece specifically for that space and its surroundings. This [destruction] is just part of the nature of the outlet and I wouldn't want to change what I'm doing to prevent this.

Obviously, artists who practice wheatpasting and choose temporary surfaces as their canvases may not be as bothered about the loss of their art as a muralist can be. The latter often needs to work for days (and sometimes for weeks) to create a piece, and – as we have seen – may be upset about an early erasure of their works. The difference between the two creative processes is clear. After all, wheatpasting – as well as other street art forms such as stickering – is easy to mass produce and allows artists to place their art in many locations with minimal effort and risk. This point emerged in the interview with City Kitty. He said, '[S]treet artists like myself that wheat paste their pieces on the street have less of a problem with this than muralists due to the ephemeral nature of the medium. One of my pieces might live on the street for an hour or a year so it has less of an audience then a mural which can become iconic and revisited numerous times'. The same goes for street poetry. Dutch artist Laser 3.14, who leaves messages on temporary surfaces such as construction site hoardings and protective wooden panels, commented during the interview, 'I don't mind [about erasure]. It creates something dynamic in the sense that, if you make a map of the city to see where my work is placed and how long they would be up, you'd see that some are there for a long time and other vanish, move around and new ones appear. I really like that idea'.

Also, several of my interviewees noted that they do not mind the destruction of their pieces because photographic documentation is an acceptable surrogate (this is exactly the opposite of what Meres One and Marie Flageul affirmed in our interviews). This argument does not come as a surprise. Even New York's Judge Block, in his 2013 preliminary decision which denied the injunction to enjoin the demolition of the *5Pointz* site, stressed the importance of photographic documentation for conservation purposes. He noted that 'the plaintiffs' works can live on in other media. The [...] works have been photographed, and the court, during the hearing, exhorted the plaintiffs to photograph all those which they might wish to preserve'.[46] As just mentioned, this point emerged in my fieldwork. Australian artist Ian Strange even told me that he actually prefers his works to be destroyed, as he likes the documentation instead: 'I think documentation is the same as the original'. Likewise, Canadian street artist Roadsworth said, 'I accept that there is a certain temporary time frame to the work I do, but I also take pictures of my work so I preserve them'. London artist Eine has a similar view: 'if you're a starting artist and you pay for all the paint and wall rights, and it gets wiped, I understand why people get upset, but at the end of the day we're living in a digital world. So yeah, just take a photograph and put it on Instagram. That's how our art lives nowadays, the digital era and photos is preservation'. The same goes for Rubin ('I accept a property owner changing his mind and whitewashing my mural. I've pictures anyway. I'm kind of used to having my murals disappear'), Gabriel Corti ('I understand it won't last forever, but as long as I get my high-resolution photos, I've my documentation and it will last forever'), Resa Piece ('as long as my artwork is in picture form, it [destruction] doesn't matter'), US mural artist Maria Rodriguez ('[I]t often happens for a number of reasons that are often out of my control. Not much we can do. Do try to document it so there is a history left'), Morley ('I do it with the knowledge that my work will live a very short life span on the street. Thankfully the pictures I post online of my work can live forever and be spread across the globe'), and again Joel Artista ('I don't waste my time; my time is very precious to me – I make a piece, there's photos of it, there's videos, there's all this and it will live forever digitally and not live forever physically and I'm not going to spend a lot of time dealing with the legal aspects and stuff like that').

Most writers also accept photographic documentation as the best way to preserve graffiti – after all, this is an art form that is still considered by many within the subculture as transient. For example, London writer Crane DPC noted in our interview: 'I quite like the fact that it's ephemeral, once I'm finished and have taken a photo, I've already moved on to my next painting. As long as I've documented it, it really doesn't matter to me how long my work lasts'. Another London writer, Noir, is on the same page. He argued in our interview: 'I accepted it [destruction] decades ago. I grew up with graffiti since 1984 so the rules of the streets still apply today. You paint your piece, get photos, and wave it [...] goodbye! The only way you could achieve this would be by owning the wall that you've installed your artwork on. But even that doesn't guarantee its lasting. I know artists that have painted their own walls and then had the council demand the area to be buffed'. New York writers Serk and David Chino are of the same opinion. While the former simply commented,

46 *Cohen v. G & M Realty L.P.*, Case No. 13-CV-5612 (FB) (JMA) (EDNY 2013).

'I accept it [destruction] totally, as long as I've the photo', and the former told me during our conversation:

> everything that we love has a limited existence. Lasts until something happens. It will come down eventually. I'd be sad, but not devastated. We're in an era in which it is expected that the wall will not last long. As long as I've my picture, it's fine. *5Pointz* created the new thing of accepting removal to give space to another better piece. When I was a kid, it was different, there have been pieces that lasted for decades. I'm one of the generation that if you painted a wall, you hope that it runs as long as possible, but in *5Pointz* rotation was a common practice.

The last point made by David Chino is quite interesting. We saw earlier that the legal action brought by twenty-one artists who painted at *5Pointz* could be considered as a testament to the evolution of these creative subcultures into less ephemeral art forms. But David Chino makes the opposite point. In his view, *5Pointz* artists – as opposed to old-school writers from the 1970s and 1980s – eventually accepted that their pieces would sooner or later disappear and be replaced by subsequent ones. It is an opinion which must be respected, but it clashes with other narrations of the New York graffiti subculture of the 1970s and 1980s, which highlighted a widespread acceptance of the ephemeral nature of this form of art.[47] It is also interesting to note that the *5Pointz* rotation rule was used as an argument by the property owner in the legal proceedings to try to make the point that destruction and replacement were widely accepted by that artistic community. Such an argument is not that strong, though – and indeed was not accepted by Judge Block. In fact, *5Pointz* also hosted pieces on long-standing walls that were more permanent (and several of the works debated in the proceedings belonged to this category),[48] and a high-quality piece could achieve permanence even if not initially placed on a long-standing wall.[49]

## ATTITUDES TOWARDS DE-CONTEXTUALISATION

In recent years we have witnessed cases involving the removal of pieces originally placed in the street and their relocation to galleries, museums, private collectors' houses, or other indoor places, often for the purpose of being sold.[50] This has occurred with

47 See, for example, Skeme's point on this issue, above fn. 34 in this chapter.

48 One of these artworks was Lady Pink's *Green Mother*. As noted by this artist in our conversation: 'because my mural was on the third storey, I felt it was going to last a very, very, very long time. You can't get ladders up there, you can't get scissor lifts, you have to spend a lot of money on getting a crane to get up there to go over it, so I figured it was going to last a really, very, very long time. And the fact that I do have a name was important to Meres One [the founder and curator of *5Pointz*] – a famous artist on the front of the building is always good for business'.

49 *Cohen v. G&M Realty* 320 F. Supp. 3d 421, 2018 U.S. Dist. LEXIS 22662, 19.

50 See also Peter Bengtsen, Stealing from the Public: The Value of Street Art Taken from the Street in Ross, above fn. 27, 426.

murals painted by famous street artists such as Banksy, Stik, Invader,[51] and Swoon.[52] The phenomenon is well represented in the provocative 2018 documentary *The Man Who Stole Banksy*, directed by Marco Proserpio, which is about how murals painted by

[51] The iconic video game–inspired mosaic tiles placed by Invader in the streets of many towns around the world have become popular with collectors. Some of them have been taken from the street and then offered for sale on eBay at a price ranging around 10,000 euros each. See Young, above fn. 28, 151.

[52] The following are some of the cases which have attracted media attention (all of them involved Banksy's artworks):

(i) In 2004 the work *Secured*, spray-painted by Banksy on a Liverpool wall in 2003, was removed and offered for sale at £100,000 in a controversial exhibition called *Stealing Banksy?* that was organised in 2014 by the Sincura Group in London.
(ii) In 2008 the piece *Old School*, spray-painted by Banksy in 2006 on an East London garage wall, was removed and offered for sale for £350,000 in the *Stealing Banksy?* exhibition.
(iii) In 2009 the piece *2 Rats*, spray-painted by Banksy during a Berlin art festival in 2003, was removed and offered for sale at £200,000 in the *Stealing Banksy?* exhibition.
(iv) In 2010 artists from a Detroit gallery removed Banksy's endangered mural *I Remember when All This Was Trees*, which was painted at a derelict site in Detroit. The property owner also took legal action asking for the artwork's restitution. The case was eventually settled as the site owner donated the piece to the gallery, which paid a symbolic sum.
(v) In 2011 the artwork *Sperm Alarm*, spray-painted by Banksy on the wall of a luxury hotel in the London area of Victoria, was removed by a person who offered it on eBay for £17,000, and then it passed into the hands of Sincura Group, which offered it for sale at £150,000 in the *Stealing Banksy?* exhibition.
(vi) In 2011 the two pieces *Wet Dog* and *Stop and Search*, spray-painted by Banksy in Bethlehem (Palestine) in 2007, appeared at the Keszler Gallery in Southampton (US) with an estimated value of, respectively, \$600,000 and \$800,000. The works had been removed from the original location and then brought to UK by Bankrobber Gallery for restoration, before resurfacing in the US, where they were eventually sold.
(vii) In 2013 Liverpool's famous *Rat* by Banksy, created as part of the 2004 Liverpool Biennial festival, was removed and offered for sale at £250,000 in the *Stealing Banksy?* exhibition. As mentioned on the exhibition's website, the piece was removed in multiple sections, with only three pieces exhibited.
(viii) In 2013 the artwork *No Ball Games*, spray-painted by Banksy in 2009 on the side of a shop at the junction of Tottenham High Road and Philip Lane in North London, was cut out, chopped in three parts, and then auctioned at an estimated sale price of £500,000 in the *Stealing Banksy?* exhibition. In March 2017 the chopped pieces were still offered for sale on the website of the Keszler Gallery, together with other original street artworks created by the British artist, including *Kissing Cops*, a piece stencilled in 2005 on a pub's wall in Brighton.
(ix) In 2013 the piece *Slave Labour*, spray-painted by Banksy a year earlier on the side wall of a Poundland store in the London area of Wood Green, was removed and then appeared for sale at the Fine Art Auctions Miami for US\$500,000. After protests from the residents of Wood Green, the artwork was returned to the UK. It was eventually sold by Bankrobber Gallery London for £750,000 at an auction organised at the London Film Museum by the Sincura Group.
(x) In 2014 the piece *Girl with a Balloon*, spray-painted by Banksy in 2004 on an East London wall, was removed and offered for sale for £450,000 in the *Stealing Banksy?* exhibition.
(xi) In 2014 the artwork *Art Buff*, spray-painted by Banksy in the English town of Folkestone during an art event, was removed, shipped to New York (by the Bankrobber Gallery), and then sent to Miami to be sold at an art fair. The piece was then returned to Folkestone after the UK High Court decision of September 2015 in *Creative Foundation v. Dreamland & Others* (2015) EWCH 2556 (Ch). In that case the judge refused to accept the argument put forward by Dreamland (which, as the tenant of the building upon which the piece had been placed,

the famous English artist are often removed, sold, and collected.[53] This phenomenon is not even recent. Several drawings made in the 1980s by Keith Haring with white chalk in the New York subway were often removed and ended up with art collectors.[54]

Some of my interviewees also told me that their works had been taken off the street. City Kitty, for example, revealed that his wheatepaste posters are often stolen. The same goes for Laser 3.14, who, as mentioned, leaves messages and poems on temporary urban surfaces, New York writer Reskew and Ian Strange. While Laser 3.14 said that some of his messages have been removed and 'hung in people's houses', Reskew noted, 'I have found out that a photo studio took my work off the street and used it

had removed and shipped the mural) that it had acquired property of the piece of work as it was discharging its repairing obligation. He instead held that when the section of the wall was removed, it became a chattel, which belonged to the landlord. For comments on this case, see Iljadica, 'Street Art Belongs to the Freeholder' (2016) 11 J.I.P.L.P. 90; Wickenden, 'Graffiti Art: The Rights of Landlords, Tenants and Artists: *Creative Foundation v Dreamland Leisure Ltd*" (2016) 38 E.I.P.R. 119.

(xii) In 2016 the piece *Love Plane*, painted by Banksy on a car park wall in Liverpool back in 2011, was removed by the Sincura Group and exhibited in a local gallery that specialised in street art.

(xiii) In 2016 the artwork *Boy with Heart*, painted by Banksy in 2009 in the Islington borough of London and then removed, was auctioned for £150,000.

(xiv) In 2019 the mural *Season Greetings*, spray-painted by Banksy at Port Talbot in Wales the previous year, was removed and purchased by Essex-based Brandler Galleries for an undisclosed six-figure sum.

(xv) In 2021 the piece *Hula-Hooping Girl*, spray-painted by Banksy on the site of a building in Nottingham the year before, was removed again by Brandler Galleries for an undisclosed six-figure sum.

(xvi) In 2021 the mural *Aachoo!!*, spray-painted by Banksy on the side of a semi-detached house in Bristol, was removed and likely relocated to an indoor location.

Also, in August 2011 an exhibition in Southampton (US) was jointly organized by Bankrobber Gallery and Keszler Gallery and included the above-mentioned murals *Wet Dog* and *Stop and Search* as well as four other Banksy murals that had been removed, including *Out of Bed Rat*, painted in Los Angeles in 2002 and offered for sale at Keszler Gallery for $400,000; *Slow Progress*, painted in New Orleans in 2008 and offered for sale at Keszler Gallery for $40,000; IKEA Punk, painted in London in 2009 and offered for sale at Keszler Gallery for $700,000; and *Laugh Now*, painted in Brighton in 2002 and offered for sale for $575,000. In this regard, see also Bengtsen in Ross, above fn. 27, 419.

53 The movie was co-written by Christian Omodeo and Fillipo Perfido, and produced by Sterven Pictures in association with Rai Cinema.

54 Keith Haring, *Art in Transit: Subway Drawings* (Crown Pub 1984), unnumbered page. Not all artworks removed from the street have been sold for mere profit purposes, though. A few times removals and sales of these pieces have generated revenues that have been used for social purposes. For example, Banksy's piece *Mobile Lovers* – painted in 2014 on a piece of board stuck to the doorway of a youth club in Bristol – was sold by said club to a private collector for £403,000. The sale saved the youth club – which had been operating for 120 years and had recently run into financial difficulties – from closure. On this case see Gander, 'Banksy's Mobile Lovers: Youth Club Owner Who Sold Artwork in Bristol Receives Death Threats' (27 August 2014) *Independent* (also reporting on a dispute regarding the ownership of the property of the artwork between the local council and the club). Also, in 2010 the *Gangsta Rat* piece stencilled by Banksy four years earlier on a wall at Moorfields Eye hospital in London was removed and then sold by the latter for £30,000. The money was invested in research into eye disease. See Will Ellsworth-Jones, The Man Behind the Wall (Aurum Press 2013) 94. Another Banksy mural – *Gorilla in a Pink Mask*, painted in Eastville, Bristol in 2001 – was removed in late 2020 with plans to sell it at an auction to raise funds to support the local community. See Zasha Whiteway-Wilkinson, 'Banksy "Masked Gorilla" Removed in Eastville: But No-One Knows Why' (18 September 2020) *Bristol Post*.

as decor for their dressing room'. Ian Strange echoed: 'have you heard about people stealing adverts of bus shelters, paint on them and put them back in? I used to do that a while back and somebody took my work and auctioned it'. New York writer Easy, sticker artist Clet Abraham, and London-based artist Osch also experienced this phenomenon. Easy pointed out that 'actually, I'm going through that right now. They go throughout New York, they cut out my tags out and put them in galleries. I've seen it online already. I've seen one of my tags hanging up in California. I had painted it on a green tarp [a large piece of waterproof cloth or plastic that is used as a cover]. They cut the tarp with my name on it and I can see it in California. I'm like "wow" – that's what they're doing'. And Clet Abraham, known for his playful modifications of street traffic signs by using stickers, said that 'often local authorities keep the signs which I've modified. They do not remove the sticker – they remove the entire sign, and probably they keep it'.

These removals and relocations have proved controversial. Indeed, these forms of art are often site specific; that is, a piece maintains its artistic meaning as long as it is kept in its original environment.[55] Everything around street artworks may be important, if not even predominant, in the whole settings which originally host the pieces. Street and graffiti artists do not simply treat the city as a canvas; they also use the streetscape as a structural element of their artworks. In other words, the place which surrounds many of these works is specifically chosen and turns out to be part of the artistic concept and representation, with the image being integrated with the texture of the street.[56]

Thus, there is a widespread belief that these forms of art are meant to be where they were originally conceived, that is, on the streets – and they lose their essence in an enclosed space.[57] Even where the removal is carried out professionally without damaging the artwork physically, its conceptual meaning may be jeopardized

[55] See Epstein, *London Graffiti and Street Art: Unique Artwork from London's Streets* (Ebury Press 2014) (reporting the opinion of London artist Stik: 'I try to make my characters react to the space they are painted in. It's all about context for me'); Ed Bartlett, Lonely Planet Street Art, Lonely Planet Publishing (2017) 150 (reporting the opinion of South African artist Faith 47: 'The context of the environment is vital, as the work needs to communicate and co-create a story with the existing history of a place. I don't want to make works that "take over" an area, but rather are a part of the fabric of that space'). Yet, it should also be noted that not all street art is site specific. Some artists do place their works indiscriminately and ubiquitously without much attention to a specific location. See Peter N. Salib, 'The Law of Banksy: Who Owns Street Art?' (2016) 83 *University of Chicago Law Review*, 2300. See also Ulrich-Blanchè, 'Street Art and Related Terms: Discussion and Working Definition' (2015) *Urban Creativity Lisbon*, 36 (noting that there are different degrees of site specificity of street art, with some works being able to be placed on any site). This point also emerged in my field research. During our conversation, London writer Crane DPC confirmed that 'there really isn't any context to what I do other than writing my name and maybe using nice colours'.

[56] Tristan Manco, *Stencil Graffiti* (Thames & Hudson 2002) 15 (reporting the opinion of street and studio artist Shepard Fairey).

[57] Nancy Macdonald, The Graffiti Subculture: Youth, Masculinity and Identity in London and New York (Palgrave MacMillan 2001) 166. See also Ellsworth-Jones, above fn. 54, 238 (wondering whether the act of removing and allegedly 'saving' a street artwork actually destroys it instead).

because the new location is not the one that had been chosen by the artist and all the extra meaning coming from the outside environment is lost.[58] As Banksy once noted, removing these works from the street and bringing them into galleries or other closed venues would be akin to locking wild animals in zoos.[59] Similar opinions were expressed by two of my interviewees, the English artist Copyright and Pablo Delgado. While the former said, '[Y]es, it becomes like taking a bird from the wild and putting it in a cage',[60] the latter pointed out that 'the pieces needed the original context to be completed. My work is not miniature anymore if it's removed from the wall that makes it small. By itself or without an element of comparison, nothing is small or big'. Likewise, Ian Strange told me that in these cases 'the power or intent of the work is removed'. Another participant I interviewed, US writer Cept, interestingly noted that while he appreciates when graffiti is recognised in the art world, he firmly believes that taking it off the wall is not acceptable. He concluded that 'what makes it graffiti is the fact that it's out there'.

Not only are some street and graffiti artists annoyed about this phenomenon, so may be the communities where the pieces are created and placed. Cases where local people voice their concerns and react against attempts to remove street artworks are not uncommon, especially when it comes to murals created by famous artists such as Banksy. Such protests have also been prompted by the belief that these works are basically gifts to the public. Losing them may be seen as a sign of disrespect towards art and in general as a cultural loss.

One may counter-argue that such removals and relocations could be justified by trying to re-create an environment similar to the one we usually find in urban open air settings, for example, by depriving the new indoor space which hosts the

58 Cedar Lewisohn, *Street Art: The Graffiti Revolution* (Tate Modern Publishing 2009) 137.

59 Banksy has strongly complained against the removal of his artworks from the street. When the controversial exhibition *Stealing Banksy?* was organised in 2014 (see above fn. 52), the following comment appeared on the artist's website: 'The "Stealing Banksy?" exhibition taking place in London this weekend has been organised without the involvement or consent of the artist. Banksy would like to make it clear – this show has nothing to do with me and I think it's disgusting people are allowed to go displaying art on walls without getting permission'. See also Ulrich Blanché, Banksy – Urban Art in a Material World (Tectum 2016) 109 (noting that when Banksy 'realised that many of the artwork backgrounds could simply be stolen and then commercialised, he began, like other known Street Artists in recent years, to choose locations with backgrounds that were more difficult to remove'); Paul Gough, "Bansky: What's the Fuss and Why Does It Matter?", in Joseph M. Siracusa (ed.), *Humanities, Arts and Social Sciences: It's Everyone's Business* (Routledge, 2016); Will Ellsworth-Jones, *Banksy: The Man behind the Wall*, 2nd rev. ed. (Frances Lincoln 2021), 182, 199 (pointing out that 'Banksy certainly would not support the gallery's action, but in an emailed interview [...] he said: "I've learnt from experience that a painting isn't finished when you put down your brush – that's when it starts. The public reaction is what supplies meaning and value. Art comes alive in the arguments you have about it"; and adding that "Banksy is trying to find another way to keep his pieces where he painted them by making them more complicated [and difficult to remove]"').

60 See also Manco, above fn. 56, 15 (reporting Blek Le Rat's opinion: 'when this art is taken away from streets, somehow it dies').

removed piece – for instance, a gallery – of its 'white cube' dimension in order to create a street art effect. This could be done by showing bricks or distressed plaster, curved walls, or ceilings to evoke an inner city or industrial sensation.[61] Yet, despite these efforts, re-creating the exact same atmosphere as in the street may be impossible because in indoor locations viewers are 'looking at the shadow of the real thing',[62] and street artworks have thus much less impact, also because of the lights, which in a museum or a gallery are fixed, but in the street change constantly, literally before our eyes.[63]

An interesting case of removal and relocation, which could be labelled as a textbook case of street art de-contextualisation, has involved Stik. The London artist himself made me aware of the details of this dispute during our conversation in his East London studio. This is what happened. In 2011 Stik had painted a community mural on containers in the Polish city of Gdańsk. The artwork featured fifty-three of the iconic Stik figures holding hands, which the artist created with local young people. Three years later the containers disappeared, and in October 2015, ten pieces of the containers re-appeared (representing sixteen out of the fifty-three figures originally painted), chopped up and offered for sale at a gallery in London as part of a 'Stik Exhibition', with each piece being offered for sale at prices ranging between £10,000 and £12,000. While the case never went to court and was subsequently settled by the artist after years of negotiations, he was very annoyed by the way his artwork had been treated. He said, '[T]he area in Gdańsk where I painted is very poor and people there are struggling with addiction and poverty. My piece was for the community. And if that community wished to sell that piece to fund a community project, I'd would have granted them permission. But I'd have done the sale in a particular manner and been careful how it would be sold, for example, with the benefit going back to the local community'.

During my research I came across other tales of de-contextualisation and learnt about how street artists feel when this occurs. Reading *The Adventures of Darius & Downey & Other True Tales of Street Art*, a book which narrates the artistic path of US artists Leon Reid IV (whom I met in his studio in Greenpoint, Brooklyn) and Brad Downey, was engaging. In particular, this excerpt from the book is interesting: 'Every street artist makes a decision at the outset. They don't make art in the hope that it may hang in a gallery that 1% of the city goes to. They give their creations for free to the whole city, putting them out there for an entire neighbourhood to walk by and see. Now, Leon's piece had been stolen from where it had been successfully installed in order to be sold to someone who would hang it in his or her living

[61] Alison Young, Street Art World (Reaktion Books 2016) 130–131 (also noting that some venues make rooftops and courtyards available for artists to paint as if they were working in the street, and that gallery owners may make the venue match the expectations of street artists and graffiti aficionados).

[62] Lewisohn, above fn. 58, 127 (reporting Blek Le Rat's words).

[63] Cedar Lewisohn, *Abstract Graffiti* (Merrell 2011) 13, 32.

room where 0,0000001% of the city could see it'.[64] A similar concept was expressed by Spanish artist Suso, who bluntly put it this way: 'when a mural is removed and relocated into an indoor location, it loses all its social content'.

But can artists rely on the moral right of integrity to oppose the de-contextualisation of their art? In some countries like the UK and US the chances of such claims are generally weak.[65] The chances of success seem to be higher if the de-contextualisation causes the mutilation of the piece, as occurred in the case of the chopped Stik's artwork. In other countries, for example, in continental Europe, the law seems more generous towards artists and may give them chances to prevent the de-contextualisation of their works, whether mutilation occurs or not.[66] There are no reported moral right cases focusing on this phenomenon yet, so it is difficult to foresee how courts would decide. The outcome of a hypothetical case would be uncertain, and very much fact specific. One of the main issues a court would need to focus on would probably be whether the relocation of the removed artwork prejudices the reputation and/or honour of the artist.[67]

What is certain is that many street artists and writers deeply dislike and find unacceptable the removal and relocation of art from the street. In the next pages I will cite the opinions of artists and writers I interviewed. As expected, many of them totally disapprove of the de-contextualisation of these forms of art, albeit with different degrees of intensity. Their discontent is confirmed by the fact that several of them refuse to authenticate artworks removed from the street.[68] As London artist Ben Eine once noted, this kind of art is 'not painted to be sold a few years later.

[64] Leon Reid IV – Brad Downey, The Adventures of Darius & Downey & Other True Tales of Street Art as told to Ed Zipco (Thames & Hudson 2008) 60–63 (also mentioning a row between artist Leon Reid IV and a person named Omar who had taken one of his artworks off the street in order to sell it, with the latter saying: 'This shit isn't yours anymore. […] Don't put it on the street and I won't take it').

[65] For example, in the US the case law does not help in this respect. In two seminal cases – *Phillips v. Pembroke Real Estate, Inc.*, 459 F.3d 128 (1st Cir. 2006) and *Kelley v. Chicago Park Dist.*, 635 F.3d 290 (7th Cir. 2011) – US courts have confirmed that VARA does not cover, and cannot be invoked to prevent, the removal of site-specific works.

[66] See the chapters on Germany, Italy, and the Netherlands in Enrico Bonadio (ed.), *The Handbook of Copyright in Street Art and Graffiti* (authored by Marc Mimler, Enrico Bonadio and Anke Moerland, respectively) (Cambridge University Press 2019).

[67] When dealing with this issue, the court would have to take into due account differences between street and graffiti art on the one hand and more traditional fine art which is usually shown in galleries and museums, on the other. Indeed, the 'musealisation' and 'gallerisation' of street art and graffiti inevitably entails control and editing tasks as well as a selection process, which may be considered by some within the subculture to be antithetical to the very nature of these forms of art and may potentially be deemed by street artists and writers to be prejudicial. See also Lewisohn, cited above fn. 58, 131. Yet, as we will see in Chapter 6, many practitioners in these communities have also accepted showing their pieces in galleries and other indoor locations.

[68] Banksy is one of them. *Pest Control*, the entity which releases certificates of authenticity for Banksy's studio pieces, refuses to give such certificates when it comes to murals removed from the street (for a couple of exceptions see Chapter 5, fn. 62, xxxviii and xxxix). Another artist who is very careful when it comes to legitimising artworks removed from the street is Stik, who 'ONLY authenticates street pieces when 100% of the money goes back to the community. Stik Studio restore, supply a COA [Certificate

I don't sign my street stuff, and, like other artists, would never authenticate it – it's not made to be sold, but to be enjoyed'.[69] Amongst the many street artists and writers I talked to who expressed disgust, the most vocal was Bogotá writer Drop. During our walk through the graffiti-friendly area of Puente Aranda in the Colombian capital he told me:

> [d]efinitely, I'd do something. It'd be flattering that they would exhibit my work in gallery but if they don't give me any credit, or anything, then I'm for sure going to take action. It can look like whatever to the rest of the graffiti community, but I don't care because it's my work. I think the graffiti community doesn't respect people that take action because it might not have happened to them yet and I think when it does happen, they'll change their mind. All of these artists that are taking action are paving the way for our business and others so that when it does happen to them, they have a precedent to follow. It's a work in progress right now and I'd like to be a part of it as opposed to against it. Some people are just too proud and have massive egos that don't allow them to take up action, because they think their street cred will be tarnished, but I don't care about it.

of Authenticity] and place the sale. Private sales are NOT authenticated under any circumstances' (see his official website at http://stik.org/fundraising/). And indeed during our conversation in his studio in East London Stik told me he had once sold one of his artworks (painted on a garage door), raising £4,000 for a charity organization called Groundwork which works with the local community.

See also Scott Reyburn, Banksy London mural may fetch $700,000, The Sunday Morning Herald, 23 February 2013 (noting that Pest Control does not authenticate street pieces because Banksy prefers street works to remain *in situ* and building owners tend to become irate when their doors go missing because of a stencil); Ellsworth-Jones, above fn. 59, 177 (pointing out that 'Banksy's argument is a clear one: the context in which he chooses to paint is critical, it is part of the piece. To take the piece out of context is to destroy the original work. He will not authenticate any piece that has been taken off a wall (although he has made very rare exceptions where the proceeds of the sale has gone to charity)'; Bengtsen, above fn. 50, 424 (commenting on the iconic mosaic tiles created by French artist Invader, and reporting his opinion: 'The Space Invaders I put up in the street aren't signed and are made from readily available mosaic tiles, which make them easy to copy. A mosaic that has been removed from its original site loses all value as it can no longer be distinguished from a reproduction'); Peter Bengtsen, 'Decontextualisation of Street Art', in Bonadio (ed.), above fn. 66, 48, 52 (noting that 'contesting authenticity in the case of a removed street artwork does not necessarily entail suggesting that an artist did not create the piece. It could simply mean that the artist no longer considers the object an authentic work of art once it has been taken out of its original context. [...] When it comes to preventing the decontextualisation and attempted sale of works from the street [...] artists can contribute to maintaining the existing negative discourse surrounding these issues – and thereby perpetuate the market's doubt about the value (both monetary and artistic) and authenticity of extracted street works generally'). This very same point has also been stressed by New York wheatpaste artist City Kitty during our conversation. He said, '[A]rtists such as Bansky battle this [decontextualisation] by not authenticating work that is stolen from the street. This will not stop people from stealing the work but [...] I believe this is the best way to battle this scenario'.

69 Bengtsen, above fn. 50, 422. Should artists agree to authenticate the removed art instead, that would mean the piece as removed and re-contextualised continues to adhere to the wishes of the artist, and can still be deemed an authentic piece of art. Yet, when it comes to illegally placed artworks, such authentication might turn out to be a boomerang against the artist, as it could be considered a 'signed confession on headed notepaper'. See Ellsworth-Jones, above fn. 54, 97.

Drop's words and thoughts are clear. He is aware of the fact that many writers would not even think about starting a legal action, or even just complain, if their piece is removed and relocated, because their street cred would be tarnished. But he wants to challenge this dogmatic position, even claiming that some hardcore writers are 'too proud' and have 'massive egos' which would prevent them from relying on the law to oppose the de-contextualisation of their art. He would be ready to be the first within his community to bring a complaint and create a legal precedent, so as to show others the right path and confirm that the law can help the subculture in some circumstances.

Thoughts of anger at the phenomenon of de-contextualisation were also expressed by writers Easy (who as mentioned has actually already experienced removals, which he was 'very annoyed' about) and Reskew ('I'd be infuriated')[70] as well as artists Stephen Palladino ('I'd feel upset'), Lamkat ('that would be disgusting and I would speak up the fight about it'), Chris Stain ('Yes, this has happened in the past. If I place it on the street, the underlying meaning is that is meant for the public and not the private sector. Yes [I would take legal action]'); Logan Hicks ('[A]bsolutely, I'd work vigorously to defend my right and would ask for an injunction against the gallery to block the sale. If it were an auction, I wouldn't authorize a certificate of authenticity. If it was a gallery, I'd reach out and shame it online. I'd deny to be the author of that work and do all that I could to block the sale'), Pablo Delgado ('if someone is using the piece to make profit, I'd look for the means to make it right, not money but for not letting people like that getting completely away with it'), and Joel Artista ('I'd definitely not want someone to take a piece I do off the wall and then put it up somewhere else without permission to do so. It's one thing to say, "Hey I'm the property owner. This is my property. I'm going to buff this whole piece and do something different". I'd say, "Ok that sucks but that's part of the world of street art". But if someone actually takes the piece off and puts it somewhere and tries to make money off of it or tries to represent it in some way without permission from the artist, I definitely think that that is wrong. They should not do that').[71] Dutch artist Fake is on the same page, stressing that the art he creates is for the public and cannot be taken away from society. He told me: 'I'd try to stop them from removing it, it's there for the people. It's not made for one person in a room, that's why I'd try to stop them. If it's already removed, I'd try to make life difficult for them, and perhaps I'd also ask for a percentage'.

[70] As mentioned above, Reskew had already experienced a case of de-contextualisation of one of his pieces.

[71] When I asked Joel Artista if he would sue if one of his murals were to be removed and relocated in an indoor environment, he replied, '[I]t would probably take a lot for me to try and take legal action, so maybe there are some cases that I would, especially if someone has made a huge amount of money out of it, or something like that. It would also depend on whether I've a pro-bono lawyer or whether I could potentially get like $100,000 out of it. It would only be in those kinds of situations, but I wouldn't put a lot of time, energy and effort into it unless it was a kind of an extreme situation'.

A 'stealing from the public' feeling[72] can again be found in the words stencil artist Jef Aerosol used in his interview with me: 'if my assistant or myself see such artwork in an art auction, I'd let the auctioneer know it's a piece that was stolen from the streets and not meant to be sold'. Similarly, Canadian street artist Roadsworth told me during our conversation:

> I don't think it's right or agree with people stealing works. I can't speak for everyone, but for me a big part of the art is where you do it and the location. Something that is supposed to live in the public, for the public view, which for me is the beautiful thing about street art and that separates it from gallery viewing. I don't think it's natural to take something that is intended to be in street and put it somewhere that isn't where it's supposed to be. Transferring street works to a gallery place is fairly insulting and I wouldn't appreciate it at all, it's just not right. I'd try to take action if I could.

Other artists also focused on the 'robbery' and 'theft' analogy. Lady Pink, for example, told me during our interview: 'it's like being robbed. It's like you're being robbed. Why wouldn't anyone be annoyed? I'm not putting it on a building and giving it away for free, so the public can walk away with it. When it's on a building, it's a permanent situation where you can interact with it and visit it, but you can't take it, you can't buy it. If it does come down and someone takes it, then I feel I've been robbed'. Likewise, English artist Andy Council told me: 'that's awful. I'd try to prevent it and take legal action. I think it's because someone is making money out of your work, they're removing it from the street and context, they're monetising. It's completely wrong, it's theft basically'. Andre Trenier and Resa Piece had the same feeling. The former said to me: 'I'd try to take action because I'd feel a sense of somebody selling something that was not theirs to sell. I'd feel like somebody was benefiting in a sneaky way from something that I worked for'. And the latter noted, 'I'd be annoyed because they are stealing my work'. Writers I met manifested similar opinions. Mastro told me: 'of course, I'd be annoyed. It [my reputation] is damaged because they are literally stealing what we put up'. Likewise, Depsone said to me: 'I'd be furious. I think this is where a line should definitely be drawn because that is crazy and straight up stealing it'.

What if the artwork has been placed in the street illegally? Understandably, some artists would be cautious about objecting to the removal and relocation of the piece, for fear of prosecution. For example, Damien Mitchell told me: 'I'd be annoyed, I'd take action. I paint my stuff in the street and there it should stay. If it was illegal, I wouldn't take action, though'. Likewise, Andre Trenier commented, 'Now, if I've done it illegally and it's on your wall and you find a way to benefit from that, I'd feel

[72] This expression is also used by Peter Bengtsen in his paper 'Stealing from the Public: On the Removal of Street Art from the Street', presented at the 2014 Lisbon Street Art & Urban Creativity International Conference.

I've a lot less legal right and ground to stand on'. Yet, surprisingly few other artists showed interest in complaining about the removal, even where their pieces had been created illegally. New York writers David Chino and Hoacs were two of them. The former said to me: 'I'm going to go after these people. You need to contact me. You need to have a conversation, my consent, to do that. If it's illegal, I'd still go after, even If I risk prosecution'. And the latter, more cautiously, commented, 'I'd take action. If it's illegal, I'd take the risk only if the value is high'. Similarly, US writer Cept told me: 'I'd take legal action to try and stop de-contextualisation. If the piece is illegal, I'd talk with a lawyer first'.[73]

Artists' disapproval of removals and relocations of their pieces may go as far as attacking the venue where the art is relocated. This is what actually happened in October 2010 in Buenos Aires (Argentina), when an exhibition of murals removed from the street without the artists' consent was organised by Peruvian artist José Carlos Martinat at the Ignacio Liprandi Contemporary Art gallery. The removed artworks, or pieces of such artworks (as some of the murals had been mutilated during the removals), were offered for sale. The exhibition was provocatively labelled by Martinat as 'vandalism against vandalism'.[74] Yet, at the opening session the artists who had painted the murals in question strongly reacted by raiding the gallery and destroying or damaging the pieces. Martinat then tried to exploit the artists' raid by noting that such action was exactly part of the conceptual work he had eventually triggered: 'the vandalized vandals were vandalizing back'.[75]

I came across the same 'revenge' feeling when interviewing Ben Eine in his studio in London. He said to me: 'I wouldn't lend my name to something that was taken off the street to go into auction. I paint on the street, I pay for the paint, scaffolding and all that, so I don't go through all this trouble just for someone to take it and turn it into profit. They aren't trying to preserve my work as they only care about stealing my work and making money, so I wouldn't support it. I'd turn up at the auction with a can of paint and paint all over it'. I was not very surprised to hear these words from him. Indeed, in the 2017 documentary *Saving Banksy* which narrates the story of an art collector's attempts to save a Banksy painting from destruction and

[73] Other artists I interviewed expressed disgust towards de-contextualisation, but at the same time they appeared not ready to firmly object to it. For example, US wheatpaste artist Morley noted that he would be 'very annoyed because the work I create for the street is meant for that context. I know that the nature of what I do means that there's not a lot that I can do, but I'd certainly let people know that I in no way endorse that kind of show'. Likewise, French stencil artist Jef Aerosol, while stressing that the removed piece should be considered as 'stolen from the streets' (as mentioned), also noted, 'I wouldn't be annoyed for myself, but I'd wonder what that person has in the brain. Anyway, I'm not very interested in that [legal action], to be honest'.

[74] Celia Lerman, 'Protecting Artistic Vandalism: Graffiti and Copyright Law' (2013) *NYU Journal of Intellectual Property & Entertainment Law*, 306.

[75] Ibidem, 306–307.

relocate it into a museum,[76] Eine gets interviewed and says, '[W]e paint stuff in the street. That's where it belongs'.[77]

In our conversation Ben Eine made clear that he could not accept someone removing and relocating its artwork, and turning 'it into profit' (Andy Council was also annoyed by 'monetisation', as mentioned earlier). The 'economic exploitation' element was a recurring point in many interviews. It was stressed by artists such as Lady Pink ('the piece does belong to me and you've just taken it and you can't take it and sell it and put it in a gallery without me owning it and profiting from it'), Lexi Bella ('absolutely, I'd take action, that's illegal, no one has the right to sell my work for profit unless I give them the authorization to do so'), Zimer ('I wouldn't be happy if someone stole my piece and tried to resell it'), Ian Strange ('if they were trying to sell it, it'd be illegal, and I'd try to catch them'), Mosstika ('I'd mind if someone takes and uses commercially my public work. I'd be ready to take legal action'), Gabriel Corti ('I'd be very upset. This is behind my back. I'd think he's making money out of it by using my talent and energy so he can profit out of it. I'd take legal action if I saw something like that'), Laser 3.14 ('I'd mind if there was a show without my permission with my work and taken out of context and worse only for profit'), Anjl ('I think that if I was in that case and the owner decided to rip it off and put it in a gallery and try to profit from it, of course I'd pursue legal action. Absolutely'), Rubin ('I'd take legal action, immediately. Especially if there is a contract that prohibits it. But even without a contract, I'd still take legal action, somebody is making money out of it without my consent'), Murrz ('I'd take full action on that, especially if you haven't paid me and I'd put time into doing it and then not getting a cent out of it. I feel like I should be compensated in some way for putting in the work'), and Kristy ('[I would fight it] because they're using it for their profit. They're using my hard-earned work and for gains. I don't own your wall. But if you're going to tear it down and sell it for your own profit, that's different'). Moreover, New York writer Reskew commented during our conversation on the above-mentioned case of removal and relocation of his own mural. He noted that 'it bothers me that they [a photo studio in New York] are indirectly making a profit out of the work by using it to enhance the appearance of their own space'.

[76] The movie has been directed by Colin Day and was first released in the US in January 2017. It documents the efforts of a collector to save and make available to the public the mural *Haight Street Rat*, painted by Banksy in San Francisco in 2010, and the difficulties he meets when dealing with city officials, museums (that turn down his offer to display the piece for free), and greedy art dealers (who are ready to pay six-figure sums to get their hands on the artwork). The difficulty of selling artworks removed from the street has also been highlighted by Bengtsen, above fn. 68, 52 (noting that 'by communicating their views on the removal and sale of street art to colleagues, collectors, fans and followers, artists can contribute to maintaining the existing negative discourse surrounding these issues – and thereby perpetuate the market's doubt about the value (both monetary and artistic) and authenticity of extracted street works generally').

[77] The same opinion was expressed by Damien Mitchell during our encounter: 'I paint my stuff in the street, and there it should stay'.

The 'economic exploitation' point also emerged in my interview with Akse (again). He highlighted that the purpose of his art is to allow the public to admire it without paying, which is clearly antithetical to any commercial exploitation coming from the sale of the removed piece. He noted, 'Yes definitely, I'd be annoyed. My street art pieces are meant for everyday people to enjoy it for free, not for people to make a financial profit out of it, neither for wealthy people to own it in their home. But I haven't reached that level of fame, so I don't have to worry about this at this time. I guess I'd [take action] not because of the decontextualisation of my art, but because someone is trying to exploit my work for financial gain'.

Thus several artists' disappointment appear predominantly directed at the lack of sharing the commercial benefits coming from the removal, relocation, and sale of the detached artwork. Italian artist Ozmo was particularly clear and told me: 'if you do it for profit, then you need to pay me'. Likewise, Reskew commented during the interview: 'if the artist credits me and makes a clear statement that it is my work, I appreciate it, though if he's making money out of it, I should get a percentage'. And William Kasso interestingly noted during our conversation:

> well, if that piece was taken out and exhibited for profit then yeah, I want my cut.[78] I want my royalties so to speak, no? 'Cause I get it, you know they are 'saving my work', and there's an expense to come with just that process, I understand all of that. They're already investing into archiving my work. But at the same time if you're doing it with the sole intention of reselling it with a higher mark up, then I want my royalties. I'm not asking for everything because again I understand there are costs associated with it. But at the same time it's still my work. I'm still the author of it, I deserve a piece of the profits. I'd take action to prevent the resale of it without me getting a piece. So I'd need a percentage of whatever it sold for, I think that's only right, you know, because I didn't get paid for putting it up. If you're going to preserve my work to resell it, then there should be a fee, there should be a percentage that comes to me as the artist, because without me you wouldn't have anything to sell.

Claw Money was even more explicit and straightforward. She said in the interview: 'let me give you two scenarios: (1) they pay me and they pay me a decent amount, I wouldn't do anything; (2) if it's underpaid or for free, for the public, I'd give a thought about suing. I could win that case, I'm well documented, I have a fashion brand, a book, a good business, all based on and around my art. I have a Public Limited Company, I come from a family of lawyers. I'm going to take action, not to stop the taking of the mural, but to ask for money. I paint for money, it's my fucking job'. Old school writer Skeme is also vocal: 'that's really crossing the line. I do a piece and you cut it out and put it in a gallery and sell; no, no, no, I'd feel

[78] The same expression was used by Bill Blast in our conversation: 'So yeah, it's annoying because you know that someone is making money of it [decontextualisation]– so where is your cut? You created it so you should get some kind of compensation for your work'.

really disrespected, cheated and all of those bad words. Yes, yes, [I would rely on legal means]. This is because now you're trying to gain from me'. Another New York writer, Keo, showed the same disgust, stressing again the 'theft' and 'stealing' element: 'if a guy rides around in his van with tools looking for artworks to steal for profit, yeah, that guy is not only a thief, he's stealing from artists who don't have a lot of money. If you want to be a thief, then rob the Rothschilds. I don't have a problem with that, but when you're robbing old ladies or hardworking people or starving artists trying to support their families, then yes I'd use any means to fight that'. London writers Transı and Crane DPC were also quite outspoken about what they consider an unacceptable economic exploitation of the removed piece, although they added that they would not care if their artwork is relocated for non-commercial purposes. The former said, 'I'd be upset, maybe I'd take action if I'd access to lawyers.[79] But if someone does it and the money goes into a charity for example for disadvantaged kids, it's ok. If it's for getting profit, I'd be a little upset'. The latter noted that 'of course, if someone was trying to make profit because of my work, it wouldn't sit right'.

Other artists I spoke with made clear that the decision to oppose the de-contextualisation of their art would need to be made on a case-by-case basis or would depend on specific factors. Mobstr, for example, noted in our interview that 'it would be frustrating to see someone else profit from your work whilst you don't. Each situation would be unique and I believe the unique factors involved would make a difference to my decision'.[80] Similarly, another English artist, Copyright, pointed out that 'taking legal action would depend on the circumstances and how time consuming the process would be for me. If it's a small thing, it might be easier to forget it and move on'.

Opinions have also been voiced which show artists' preference for the piece 'dying' in the street rather than being removed and brought into an indoor environment for profit purposes. After all, there is still a relatively widespread belief within certain sectors of the street art and graffiti subcultures that these forms of art are ephemeral and should remain on the street until they vanish 'naturally', either because the pieces are buffed by the authorities, gone over by someone else, or whitewashed by property owners[81] or even by the very artists who created them in the first place. The latter is actually the case of the famous Italian artist Blu, who in 2014 painted over and cancelled two of his iconic murals in the Kreuzberg area of

[79] Andre Trenier – who as mentioned has expressed interest in suing if his mural is removed and placed in an indoor location – has also stressed this point during our conversation: 'If I'd the legal means, sure. If I'd money to throw at it, why not?'

[80] Yet, Mobstr also pointed out that the fact that someone removes and relocates one of his artworks could be seen as sign of appreciation as well. He indeed added that 'if people are going to such lengths, then it must mean that your work is very much liked and in a strange way it can be seen as a compliment'. We will see later in this chapter that a few other artists have the same opinion.

[81] Bengtsen, above fn. 50, 422.

Berlin to prevent their commodification and to protest against gentrification in that area.[82] Indeed, a local real estate company had advertised their future apartments as having a view of the murals, which Blu could not accept because he deeply disliked his art being exploited for the valorisation of the lot.[83] Blu also strongly complained about an exhibition in 2016 in the Italian city of Bologna of some of his murals that had been detached from the walls of a derelict building. The removed artworks were showcased together with works by other artists at the exhibition *Street Art: Banksy & Co: L'Arte allo Stato Urbano*. In protest against the exhibition, Blu erased many of his remaining murals in Bologna. A certain preference for destruction was also expressed by Alice Pasquini in her interview with me. She commented, 'In Venice I met a guy who then told me: I saved one of your artworks painted on a door – can you give me a certificate of authenticity? I replied: no! I don't give you any certificate. Better to destroy the door with the artwork than allowing you to sell it'.[84] Spanish artist Suso told me he had a similar experience. Likewise, US street and contemporary artist Swoon, interviewed by Cedar Lewhisohn, commented that 'when I paste something to the wall, I'm sort of hoping that that object will ultimately be destroyed. I want it to be outside and part of the city landscape and to rot away, so that it's never going to stick around and be a permanent thing. The sort of change that happens when people start to view it as an object of value, then take it into their personal possession, was never what was intended for that specific installation'.[85]

Not all artists and writers I talked to manifested outrage at this phenomenon. Some of them expressed more neutral feelings. We have already seen earlier that writers Trans 1 and Crane DPC do not mind if the removal and relocation happen

[82] Street artists' concerns about processes of gentrification triggered by the boom of art in the street also emerged in the interview I conducted with Damien Mitchell. He told me: 'I don't want to paint too much in my neighborood because I want to avoid gentrification'. Such processes have also been highlighted by Banksy in his book *Wall and Piece* (Vintage Publishing 2005) 130. The Bristol artist even acknowledged that his own art may contribute to such gentrification. In *Wall and Piece* he copy-pasted an email sent to his website by a resident of Hackney, East London: 'I don't know who you are or how many of you there are but I am writing to ask you to stop painting your things where we live. In particular xxxxxx road in Hackney. My brother and me were born here and lived here all our lives but these days so many yuppies and students are moving here neither of us can afford to buy a house where we grew up anymore. Your graffities are undoubtedly part of what makes these wankers think our area is cool. You're obviously not from around here and after you've driven up the house prices you will probably just move on. Do us all a favour and go do your stuff somewhere else like Brixton' (130).

[83] Antje Akkermann, 'And I Want to Paint It Black!? What Strategies Are There to Undermine the Reclamation of Street Art for Profit and Support Public Engagement for the Interest of Citizens?' (2015) 1(1) *Street Art and Urban Creativity Scientific Journal*, 63.

[84] Alice Pasquini confirmed she gets annoyed by the phenomenon of de-contextualisation. She admitted, 'I stopped painting on urban surfaces that can be removed because they often get stolen'. Similarly, Copyright noted during our conversation: 'I try to avoid painting on anything easily removable; for example, I'd prefer a brick wall which cannot be removed over some wooden boards'.

[85] Lewisohn, above fn. 58, 141.

for non-commercial purposes. New York artist John Fekner is on the same page: 'I've no problem with that. That's my problem, I've put it illegally. They can do whatever they want. After putting my stuff on wall, I've no control on that anymore. People can use my work, like as a donation or for charity, not for commercial purposes though, that would be another issue entirely'. Other interesting opinions were expressed by Eine (who does not approve removals 'unless all the money is going to charity I support') and Serk (who would not be happy about the removal, 'especially if it's sold for a significant amount' – however, he would not take legal action).

An even softer approach was shown by Italian writer Fra32, who pointed out during our conversation that a street piece may suffer from any kind of damage, and artists and writers need to accept it: 'if you paint in the street, anything can happen. If you don't like it, you stay at home'. Likewise, New York artist Zimer said to me:

> if I put it up without permission, then it [de-contextualisation] is a fair game. It might change the context of my piece, but it would be hard to change the message. No, I don't consider to use legal means. No one can harm my sensibility as a man or as an artist. There is no room for feelings or weakness in the streets. You gotta be tough or the culture won't take you seriously, they might kick you out of the game entirely if you're too weak. And to be honest, the professors at architecture school were even tougher and meaner than the street guys, so with my upbringing, I've no problem handling all of that.

Curiously, some artists said they would even be happy if their piece is removed and relocated, or anyway still like their artistic practice despite the removal. City Kitty, for example, said to me: '[i]t [taking artworks from the street] can be annoying, but it's my decision to continue to produce work to place on the streets. I still enjoy the outlet enough to continue to make this work. It is nice that people like a piece enough to want to have it but more often than not the piece is destroyed in the process'.[86] Zephyr also confirmed with me that this actually happened to him. He noted, 'No, I don't think I'd start a legal action because I think that my willingness to put it into the public sphere created the opportunity for whatever happened. So, I'd share the responsibility. [...] So, when I walked in that show in the museum and saw my piece, I'm like 'oh shit'. I saw this stuff of mine that was stolen, but it ended up in a museum and so I was so glad. I was glad that it got stolen because it ended up in a museum through a series of events'. Even New York writer Reskew, who – as we have seen – felt anger when he found out that his piece had been removed to be relocated into a photo studio, then tempered his feeling. He said to me: 'at first I was very angry, but when I spoke with them, I realized my work had been saved

[86] This does not mean, however, that City Kitty would not be bothered by the removal or relocation of his art. He added during the interview: 'I'd be annoyed if someone removed a piece and showed it in another context, but it also depends on the context. The pieces I paint that are for sale are different then the work I put on the street, so I'd be annoyed if someone was trying to sell this work since it isn't the original intent'.

from going in the garbage because the building I did it for was being torn down'. It is also interesting to highlight the opinion of Greg Lamarche in this regard. He commented during our conversation:

> truth be told, if someone took the energy to lift the bricks and reassemble them, then more power to them. That wouldn't bother me. I try to stay pretty away from auctions. I don't have a problem. There are two different things, even if you bring stuff from the street to the gallery there is always the thought that you're dumbing it down or taking of the edge. And yeah to a certain extent that's true, but that could be said about a lot of things. So I still think that graffiti can be exhibited inside a gallery and museums because we're talking about a totally different audience which you're exposing things to. And sometimes I think it's nice to take things from their natural habitat and put them under a light and look at them and appreciate them. Sure, there's always going to be what is going on in the streets and that's never going to stop and so there will always be level of people being 'I don't like this and that'.

Thus, there are street artists and writers who do not dislike the idea of their work being detached and relocated, as it would give them more visibility and allow more people to view and enjoy it. Danish writer Bates, for example, noted in our interview: 'I'd have mixed feelings about it. First it was made to be in the street on the location I did it, but if it ends up in modern museums, maybe more people would approve the talent and more people would appreciate it and see it'. Mobstr and Ozmo have a similar opinion. While the former would be frustrated and noted that the decision to oppose de-contextualisation should be taken on a case-by case basis, he also noted that 'if people are going to such lengths, then it must mean that your work is very much liked and in a strange way it can be seen as a compliment'. And Ozmo told me he would not be bothered about the removal because it would give him more artistic credibility.[87] He added that when street art, especially if created illegally, enters a museum, it 'simply' becomes contemporary art. Similarly, while as mentioned Stephen Palladino would be upset if one of his murals is de-contextualised, he told me that once he tagged a mattress in the street and the part of the mattress with the tag was removed – that made him feel 'flattered'. Australian artist Crisp is on the same page. He commented in our interview:

> I also do sculptures that then I glue, they get stolen a lot. A guy in New York has stolen half works I glued and then often posted on Instagram. This guy has taken eight of my pieces. He systematically steals, has a good collection. I've contacted him, I said: 'I know you've taken them, and that I didn't create them for a guy to take them in their house. Can you stop doing that? And he replied: 'I'm just a big fan of your works, you shouldn't be concerned about it'. Also, in Miami I put up twelve masks in one night and nine of them were stolen by the end of the evening: in a sense they show appreciation.

87 Yet, as mentioned above in this section, Ozmo clarified that if his artwork is de-contextualised for profit, then he expects an economic recompense.

Another artist, Giacomo (Run) Bufarini, also likes the idea and believes that a de-contextualisation of his art would give him massive exposure and visibility. He told me that 'if they remove my mural, it's a big advertising move which will hit the headlines. If the Guardian publishes an article on my removed piece, here we are, I can get five exhibitions in the best galleries!' Similarly, Dutch street artist Fake said in our interview that 'it might be good publicity and perhaps I'd also ask for a percentage'.

It should also be noted that far from being comparable to 'art thefts', removals and relocations of street artworks could in some exceptional circumstances be accepted and considered as examples of ex-situ conservation.[88] This is especially the case where the extraction of the work from the street (e.g. from a wall) and relocation to a controlled and secure environment are competently and safely carried out, and more importantly free access by the public in the new protected location is guaranteed.[89] This seems to have happened with the mentioned exhibition of Blu's detached murals in Bologna. Firstly, the conservators used a very sophisticated and effective technique of art restoration, adapting a process of removing paintings developed in Bologna in the eighteenth century. This technique consists of taking down a one-millimetre film from the concrete wall and pasting it on a canvas, while conserving the original wall appearance.[90] Secondly, although there was an entrance fee for the main exhibition, Blu's detached murals were inserted in an area of the museum which was freely accessible by anyone. Thus, despite the harsh response from Blu, the removal and relocation had some merit and served a public interest, especially considering that the pieces that had been detached were alternatively doomed to fade and be lost forever. As has been noted, there may be long-term benefits from the preservation of removed street artworks, if such pieces remain accessible to the public in museum collections, allowing researchers and art enthusiasts to admire them and understand the techniques used by the artists.[91]

88 On the distinction between ex situ and in situ conservation methods, see Rita L. Amor Garcia, 'When Documenting Doesn't Cut It: Opportunities and Alternatives to Intangible Conservation' (2017) 3(1) *Street Art and Urban Creativity Scientific Journal: Intangible Heritage*, 57–58; Enrico Bonadio, 'Does Preserving Street Art Destroying Its Authenticity?' (2019) 1 *Nuart Journal*, 36–40. Protecting street artworks by covering them with perspex glasses in their original location is considered an in situ intervention.

89 Therefore, the guy who claimed to have 'saved' the artwork painted by Alice Pasquini on a door in Venice and asked her for a certificate of authenticity may not be considered as having engaged in an acceptable ex situ preservation. The main reason for which he removed the artwork – it seems – was to just make a profit by reselling it.

90 See the interview with one of the exhibition's curators, art historian Christian Omodeo, published in the online magazine *Widewalls* on 16 May 2016 (available at www.widewalls.ch/street-art-bologna-christian-omodeo-interview/).

91 Peter Bengtsen, The Street Art World (Almendros de Granada Press 2014) 100–102 (also noting that in case a fee is required to enter and enjoy the removed street art, the scenario would be different; and adding that while one may note that the fee is necessary to cover the costs of the exhibition, and maintenance of the piece, this may still betray the spirit of street art, which is free to enjoy – with the result that the audience will be different from the one which usually walks down the street and comes across street artworks).

Another of my interviewees, Keo, also pointed out that the removal and relocation of street artworks may be acceptable in these circumstances. While he said that he would feel disgusted at what can be considered a theft, he also noted that 'if it's salvaged, it's a different story'. I have come across similar interviews in the street art literature. Peter Bengtsen, for instance, reports the opinion of Brooklyn-based artist Bast, who believes that his art is 'free for all. If you can get it off the wall and save it from the elements, how amazing is that!'[92] Even artists themselves may take works from the street. London artist Pure Evil revealed in an interview with Alison Young that he has 'taken a lot of stuff off the street' and believes that anybody who has not is a hypocrite. If the piece is fading, he noted, he takes it and brings it home – after all, he considers it 'free art'.[93]

[92] Bengtsen, above fn. 91, 98.
[93] Young, above fn. 28, 153.

# 5

# The Subcultures between an Anti-Establishment Ethos and the Mainstream

A characterising feature of street art and graffiti is their anti-establishment nature. Artworks are often placed in the streets to oppose war, criticise consumerism, question the function of modern media, and in general send anti-system messages. The resistance to legal and political authority is considered to be a hallmark of these art forms.[1] This chapter will look into whether such characteristics suggest that copyright is not suitable to govern these creative communities. In other words, is it paradoxical to allow street artists to ask for copyright protection from the very state they want to criticise?[2]

The chapter's focus will also be on some practices which have been traditionally typical of fine and studio art circles, that is, exhibiting in galleries, taking commissions, and doing merchandising – activities which have become the new normal for an increasing number of street artists and writers. This may be somewhat surprising. But looking at not only the current scenarios but also the history of these artistic movements will help provide an understanding that the anti-establishment ethos which pervades these subcultures can sometimes co-exist with behaviours which may be considered by some as having 'sellout' connotations. We will also see how practitioners of these forms of art – who frequently use street penetration strategies similar to those adopted by advertisers – often end up having commercial careers in mainstream sectors of society. Needless to say, when street and graffiti artists do engage in all these behaviours, getting more involved with copyright, and accepting its rules, is the inevitable consequence.

1 Jeff Ferrell, 'Urban Graffiti: Crime, Control and Resistance' (1995) 27 *Youth and Society*, 77; Chris Dent, 'Regulating the Artist: Laws, Norms and Practices', in Jani McCutcheon and Fiona McGaughey (eds.), *Research Handbook on Art and Law* (Elgar 2020) 47; Marta Iljadica, Copyright Beyond Law: Regulating Creativity in the Graffiti Subculture (Bloomsbury 2016), 129 (reporting the opinion of a writer describing writing 'as a "fuck you" to the government' [...] as well as commercial or corporate interests').

2 Jamison Davies, 'Art Crimes? Theoretical Perspectives on Copyright Protection for Illegally-Created Graffiti Art' (2012) 65 *Me. L. Rev.* 27, 45.

## THE ANTI-ESTABLISHMENT ELEMENT

Some street artists could be very rich, but have chosen not to go down that route because of their anti-consumerist credo. The famous Italian artist Blu, considered one of the most talented, is one of them. Despite the fame, Blu has decided not to extract economic profit from his art – and I am convinced that many corporations and advertisers would pay him serious money to be able to exploit his art. Another such artist is Stik, who prefers to use his art to support social causes and civil rights. He has collaborated with various organisations to promote free health services, the fight against homelessness, and the protection of LGBTQ+ rights. As he confirmed in our conversation in his studio in East London, he turned down lucrative offers for commercial collaborations with various companies. He also informed me that he received £10,000 from an out of court settlement (a company had exploited one of his artworks without permission). He added that he used this amount for a project with *The Big Issue* street newspaper, which is sold exclusively by homeless people or those struggling with homelessness. Through his donation, 75,000 additional prints of the magazine (each containing a Stik figure poster) were produced and distributed. The same could be said of Banksy, whose art often carries strong political protest messages. He could certainly earn much more money than he actually makes,[3] for example, via regularly licensing his copyright and trademarks to purely commercial entities. Instead, he chooses to use his art to support charity organisations such as the London-based Loves Welcome, a creative social enterprise that helps refugee women, or donate the proceeds of the sales of his canvases to non-profit organisations.[4]

The reasons many artists within these communities refuse the commodification of their art are various, including the willingness not to betray the cause of the subculture they belong to[5] and more generally to keep creative freedom and

[3] In an interview with *The Sunday Times* of 28 February 2010 Banksy noted, 'I don't make as much money as people think'.

[4] This happened in 2011 when the Covid-themed painting *Game Changer*, depicting a young boy playing with a superhero nurse doll, was sold at a Christie's auction for £16 million, with the proceeds being given to an NHS charity.

It should be pointed out that there are also artists within these communities who are not anti-establishment. This has emerged in some of my interviews. New York artist Joel Artista noted that 'knowing a lot of street artists, there's definitely this kind of anti-establishment sentiment. But I'd definitely not say that it's universal. I mean, I definitely think there's tons of street artists that if Coca Cola wants to sponsor an ad [would love to collaborate], you know they're just there doing their art, they want to get their art out there and they're not particularly anti-consumerist. They're not really politically radical'. A similar opinion was expressed by New York writer Reskew and Dutch artist Fake in our conversations. While the former said that his 'art is not anti-establishment, it is not anti-anything. It's about my personal expression, not about any statements to be made', the latter commented, 'I try not to be anti-establishment because it's the easy way, so many artists do that. I try to tell other stories of the people around you'.

[5] Lynley Farris, *Challenging Conceptions: The Fine Art of Graffiti* (ProQuest 2011) 49.

independence.[6] After all, this is also true of other artistic movements such as muralism, which often has anti-establishment features.[7] And even those who have decided to compromise and take commercial jobs have sometimes lamented the loss of cultural value. US street artist Swoon is an example. Her opinion is documented in Alison Young's book *Street Art World*: '[w]hile the work gaining value has allowed me to survive and has allowed me to do many projects that are entirely funded by sales of my artwork, on the other hand it has had the negative relationship of people seeing it as an object of value and not as this moment of beauty and freedom. I think that's regrettable'.[8]

Writers often have a more radical view, which positions many of them outside the circle of corporate style and consumption,[9] pushing them to be at war with the government, the police, train authorities, the media, and the business establishment. This is reflected in the war-inspired terminology used within the subculture, especially in the early years. Writing on walls or other urban surfaces becomes 'bombing', a tag is a 'hit', and well-produced pieces are 'burners'.[10] The 'keeping it real' creed is thus still dominating parts of this subculture, which means that writers who accept commercialising their art may lose respect within the community because they forget the 'remember where you come from once you achieve notoriety' factor.[11] Oldschool writers may therefore strongly dislike and snub those who get involved in commercial ventures because they 'bastardise' the whole movement.[12] This is because an overtly commercial agenda may lead to an erosion of subcultural graffiti's original anti-consumerist remit,[13] clash with entrenched expectations within the scene, and tarnish the image of this community.[14] Yet, as we will see in this chapter, not all writers share this strong view.

6 Tristan Manco, Stencil Graffiti (Thames & Hudson 2002) 88.

7 Eva Sperling Cockcroft, John Pitman Weber and James Cockcroft, Toward a People's Art: The Contemporary Mural Movement (University of New Mexico Press 1977) xxiii, 38 (noting that this form of art is addressed to oppressed people, minority groups, and the working class – all sectors that are in no way part of the traditional art world or of the bourgeois; stressing that muralism does not follow the 'put a price on your art' approach; and also reporting the thoughts of a muralist named Tania: 'A wall belongs to everybody – it can't be traded on the art market [...] it's nobody's property and it's everybody's property, the way art should be').

8 Alison Young, Street Art World (2016 Reaktion Books) 173.

9 Jeff Ferrell, Crimes of Style: Urban Graffiti and the Politics of Criminality (Northeastern University Press 1996) 197.

10 Cedar Lewisohn, Street Art: The Graffiti Revolution (Tate Modern Publishing 2009) 87.

11 Janice Rhan, Painting Without Permission: Hip-Hop Graffiti Subculture (Praeger 2002) 20, 159.

12 Rhan, above fn. 11, 9; Patrick Rabiega and Mariekie Burger, 'Commercial Graffiti: Self-Expression, the Allure of Danger, or Graffiti Made "Pretty"? (2017) 1(43) *South African Journal for Communication Theory and Research*, 43.

13 Samuel Merrill, 'Keeping It Real? Subcultural Graffiti, Street Art, Heritage and Authenticity' (2015) 21 *International Journal of Heritage Studies*, 383.

14 Peter Bengtsen, The Street Art World (Almendros de Granada 2014) 70. See also Cathay Smith, 'Street Art: An Analysis under U.S. Intellectual Property Law and Intellectual Property's "Negative Space" Theory' (24)259 *DePaul Journal of Art, Technology & Intellectual Property Law*, 284.

## IS COPYRIGHT ANTITHETICAL TO THE 'KEEPING IT REAL' MANTRA?

As mentioned, some commentators noted that the anti-establishment nature of much street and graffiti art cannot be reconciled with legal systems, in particular copyright regimes. It has been argued that the graffiti community cannot be amenable to the conventional protections offered by copyright[15] and that it is not 'well adapted to protecting creativity that is resistant to commodification'.[16] Primary within this community – it has been further stressed – is 'the core value of rebellion', with many artists considering 'themselves apart from mainstream culture, especially the legal system that […] is the nemesis of illegal graffiti'.[17] Therefore, the anti-system nature of these subcultures would mean that relying on the law to oppose unauthorised uses of the art would be antagonistic to their transgressive characterisation[18] and that fighting a 'beef' in court would amount to 'selling out to the man'.[19] Also, it would make no sense to open up intellectual property laws to a form of art that is meant to flout the establishment and has its own rules instead[20] (we will look at such 'social norms' in Chapter 6).

The relationship between these artistic movements and copyright has also been analysed by philosopher Andrea Baldini in his book *A Philosophy Guide to Street Art and the Law*. Baldini notes that street and graffiti art is subversive by nature, which makes these subcultures irreconcilable with copyright. The penetration of copyright into these communities, Baldini adds, would be capable of corrupting, destabilising, and jeopardising the very heart of these artistic movements because this intellectual property right would have the power of turning everything it touches into a hot commodity.

A few of my interviewees, both writers and street artists, also highlighted this very point. Italian writer Fra 32, for example, told me that if a big company starts selling a shirt reproducing his graffiti, he would be 'pissed off' but would do absolutely nothing. He added: 'I believe graffiti has a political value, in the sense of opposing society and property. Invoking copyright doesn't make any sense: what's the point if you claim copyright like fine artists do? When copyright and money enter the scene, the whole movement is weakened. I don't want money

15 Al Roundtree, 'Graffiti Artists "Get Up" in Intellectual Property's Negative Space' (2013) 31 *Cardozo Arts & Entertainment Law Journal*, 959, 973, 978.

16 Marta Iljadica, Copyright Beyond Law: Regulating Creativity in the Graffiti Subculture (Bloomsbury 2016) 137, 288 (also noting that 'copyright law is ill-suited to regulate particular, especially subcultural, forms of creativity' and pointing out in the book's introductory section, 'A Note on Pictures', that 'much of creativity and many of the pleasures of creation and belonging [within the graffiti community] exist beyond copyright. Copyright does not reach, and cannot speak to, these pleasures').

17 Roundtree, above fn. 15, 966.

18 Davies, above fn. 2, 38, 45.

19 Roundtree, above fn. 15, 978; Cathay Smith, Street Art: An Analysis Under U.S. Intellectual property Law and Intellectual Property's Negative Space Theory, DePaul Journal of Art, Technology & Intellectual Property Law, Vol. XXIV, No. 259, 284.

20 Nicole A. Grant, Outlawed Art: Finding a Home for Graffiti in Copyright Law (2012), htttp://ssrn.com/abstract=2030514, 27.

to enter the subculture'. London writer Noir and former New York writer Dejer have a similar opinion. The former confirmed with me that relying on copyright would be 'hypocritical', and the latter highlighted the risk of a 'mainstreamization' of graffiti. Some street artists made the same point. London-based Delgado noted in the interview: 'I think it's a contradiction'.[21] Similarly, English street poet Mobstr replied to my question on this very issue that 'street art like human behaviour is riddled with hypocrisy'. And Daleast simply told me that 'vandals don't care about copyright'.

But is this what *all* street artists and writers really think? If we look again at the legal actions which have been brought by some of them, especially in the US, we get a different picture. In Chapter 3 I mentioned some of these cases, including the legal complaint filed by the artist Ahol against popular teen clothier American Eagle Outfitters. The latter had used Ahol's mural (consisting of his signature 'lazy eyeball' motif) in its advertising campaigns without his consent. The artist claimed that his reputation rests on the assumption that he does not sell out to corporate interests, and that the misappropriation of his art by such a company changes the original working-class-oriented meaning of his work.[22] Similar complaints and objections have been brought by Rime (against the fashion company Moschino),[23] Revok (against the fashion company Cavalli),[24] Norm,[25] and Dash Snow's fiancée[26] (both against the fast food giant McDonald's) as well as Futura 2000.[27] And in the cases brought against Moschino and Cavalli, both Rime and Revok made the point that 'nothing is more antithetical to the outsider "street creed" that is essential to graffiti artists [...] than associations with European chic, luxury and glamour – of which [Moschino/Cavalli] is the epitome'. The two writers also noted that they are 'diligent in controlling distribution channels' of their works 'because such channels greatly affect an artist's reputation and the overall market for an artist's work', adding that they do not 'make their art available [...] in retail stores', and like their target audience they 'eschew any connection to commercial consumerism'. Likewise, in the above cases against McDonald's both plaintiffs claimed that nothing is more antithetical to the artists' 'outsider "street cred" than association with corporate consumerism of which McDonald's and its marketing are the epitome'. In his complaint the writer Norm also argued that being associated with McDonald's may make him lose other

[21] Delgado, however, added that 'nowadays street art is about many things, it is not counterculture anymore. It can be, but now it's a popular movement that brings many sides and experiences about the subject'.

[22] Gabe Friedman, Can Graffiti Be Copyrighted? *The Atlantic*, 21 September 2014.

[23] *Joseph Tierney v. Moschino S.p.A. et al.*, Docket No. 2:15-cv-05900 (C.D. Cal. Aug 05, 2015).

[24] *Jason Williams et al. v. Roberto Cavalli, S.p.A. et al.*, Docket No. 2:14-cv-06659 (C.D. Cal. Aug 25, 2014) (this case was started by Reyes, Steel and Revok).

[25] *Eric Rosenbaum v. McDonald's Corp., et al.*, CV 16–2063 FMO (United States District Court, Central District of California).

[26] *Jade Berreau v. McDonald's Corporation et al.*, 2:16-cv-07394 (Central District of California).

[27] See above fn. 2, Chapter 3 (mentioning a trademark dispute started by Futura 2000).

business opportunities. Points similar to those mentioned above were made by the artists in other cases mentioned in Chapter 3.[28]

These legal complaints show that a writer or a street artist can be anti-establishment and at the same time rely on copyright (remember that traditional works such as fine art paintings often carry anti-establishment and rebellious messages, and nobody doubts they are protectable by copyright). Not only is copyright compatible with anti-establishment messages – it could even be the tool to keep that message 'as such'. Indeed, this intellectual property right allows artists and writers to object to and (try to) prevent what many of them do not accept, namely a commercial exploitation of their art which is antithetical to that message. Therefore, resorting to copyright laws may protect the reputation of artists and writers who do not want to be associated with marketing and profit-oriented activities. Thus, these laws, by making available injunctions and other remedies against unauthorised exploitations of artworks, could be the right instrument of reaction for those artists who reject sellout labels and want to keep control of the art they create.[29]

We have seen in Chapter 4 that such control can also be achieved by asserting the moral right of integrity.[30] So, both copyright and moral rights laws seem suitable to protect subcultural creativity and make it resistant to commodification. This can also be seen from how the artist Blu has managed information related to one of his most famous works, that is, the universally acclaimed wall paint video animation *Muto*, originally uploaded on YouTube in 2008 and with almost 13 million views at the time of this writing. The video is preceded by a Creative Commons licence disclaimer which informs that: '[y]ou are free to copy, distribute, display this work for non commercial purposes. No commercial websites or televisions are allowed to display this film without the author's permission. Any modification of the original work is not allowed without the author's permission'. Similarly, Banksy's organisation, Pest Control, has included in its website the following disclaimer: 'You are welcome to use Banksy's images for non-commercial, personal amusement. Print them out in a colour that matches your curtains, make a card for your gran, submit them as your own homework, whatever. But neither Banksy or Pest Control licence the artist's images to third parties. Please do not use Banksy's images for any commercial purpose, including launching a range of merchandise or tricking people into thinking something is made or endorsed by the artist when it isn't'

In this way Blu and Banksy have made clear that they want to keep some form of control over their creation, especially to prevent commercial co-option. It should be noted that artists are able to do so exactly because copyright laws empower them: without copyright, they could not do that. So, one may note that there is no

[28] See in particular fn. 11–18.

[29] Grant, above fn. 20, 25.

[30] Yet, several street artists and writers who brought suits in the US did not invoke such right.

contradiciton between relying (directly or indirectly) on copyright and moral rights and at the same time keeping a strong anti-establishment position.

Many street artists and writers I approached confirmed that they do not find any contradictions here – with some stressing the importance of protecting free artistic speech and democratic values. New York artist Zimer, for example, noted that 'governments are supposed to be challenged so you should always be able to criticise them. Needing services that only the establishment can provide doesn't disqualify your voice'. Other New York artists I interviewed are on the same page. Paul Richard noted that 'no, there is no contradiction with street artists who want copyright protection'. And while Al Diaz told me that 'it's my right as a citizen to voice my opinion. It's part of our constitution, it's an artistic venture, it's not just a statement against the government. I'm entitled to protect something that's mine', Logan Hicks pointed out, 'Contradiction? Not at all! Why should there be? The law should protect all, not just one set of people. Freedom of speech is open to all people. The law should be equal for everyone'. Such need for the laws has also been highlighted by Reskew, who admitted during our conversation that 'for vandals, yes, it [relying on copyright] is very ironic', but at the same time it is 'very wise to play their game perhaps. If the common person does not have the law to back them up when in need, how will they fend for themselves? Until the world can be purely cooperative, we need the help of laws'. It is also interesting to report the opinion of Andre Trenier. He told me during our encounter:

> if that same copyright enforcement protection is available to people with other opinions and people who are against the voices that I'm trying to speak for, then I think that the same protection should apply both ways. I don't feel that this is hypocritical because I think that it just benefits someone wanting to take advantage. I can be critical of a government because a government is supposed to be the collective voice, so it needs differences of opinion to maintain a positive course, because it can very quickly become a dictatorship or something controlled by a ruling class of upper-class people, which in a lot of ways, we still end up with. The poor usually have less of a voice and less of a way to enforcing and bringing their voice to other people. So, the artwork that a lot of anti-establishment artists do will voice the people who do not have a voice. But by voicing those opinions, that doesn't mean that I relinquish my rights.

This line of argument is shared by other artists I talked to, including Bristol artist Andy Council ('there should be protection even if there is rebellion, there is free speech'), Copyright ('there's an assumption that all street artists must be anti-corporate anarchists, and sure some are. […] Maybe we threaten people by living outside of society norms, but we still deserve the same rights as everyone else'), and Ben Eine ('very much so [graffiti should be protected], even if it is anti-establishment, because we live in a democracy'). Likewise, Laser 3.14 noted, 'I don't think there's a contradiction there. A government is made of a lot of layers and aspects, and works through different kind of policies and one can criticize one or a couple of those policies and celebrate others. I think it's easy to be anti-government as a whole, but it's more interesting to be critical about certain policies and use that critique in one's work. I myself don't like over-consumerism, but I can see the benefits of capitalism'. And Damien Mitchell echoed this sentiment: 'you can believe in copyright law and then do not approve of other governments' measures'. Morley and Lexi Bella could not see any contradiction, either. The former opined: 'I think protecting yourself as an artist is the only way to battle corporations that would look to take advantage of you. If you want to fight a consumerist culture you need the tools to do it'. And the latter said to me: 'that's covering your ass and playing by their rules, and using their rules to protect yourself and know your rights and value'. Similarly, during our conversation in Harlem, Kristy explained her view on the difference between being anti-capitalist and being anti-governmental while choosing to rely on copyright:

> [t]he thing is that you should be able to control what somebody uses your work for. I'm anti-corporate and anti-capitalist, but I'm not anti-government. I don't agree with everything the government does, but I think our government serves some good purposes. So that would be one good purpose to help artists protect their work legally from people giving another purpose to their work. There are different branches of the government. But the government is 'here' and capitalism is 'there' and they overlap in some ways, but they are not the same.

Other interviewees gave a more business-oriented explanation. Claw Money for instance told me that 'if you do it for profit, you have to pay taxes as a citizen, if you're doing art for a living, you need to have a business, you need to comply with the law, is it hypocrite? I don't think so, you need to "play the system"'. Likewise, writer and graffiti promoter Good Guy Boris expanded on the need to protect artists' businesses:

> [n]o, in my opinion the artist who claims copyright doesn't sell out. Everybody does his best to put bread on the table, so the morals of each one of us are different. If you like something, you do it as long as you don't hurt anybody else. I think it's important that they should have the opportunity to be protected if they want it. Graffiti today is an industry and each industry needs business and each business needs legal help. I'm doing business with graffiti, I'm selling books, promoting graffiti and street artists, creating campaigns for exhibitions. These things need legal help, for example I often need an accountant and lawyer to create a contract between me and the artist.

There are also more nuanced positions. A couple of my informants, for example, distinguished between the controversial 'means' and the acceptable 'end'. Indeed, US writer Cept noted that 'yeah, there seems to be a contradiction, but at the same time it's fair to sue corporations; the *means* may be contradictory, but the *end* is in line with the graffiti subculture'. Greek artist Sonke is of the same opinion: 'that's a very tough question. I think in this occasion the *end* justifies the *means*'. US artist City Kitty's take on this issue is also interesting – he focuses on whether the artist has copied from someone else. He told me: 'I think that protecting one's art and personal creation is important. I only think this is a contradiction when artists appropriate already copyrighted recognisable images (such as cartoons or pop culture references) in their own work and then want copyright protection'.

## SELLING OUT, THE 'ROBIN HOOD' APPROACH, AND THE PARADOX OF 'CONSUMERIST ANTI-CONSUMERISM'

As we have just seen, many artists and writers I encountered believe that copyright is suitable to regulate creativity within these communities, and they welcome its rules. The acceptance of copyright is certainly more evident within circles of artists and writers who have widely opened up to the mainstream and its commercial opportunities. Although many practitioners of writing still do not accept it,[31] it cannot be denied that a part of these subcultures has been absorbed by some aspects of the mainstream, propelling what has become a fully fledged industry – with speciality paints being produced and sold; formal support from institutions, governments and corporations; and even a range of university degree programs.[32]

Nowadays, many street artists and writers get paid to create pieces (I will come back to commissions in the next section); often carry business cards; and leave telephone numbers, email addresses, or social media details next to their murals so as to advertise what for many has become a regular job.[33] And they often do that without paying attention to sell out criticisms.[34] Ronald Kramer has reached similar findings in his own ethnographic research. One of his interviewees, the US writer Demer, interestingly noted that 'if graffiti writers can get paid and be involved in it, then I'm definitely all for it. People say it's "selling out", but I think that's a ridiculous term. If you love what you're doing and you can get paid to do it, there is nothing better than that'.[35]

Commercial opportunities are seized by an increasing number of street artists and writers, especially (but not only) at a later stage of their career when their horizons are broader.[36] Early New York writer Futura 2000, now a successful studio artist with collaborations with famous brands such as Nike, Uniqlo, and Louis Vuitton,

[31] See also Andrea Mubi Brighenti, 'At The Wall: Graffiti Writers, Urban Territoriality, and the Public Domain' (2010) *Space and Culture*, 318 (noting that 'the more you content yourself with legality and legal arrangements of some sort – for example, public institutions granting you a wall out of town where you can practice, or shopkeepers hiring you to paint their place – the more you become something different from a writer').

[32] Roger Gastman (ed.), Wall Writers (Gingko Press Incorporated 2015) 23.

[33] This is exactly what New York street artist Resa Piece does. She pointed out in our conversation that 'someone will see the mural and their business owners want me to paint their storefront or something. So I get exposure'. It is for this reason that she always signs her murals: 'because that's how I get other jobs, you know'.

[34] See also Rabiega and Burger, above fn. 12, 49.

[35] Ronald Kramer, *The Rise of Legal Graffiti Writing in New York and Beyond* (Palgrave MacMillan 2017) 74.

[36] It has also been pointed out that commercial graffiti may advance artists' skills and techniques. See Rabiega and Burger, above fn. 12, 49.

is certainly one of them: he simply believes that artists should be free to do what they want to do.[37] Cey Adams – who has also had success as a graphic designer and worked with popular US hip-hop bands and stars such as Run DMC, Beastie Boys, Public Enemy, Notorious Big, and Jay-Z – is of the same opinion, and curiously focuses on people's enviousness. He commented in an old interview with Ivor Miller: 'I think the issue of selling out comes from jealousy. It is no different from a theatre actor going into film. People get jealous and don't understand how to find a way to get there themselves, because if they did, they wouldn't have time to point fingers. There's nothing wrong with success! [...] my perspective is that there is room for graffiti artists to evolve in mainstream society and still keep their integrity. [...] it's your right to earn a living being creative'.[38] I was not surprised to hear Cey Adams expressing such an opinion. He reiterated this point during our own conversation in his studio in New Jersey, where he added that there has been an evolution in the graffiti subculture: 'back in the days, many writers hated selling out, now many accept it'. US artist Gaia made this very same point in our conversation. He noted that 'there is nothing wrong in selling out – it's good. You can feed your family, and get profits. [...] I've made quite a lot of money from movie licensing and even got a large settlement from an illegal piece I had produced that was improperly reproduced in the lobby of a building'. Many of my interviewees confirmed that they regularly collaborate with established brands. Keo, for example, has done commercial jobs for companies such as Nike, Adidas, and Puma, which paid him to paint for commercials, films, and music videos.

Yet, several artists within these communities can still face what has been called the 'sellout' dilemma: on the one hand, they accept making profits by exploiting their art, but on the other they do not want to betray the anti-consumerist principles dear to them and thus lose street credibility and a reputation within the scene.[39] This is well explained by psychologist Yoav Litvin,[40] who notes that in capitalistic societies it is often difficult for artists to survive without accepting working for corporations or the government. He calls it the 'artist's dilemma': if you choose to be involved with any sort of business, you may risk losing moral ground and be seen by peers and audiences as a sellout, 'arguably the worst insult that can be lobbed at an artist'.[41]

It is probably to mitigate the effects of this dilemma that several artists try to hide themselves behind what in our interview Zephyr called the Robin Hood approach, namely using the money and other advantages that come from the commercialisation of their art to support their own projects and thus further the interests of the creative subcultures they belong to (Litvin also mentions the Robin Hood approach

37 See Lewisohn, above fn. 10, 67.

38 Ivor L. Miller, Aerosol Kingdom: Subway Painters of New York City (2012) University Press of Mississippi, 161, 181.

39 Ulrich Blanché, Banksy: Urban Art in a Material World (Tectum 2016) 48.

40 Yoav Livtin, 'The Artist's Dilemma: What Constitutes Selling Out?' (1 December 2015) *The Conversation*.

41 Ibidem.

and brings, as Zephyr did in our conversation, the example of US street and studio artist Shepard Fairey). My interview with Stik is also relevant here. I asked him whether he feels that he has gone mainstream. He replied that he engages with the mainstream, but he does so by co-opting it for social causes. In his research Kramer also interestingly argues that accepting work on mainstream projects helps establish connections with those who possess the capital, for example, big corporations, to make sure that any possible economic benefit deriving from commodification can be channelled back to the graffiti community.[42] In this way writers can take advantage of such commercialisation for their own purposes – they do not just look passively at the exploitation of their art.[43] And by creating their own brands and businesses, writers can get profits while representing the subculture they are part of.[44] Thus, painting graffiti for money would not compromise writers, nor make their pieces 'inauthentic'.[45]

There is another angle which needs to be highlighted. Artists who regularly convey anti-establishment and anti-consumerist messages may end up increasing the sales of their studio works such as canvases (as well as merchandise based on their art) exactly because of these kinds of messages,[46] a sort of paradoxical 'selling rebellion to rebels' outcome. Banksy is the best example. Having for years embraced anti-consumerism and conveyed such message through sarcastic imagery, perhaps involuntarily he has made himself and his anti-commercial art *commercially* successful.[47] The title of his

42 Ronald Kramer, 'Painting with Permission: Legal Graffiti in New York City' (2010) 2(11) *Ethnography*, 248; Kramer, above fn. 35, 76. See also Jeffrey Ian Ross, John F. Lennon, and Ronald Kramer, 'Moving beyond Banksy and Fairey: Interrogating the Co-optation and Commodification of Modern Graffiti and Street Art' (2020) 9(1–2) *Visual Inquiry*, 9 (noting that artists 'may take money from advertising companies to help fund their illegal street art campaigns'); Miller, above fn. 38, 179 (reporting Futura 2000's words: 'we are not out to sell, sell, sell. We want to control our product, have fun, and maintain a mystique').

43 Kramer, above fn. 42, 76.

44 Kara-Jane Lombard, 'From Subways to Product Labels: The Commercial Incorporation of Hip Hop Graffiti' (2013) 2(20) *Visual Communication Quarterly*, 95.

45 Kramer in Ross, above fn. 35, 116.

46 Bengtsen, above fn. 14, 126.

47 It should also be remembered that Banksy, especially in the early years of his career, accepted some forms of commercial collaborations. He designed, for example, the art for the cover of the *Think Tank* album that was released by the British pop band Blur in 2004. Also, the *Turf War* exhibition organized by the Bristolian artist received financial support from Puma: visitors were given three postcards and a single black latex glove bearing the Puma brand and could also buy official Banksy T-shirts with the Puma brand on the sleeve. See Ellsworth-Jones, Banksy: The Man Behind the Wall (New York: Aurum Press Ltd, 2013) 127–128. It would however be a mistake to conclude that Banksy is just interested in finalising commercial transactions. Not only does he support charities by sharing part of the proceeds he obtains from the sale of his studio works. What he did with his company Picture on Walls, which was tasked with producing and selling limited editions of his prints, confirms that he has also been keen to guarantee that as many people as possible could access and possess his art. Indeed, Pictures on Walls used to sell prints at relatively affordable prices (e.g. £100). See Luke Dickens, Pictures on Walls? Producing, Pricing and Collecting the Street Art Screen Print (2010) City, Vol. 14, 1–2, 70 (pointing out that '[a]ware of the dangers of being seen to be "totally corporate", Banksy and Lazarides were keen for their POW project to

2010 acclaimed film documentary – *Exit through the Gift Shop*, which was nominated for the Oscar Academy Award for Best Documentary Feature,[48] epitomises Banksy's ironic take on commercial exploitation of art. As noted by Ulrich Blanché, artworks which criticise capitalism, the traditional art world, and advertising end up publicising the artist's brand,[49] a fact Banksy himself self-ironically addresses in several of his pieces and even admitted in one of his rare interviews. He once noted that 'it's hard to know what "selling out" means – these days you can make more money producing a run of anti-McDonald's posters than you can make designing actual posters for McDonald's. I tell myself I use art to promote dissent, but maybe I am just using dissent to promote my art. I plead not guilty to selling out. But I plead it from a bigger house than I used to live in'.[50]

Blanché highlighted how Banksy has depicted opponents of capitalism as consumers, making fun of the 'commercialization of non or anti-commercial ideas and art forms'.[51] Blanché brought the example of a mural painted by the famous Bristol artist in 2009 in Croydon (South London), depicting a spike-headed punk puzzling over a set of instructions for assembling an IKEA-style product (the logo on the box is also disassembled, IEAK). Next to the punk is a box bearing the words 'LARGE GRAFFITI SLOGAN'. Blanché also reminds us of Banksy's *Destroy Capitalism* artwork printed on T-shirts that were presented at his *Barely Legal* exhibition in Los Angeles in 2006 and later made available as a digital image through his website. The imagery includes different kinds of 'rebels' (e.g. a punk, again) queuing to buy a *Destroy Capitalism* shirt priced at $30. The result is paradoxical. Banksy's criticism of consumption culture – printed on commercial products – is being sold, with the artist visualising it in his own artwork and showing people who criticise consumerism, like himself, as sometimes willing or involuntary producers and consumers of anti-consumer products'.[52] In addition, the copyright © symbol is displayed in the product, with the fine print underneath reading: 'Registered trademark, not to be reproduced without prior written permission. Copyright 2007'.[53]

be focused on "bringing art to the masses". […] Their attitude on this issue was intended to express their stated belief that access to art should be as non-elitist as possible – a sort of corporate social responsibility agenda – which seemed to unsettle the notion of a profit-driven rationale').

48 The movie was directed by Banksy himself and produced by Jaimie D'Cruz, and it tells the story of the Los Angeles-based artist Thierry Guetta, also known as Mr Brainwash.

49 Blanché, above fn. 39, 196.

50 Interview with Banksy by Ossian Ward, in *Time Out London*, 1 March 2010. See also Will Elsworth-Jones, *The Man behind the Wall*, 2nd ed. (Frances Lincoln, 2021) 8 (noting that Banksy 'too is a capitalist – albeit a reluctant one'). Moreover, it is worthwhile to note that the same kind of dilemma has also been highlighted with reference to muralism. See Cockcroft, Weber, and Cockcroft, above fn. 7, 234 (noting that 'in essence, all forms of opportunism in community art come down to the single question: is the artist using art to serve the people and the people's struggle? Or is the people's struggle being use[d] to serve the artist?').

51 Blanché, above fn. 39, 110.

52 Ibidem, 195.

53 Ibidem, 110–112.

## COMMISSIONED WORKS

Street artists and writers are frequently commissioned to create art. Contrary to what one may think, graffiti works were also sometimes commissioned in the early days of the movement in New York. Even cases of ghost writing occurred in those initial years. Jack Stewart, for example, reveals that Tracy 168 earned money doing pieces on trains for people who wanted to see their names go by and that he and other writers got commissions to do graffiti-style decorations on walls and gates for stores, skating rinks, bars, and restaurants.[54] The iconic film *Wild Style*, which narrates the lives of New York graffiti writers of the early 1980s, also refers to a $200 commission (for spray-painting a canvas) which the protagonist Zoro, played by Lee Quiñones, accepts from a wealthy art collector. The same happens in *Downtown 81*, a US film of the early 1980s featuring a young Jean-Michel Basquiat wandering around Manhattan and trying to sell art to raise money.[55] In one scene, Lee Quiñones and Fab 5 Freddy paint graffiti on a wall and tell Basquiat that they are working legally and on commission.

Nowadays, commissions of street and graffiti artworks are obviously more common and are accepted by many within these subcultures. There are specialist agencies and collectives such as Graffiti Life and Graffiti Kings in London that provide commissioning services for clients that want to hire artists for both temporary and permanent works. Sketches of commissioned murals are usually presented and approved by the commissioner, who may also request changes during the execution.[56] Thus, such commissions often produce a dialogue between the commissioner and the artist, which inevitably gives artists less artistic freedom during the execution of the work.[57]

Commissioners may include private property owners who are willing to embellish their space; local councils which want to reinvigorate neighbourhoods; businesses such as restaurants and cafés which aim to promote their services; and even big brands. This was confirmed by many of my interviewees. New York artist Andre Trenier said to me: '[I do commissioned works for] businesses, shops restaurants and other different clients'. Similarly, Depsone noted, 'I do a lot [of commissions] and that's basically all I do now, but usually small ones, for like small-scale shops and stuff like that. It's pretty much my job'. Italian artist Ozmo

54 Jack Stewart, Graffiti Kings: New York City Mass Transit Art of the 1970s (Abrams 2009) 203.

55 Stewart, above fn. 54, 203.

56 See Martha Cooper and Joseph Sciorra, *R.I.P.: New York Spraycan Memorials* (Thames & Hudson 1994) 12 (focusing entirely on memorial walls, which are commonly commissioned, and noting that the family of the deceased person usually gives artists precise instructions which follow the aesthetic tastes and sometimes also religious sensibilities of the deceased's friends and siblings). Memorial murals almost always consist of portraits painted based on pictures of the deceased person, with other elements being added such as RIP ribbons and skulls.

57 Lombard, above fn. 44, 92.

also welcomes commissions. He said to me: 'if the project and the sponsor are interesting and show respect towards my art, I do commissions (I don't necessarily do it for money). I've painted for Absolut Vodka and Prada. It give me extreme visibility, even better than painting in Times Square in New York!' The same goes for Dutch artist Fake ('I do commissioned works for companies and private owners'), Bill Blast ('Yeah, I 've done TV stations. I've done a mural inside an office. I got commissions for this. It's the way I put food on the table'), Kristy ('I do sometimes, but rarely on walls, so if it's commissioned it's usually inside somebody's space. Mostly for bars, restaurants, and private owners'), and Rubin ('[T]hey commission me to do murals. Everything from mainstream companies to local business').[58]

Also, as we have seen in Chapter 3, several artists I spoke with confirmed that when it comes to taking jobs on commission, they make sure to keep ownership of the copyright over the commissioned work, especially via contractual arrangements. This seems to be a widespread habit – with some exceptions, though. Indeed, Australian artist Crisp told me: 'yes, I do, but no written agreement, never. I've once done a written agreement at a live painting for Mercedes. I painted the same car seven times. They paid me for that. It's a big brand, but I was able to accept the offer as it was a more environmentally friendly product, it was a smart car. Artists need to make a living – I need to live as well'.[59] This comment by Crisp also shows how artists may want to accept commissions where they share the same values as the commissioner. This point emerged in other interviews. Alice Pasquini told me that she painted walls on commission, even for big corporations like Nike. On the latter commission she said that 'it was a big billboard, an authorised campaign, but without brand. I wouldn't do it if the brand is exposed'. English artist Copyright and Giacomo Run Bufarini are on the same page. While the former noted in the interview that 'I've licenced artworks for collaborations with brands I admire', the latter informed me that he painted a mural for Absolut Vodka, but in general he would like to keep his artistic freedom. He added, 'I need to live and I've three daughters, and I like living nicely. But I don't accept everything. I also want to be able to

58 However, a few of my interviewees, especially writers, showed no interest at all in commissioned works. One of them is New York writer Serk. He said, 'I'm not interested. I don't see it as a job or as an additional income'.

59 Not all artists I talked to accept commissions. French artist Jeff Aerosol told me: 'people offer these commissions, but I usually refuse unless they are friends of mine or collectors who have already purchased pieces from my galleries. I'm not really interested in doing that, except if the wall is outdoor and seen by passer-by, then I can consider doing that, but it doesn't happen often'. Daleast is of the same opinion. He pointed out during our conversation: 'I don't do much [commissioned works] – maybe in the future. I'm more focused on art projects'. Writers Easy and Crane DPC also dislike commissions. The former said to me: 'I don't really do that stuff. Had a lot of offers but turned them down. I'm not interested in doing that really. It's money, but it's not about the money all the time'. And the latter commented, 'I don't paint commissions – as soon as you do it, it becomes work – what I do is solely a hobby. If I did, I wouldn't feel the need to get written agreements, as the type of work I'd be doing just wouldn't warrant it'.

choose'. A similar opinion was expressed by Mosstika during our conversation in Brooklyn: 'I had a proposal five years ago for a living installation from a company. I paid lawyers, but then the company retreated. I'm not a huge fan of this commercial stuff but since I'm a full-time artist, I'd be happy to get some money, only for a piece of art of which I'm proud of, though. I'd do that just for money – I wouldn't put it on my website'. US artist Paul Richard also had some reservations, but more based on whether the property upon which the art must be placed is private or public. He told me during our conversation in his studio in Brooklyn: 'I have been commissioned to do art on public property. But I might not accept commissions to put art on private property. I don't like the ambiguity of that arrangement. I might prefer to put the art on a canvas or panel and let the property owner do what he wants'.

## ACCEPTING THE INSTITUTIONAL ART MARKET

A relatively high number of street artists and (to a lesser extent) writers also create and show studio works in traditional fine art venues. Many of my interviewees confirmed that. Graffiti- and street art–inspired pieces can now be appreciated in venues such as the Museum of Graffiti in Miami (opened in 2019), the Urban Nation Museum in Berlin (opened in 2017), and a multitude of galleries in many cities of the world. Well-attended exhibitions of these forms of art have taken place, for example, those in London in 2008 (at the Tate Modern, sponsored by Japanese carmaker Nissan) and Los Angeles in 2011 (*Art in the Street* at the Museum of Contemporary Art). Bristol also hosted successful indoor exhibitions of street and graffiti art. An important one was the 2009 exhibition *Banksy versus Bristol Museum* at the Bristol Museum & Art Gallery, which showcased many of the Bristolian artist's works. It was visited by 300,000 people.[60] Banksy's comment on that exhibition was emblematic and, as the messages conveyed by his art often are, sarcastic: '[t]his is the first show I've ever done where taxpayers' money is being used to hang my pictures up rather than scrape them off'.[61]

Not only do many street and graffiti artists expose their studio artworks – they also sell them, even via auction houses. Banksy is one of them, and his studio pieces have been sold for significant amounts of money – with one of them even being segmented into 10,000 non-fungible tokens (NFTs).[62] The Bristol artist is also

[60] Ulrich Blanché, '*Banksy v. Bristol Museum* – Street Art or Street "Flavored" Art?' in Pedro Soares Neves and Daniela V. de Freitas Simões (eds.), Lisbon Street Art & Urban Creativity - 2014 International Conference, 18–20. On this exhibition see also Paul Gough (ed.), *Banksy: The Bristol Legacy* (Sansom & Co 2012).

[61] 'Banksy at Bristol Museum' (12 June 2009) *The Guardian*.

[62] Many of Banksy's artworks have fetched high prices. Sales and auctions of the following Banksy pieces, most of them created in studio and not bound to an outdoor environment, are noteworthy. This first list includes Banksy's pieces which were sold for more than £1 million.

i. *Love Is in the Bin*, sold in 2021 for £18,582,000 (self-mutilated canvas, originally auctioned as *Girl with a Balloon*);
ii. *Game Changer*, sold in 2021 for £16,800,000 (canvas);

responsible for pioneering the street art prints business, having launched in 2002 the already mentioned company Pictures on Walls together with his former agent Steve

iii. *Love Is in the Air*, sold in 2021 for $12,900,000 (canvas) (as mentioned, the artwork has then been segmented into 10,000 NFTs);
iv. *Devolved Parliament*, sold in 2019 for £9,879,500 (canvas);
v. *Show me the Monet*, sold in 2020 for £7,551,600 (canvas);
vi. *Forgive Us Our Trespassing*, sold in 2020 for £6,300,000 (canvas);
vii. *Mediterranean Sea View*, sold in 2017 for £2.230,000 (tryptic of oil paintings);
viii. *Sorry. The Lifestyle You Ordered Is Currently Out of Stock*, sold in 2020 for £1,780,000 (canvas);
ix. *Monkey Poison*, sold in 2020 for £1,600,000 (canvas);
x. *Keep It Spotless*, sold in 2007 for £1,300,000 (household gloss and spray-paint on canvas);
xi. *Girl with Balloon and Morons*, sold in 2020 for £1,230,000 (double print);
xii. *Vote to Love*, sold in 2019 for £1,155,000 (spray-painted heart over a UKIP poster, replacing its message to 'Leave' the European Union with 'Love').

This second list includes other sales of Banksy's artworks that were sold for less than £1,000,000, organised chronologically.

xiii. *Heavy Weaponry*, sold in 2004 for £32,000 (spray-paint on canvas);
xiv. *Vandalised Phone Box*, sold in 2005 for $605,000 (sculpture);
xv. *The Rude Lord*, sold in 2006 for $658,025 (oil on canvas);
xvi. *David*, sold in 2007 for £204,500 (sculpture);
xvii. *Bombing Middle England*, sold in 2007 for £102,000 (acrylic and spray-paint on canvas);
xviii. *Space Girl and Bird*, sold in 2007 for £288,000 (spray-paint on steel);
xix. *Bomb Hugger*, sold in 2007 for £31,200 (print);
xx. *Testing*, sold in 2008 for £636,500 (oil on canvas laid onto board, five parts);
xxi. *Queen Victoria*, sold in 2008 for £277,250 (oil on canvas);
xxii. *Insane Clown*, sold in 2008 for £241,250 (spray-paint stencil on Hessian);
xxiii. *Laugh Now*, sold in 2008 for £228,000 (spray-paint on painted board);
xxiv. *Ruined Landscape*, sold in 2008 for $385,000 (oil and spray-paint on canvas);
xxv. *Pie Face*, sold in 2007 for £192,000 (oil on canvas);
xxvi. *Simple Intelligence Test*, sold in 2008 for £636,500 (oil on canvas);
xxvii. *Warning Sign*, sold in 2008 for £ 181,250 (spray enamel on composite plastic);
xxviii. *Think Tank*, sold in 2008 for £156,000 (stencil and spray-paint on steel);
xxix. *Happy Coppers*, sold in 2008 for £144,000 (acrylic and spray-paint on cardboard);
xxx. *You Told That Joke Twice*, sold in 2010 for £169,250 (acrylic, enamel and oil stick on canvas);
xxxi. *Very Little Helps*, sold in 2010 for £82,850 (canvas);
xxxii. *Bird with Grenade*, sold in 2011 for £145,250 (oil and spray enamel on canvas);
xxxiii. *Gas Mask Boy*, sold in 2011 for $178,000 (oil on canvas);
xxxiv. *Submerged Phone Booth*, sold in 2014 for £722,500 (sculpture);
xxxv. *Happy Shopper*, sold in 2014 for £506,600 (sculpture);
xxxvi. *Rembrandt*, sold in 2014 for $541,761 (painting);
xxxvii. *Balloon Girl*, sold in 2015 for £56,250 (print, originally painted on a wall in East London, Great Eastern Street);
xxxviii. *Silent Majority*, sold in 2015 for £445,792 (the piece had been painted at the 1998 Glastonbury Festival on the side of a festival worker's trailer and was authenticated by Banksy before the sale);
xxxix. *Swat Van*, sold in 2016 for £218,500 (the piece had been painted on the side of a van and shown at Banksy's *Barely Legal* exhibition in Los Angeles in 2006; it was later authenticated by Banksy before the sale);
xl. *The Caveman*, sold in 2018 for $680,000 (stencil and colored spray on concrete wall in metal frame);

Lazarides (that company lasted until 2017). Moreover, Banksy asserts the 'resale right' over his studio pieces under the UK Artist's Resale Right Regulations 2006.[63] This intellectual property right allows artists to claim royalties each time their work is resold through an auction house or art market professional. After all, the exhibition and sale of canvases by street and graffiti artists is nowadays largely accepted within these subcultures. And indeed I was not surprised to learn that Revok, Reyes, and Steel pointed out in their copyright-based complaints against fashion company Cavalli that they sell original art pieces (for prices in the range of $50,000) and limited edition prints.[64]

This should be no surprise also because some writers have been involved with traditional art circles from the very beginning of this movement in New York. In 1972 Hugo Martinez, a student at City College of New York, gathered a group of writers of mainly Latino background – including Henry 161, Snake, SJK 171, and Coco 144 – who had been widely tagging subway trains and other urban surfaces, and founded the United Graffiti Artists (UGA). At the beginning UGA had its own studio loft in upper Manhattan, where writers could work, also on canvases. Martinez was convinced that graffiti was a form of art and that the energy writers were putting into it needed to be transferred onto canvas to give the form the social recognition it deserved.[65] In December of that very same year, Martinez organized an exhibition of graffiti works in a classroom at City College, whose walls had been covered with wrapping paper. The event – called *City College Writer's Exhibition* – was the first ever show of graffiti paintings in an indoor venue, and was covered by the *New York Times*.[66] Then in early 1973 Martinez had the idea to collaborate with the Joffrey Ballet, one of the major dance companies worldwide. In April UGA writers joined the performance titled *Deuce Coupe* (they painted a rolling backdrop on stage as dancers were performing). In the book *Wall Writers*, edited by Roger Gastman, writer JEC is reported as saying about that event: 'it was just an amazing thing'.[67] Also, in September 1973 Martinez organized another exhibition at the Razor Gallery in SoHo where canvases by Mico, Bama, Flint 707, and others were priced at $200

xli. *Bacchus at the Seaside*, sold in 2018 for £669,000 (painting);
xlii. *Mona Lisa*, sold in 2018 for £731,250 (spray-painting); it had been previously sold in 2008 for just £168,500;
xliii. *Monkey Detonator*, sold in 2018 for $587,544 (stencil);
xliv. *Laugh Now*, sold in 2019 for $764,000 (spray-paint on wooden palette);
xlv. *Girl with Balloon* – Colour AP (Gold), sold in 2019 for £395,250 (print);
xlvi. Untitled (*Fuck the Police*), sold in 2019 for $561,238 (acrylic and spray enamel on board);
xlvii. *Girl with Balloon* – Colour AP (Purple), sold in 2020 for £791,250 (print).

63 See, for example, the sale by Christie's of Banksy's stenciled canvas *Keep It Real* (acrylic and spray enamel) for £34,850, to which the resale royalty rate applied, as mentioned by Christie's website at www.christies.com/en/lot/lot-5128455.

64 *Jason Williams et al. v. Roberto Cavalli*, S.p.A. et al., Docket No. 2:14-cv-06659 (C.D. Cal. Aug 25, 2014) (this case was started by Reyes, Steel, and Revok).

65 Kramer, above fn. 35, 29.

66 See the website of Beyond the Streets at https://beyondthestreets.com/pages/uga.

67 Gastman, above fn. 32, 123.

to $3,000 and several were sold.[68] This was the first time graffiti works were exhibited in a gallery setting. Again, the book *Wall Writers* reports an interview with Coco 144, who commented on that show at the Razor Gallery: 'this is one of the things I never imagined, that this was gonna happen, and you know how good it made me feel about myself and how good it made everybody else that participated in it feel. You're trying to get some recognition and then all of a sudden you're on this stage and you got these people just standing up. It's something I can't even explain in words. Just living it was grand'.

UGA has not been the only collective which in that period got involved in typical fine art settings. In December 1974 Jack Pelsinger, a theatre director, founded another collective of writers, NOGA (Nation of Graffiti Artists). NOGA was more open than UGA, and writers of all ages and races were allowed to join it. In March 1976 it held its first large exhibition at the Bank Street College of Education in New York, with paintings by twenty-five NOGA writers – and a table was also arranged where writers drew customers' names in graffiti style on small canvases for $5 each, and some bigger canvases were sold for $300.[69] In September 1976 NOGA writers were also invited to paint a mural at Prospect Hospital in the Bronx.[70] In general, NOGA's mission was to re-channel graffiti creativity towards legal spots, either in galleries or in connection with privately commissioned wall murals. Pelsinger indeed saw commercial potential in graffiti.[71] Craig Castleman also confirms that NOGA (as well as UGA) had this important function in the early years of graffiti in New York. He notes that these collectives' mission was 'to win their members recognition as serious artists by encouraging writers to produce graffiti-style works on canvas and various other media with a view toward their sale to art collectors'.[72] During my research residency in New York I had an encounter with Christopher Chambers, an artist who had joined NOGA and who later would found the AVANT street art guerrilla collective with David Fried, Peter Epstein, and Marc Thorne.[73] Chambers confirmed that he was encouraged to also paint on canvases, but he did not obtain economic recompense at the beginning. He told me: 'I was involved in NOGA, which I'd define as a neighbourhood centre to get kids out of crime. It was located in Amsterdam Ave and 88th Street. I used to go there, draw my stuff on walls, canvas, whatever. There were people of all races. We did not get any money, just recognition within the community. Money came in later'.

68 Gastman, above fn. 32, 214.

69 Craig Castleman, Getting up: Subway Graffiti in New York (MIT Press 1984) 131.

70 Ibidem, 131.

71 Kramer, above fn. 35, 29.

72 Castleman, above fn. 69, 117.

73 AVANT was active in New York in the early 1980s, having created thousands of acrylic on paper paintings and plastered them on walls, bus stops, and other urban surfaces. See www.avant-streetart.com/avant_street_art_history_nyc_80s.htm.

The following years saw an intensification of experiences in galleries. As mentioned in Chapter 3, in 1978 Austrian American artist Stefan Eins founded the Fashion Moda gallery in South Bronx, where writers could paint on the walls and facade.[74] The first big show at Fashion Moda, *Graffiti Art Success for America*, took place in October 1980 – it was curated by writer John Crash Matos, featuring pieces by Lady Pink, Futura 2000, John Fekner, Zephyr, Noc 167, and Mitch, amongst others. The show gave writers new opportunities, permitting them to connect with collectors, curators, and critics. Fashion Moda was not a purely commercial gallery, though. Using writer Daze's words, as reported by Henry Chalfant and Sacha Jenkins in their book *Training Days: The Subway Artists Then and Now*: 'it was more an artist-run alternative space that was project-based. There wasn't a commercial pressure to sell, sell, sell'.[75] In the meantime, in 1979 Lee Quiñones and Fab 5 Freddy had exhibited at Claudio Bruni's Galleria La Medusa in Rome, the first international exhibition by US graffiti artists;[76] and in spring 1980 art collector Samuel Esses had invited Zephyr, Futura 2000, and other writers to his studio in Manhattan to paint canvases.[77] In June 1980, the *Times Square Show*, organised by Fashion Moda Gallery with Colab (also known as Collaborative Projects, Inc), constituted another seminal introduction of graffiti into the traditional fine art world, one of the first major encounters between fine artists and writers.[78] The exhibition also included fashion, music, videos, and performances. Writers' penetration into the world of New York galleries continued through the mid-1980s. The Fun Gallery, founded by Patti Astor and Bill Sterling in 1982 and located in Manhattan's East Village, organised several graffiti exhibitions featuring writers such as Fab 5 Freddy, Dondi, Lee Quiñones, and Zephyr until its closure in 1985 (Keith Haring and Jean-Michel Basquiat also exhibited there sometimes).[79] The *Post-Graffiti* exhibition at the Sidney Janis Gallery in Manhattan in late October–November 1984 is also worth noting, with artworks by Daze, Crash, Futura 2000, Toxic, A-One, and others.[80]

Thus, in these venues New York writers, many of them coming from poor and ethnic backgrounds, had the chance to enter into contact with, and be influenced by, traditionally trained artists. As Cey Adams noted in our conversation

74 Francesco Spampinato, 'Fashion Moda: A South Bronx Story' (2013) 55 *Waxpoetics*.

75 Henry Chalfant and Sacha Jenkins, Training Days: The Subway Artists Then and Now (Thames & Hudson 2014), 52–54; see also Francesca Alinovi, Arte di Frontiera (Mattote 1984) 12.

76 Castleman, above fn. 69, 117.

77 Snyder 'Graffiti and the Subculture Career', in Jeffrey Ian Ross (ed.), Routledge Handbook of Graffiti and Street Art (Routledge 2016) 205.

78 Anna Waclawek, Graffiti and Street Art (Thames & Hudson World of Art 2011) 63.

79 During my conversation with New York artist Christopher Chambers, he informed me that another venue which exhibited graffiti works at that time in Manhattan was the 51x gallery, opened by painter Rich Collicchio.

80 This was also the first time the expression 'post-graffiti' was used. See Luke Dickens, 'Pictures on Walls? Producing, Pricing and Collecting the Street Art Screen Print' (2010) 14 (1–2) *City*, 53 (noting that 'the term "post-graffiti" was adopted by a number of commentators seeking to describe a more general attempt by urban authorities and cultural magnates to displace graffiti writing from the street to the gallery').

in his studio in New Jersey, 'the idea was to turn graffiti writing into something positive you could benefit from, something that you can have control over. If you exhibit in a gallery, you may have chances to sell canvases, which allows you to pay the bills to get recognition from the establishment. A way to make a mark in society'. Similarly, the book *Wall Writers* reports an interview with Snake I: 'When we started to really see what was ahead on the future of this, then we got more attached to only doing it on canvas'.[81] Certain scenes within the 1983 cult movie *Style Wars* also epitomise the transition of graffiti into galleries and other art establishment venues. The film features a gallery exhibition of graffiti-inspired canvases, with writer Daze saying in an interview during the show: 'the real subway graffiti that started on the trains is slowly dying out and this [canvases and galleries] is taking its place'. Another scene set at the same party shows young New York writers talking to each other about the new world of galleries and the benefits of entering the professional art world: 'forget about the trains [...] I want to make money, [...] it feels good, [...] when was it last time you made $2,000 in a month?' These are indeed the times when the most famous New York writers became high in demand. As has been noted by Roger Gastman and Caleb Neelon in their book *The History of American Graffiti*, writers 'walked past the velvet rope at fancy clubs and parties. They were making money – pretty good money – from their painting. They hung out with rock-stars'.[82] Art critic and researcher Francesca Alinovi in her 1984 book *Arte di Frontiera* narrated a similar scenario: 'tough kids with a kind, mocking air who smear the city with their symbols and graffiti but who go to galleries in order to be seen [...] taking part as the latest fashion at the most elegant parties'.[83]

This trend was not confined to New York. Early English writers of the 1980s also attended galleries and other conventional art venues, for example, the Arnolfini art centre in Bristol. In 1985 Arnolfini organized a show where writers 3D (also a member of the successful DJs collective and sound system Wild Bunch and then the Massive Attack band), Inkie, Nick Walker, and others spray-painted live on the gallery's walls while the Wild Bunch played music.[84]

We have seen that to some extent the graffiti and street art subcultures have had opportunities to 'merge' with the fine art world – and this happened from the very beginning, with some early New York pioneers helping make the path for subsequent generations. In other words, a portion of street and graffiti art has always moved between the street and the galleries.[85] In the current era this merger is even more evident. Many of my interviewees confirmed that they do create art in both the public environment and the studio, with some of them even considering

[81] Gastman, above fn. 32, 115.
[82] Roger Gastman and Caleb Neelon, History of American Graffiti (Collins Design 2001) 132.
[83] Alinovi, above fn. 75, 13.
[84] Felix Braun, Children of the Can: Bristol Graffiti and Street Art (Tangent Book 2012) 40–43.
[85] Lewisohn, above fn. 10, 24.

themselves to be fine artists. As mentioned in Chapter 1, during our conversation Lady Pink candidly said, 'I'm a fine artist'.[86] Likewise, Roadsworth noted, 'I'd call myself an artist because I do all kinds of things, street art, public art – and I paint canvases. I don't call myself a street artist, although many people call me like that because I'm known as a street artist. I don't care what people call me to be honest. I just call myself an artist to keep it simple'. Several others I talked to have a fine art background, having studied in art schools. Don Rimx, a Puerto Rican muralist based in Miami, said that he studied art in college back in Puerto Rico and that he 'was trained as a classical painter'. When I asked him whether such background had an influence on his style, he replied, '[D]efinitely. And learning about the history of art was also important to me'.

But can art which is done in studio still be considered graffiti or street art? While one may note that studio artworks are just 'street art–flavoured' pieces (with spray-paint drips sometimes used to instill in the piece a 'street' element)[87] which cannot be compared to 'true' art in the street, others have made the point that street artists and writers do not stop being what they are simply because they also do works in galleries. New York street art duo Faile, for example, has been reported as saying, 'We always created work for the street and for the studio – the two have a symbiotic relationship that informs each other. We never set out to be "street artists" per se; we just wanted to be artists'.[88] As Alison Young also put it: '[l]ocation need not be confined. Consider a Banksy canvas for sale at Sotheby's auction house or a work by Pure Evil displayed on the walls of a hip London coffee. They may not be as obviously connected to the street as a Banksy stencil or a Pure Evil tag on the walls of London, but neither their use of canvas or screen printing nor their display in an auction house or coffee shop disqualifies them from the genre of street art'.[89] Thus, an argument could be made that street and graffiti artists who exhibit in galleries do not lose their status, in the very same way that fine artists that happen to place their works in public spaces do not automatically become street artists.[90] Cedar Lewhisohn makes an interesting comparison with land artists such as Richard Long, who does not stop being a land artist when he shows his pieces in galleries.[91]

[86] This point was also stressed by Stefan Eins, the founder of Fashion Moda Gallery. When I asked him during our encounter in Manhattan if his South Bronx–based gallery accepted all categories of artists, including writers, artists who used to place works on the street, and fine artists, he replied, 'I'd call graffiti artists "fine artists"'.

[87] Alison Young, Street Art, Public City: Law, Crime and the Urban Imagination (Routledge 2013) 130–131 (also noting that some indoor venues make rooftops and courtyards available for artists to paint as if they were working in the street); Claudia Walde, *Sticker City: Paper Graffiti Art* (Thames & Hudson 2007), unnumbered page (noting that indoor venues which organise street art and graffiti exhibitions place canvases and other works 'in a deliberately chaotic way, to avoid the geometrical order of the traditional gallery space. Often street signs are integrated into the scene, or the walls themselves are painted with apt motifs').

[88] Ed Bartlett, Lonely Planet Street Art (Lonely Planet Publishing 2017) 98.

[89] Young, above fn. 87, 43.

[90] Peter Bengtsen, Street Art World (Almendros De Granada 2014) 17.

[91] Lewisohn, above fn. 10, 24.

But not all writers and street artists approve of these forms of art moving into institutional venues, which confirms once again that these creative subcultures are in no way homogeneous. Some of them do not like it, and prefer to focus on placing art in the street. For example, Damien Mitchell pointed out in our conversation: 'I've done two exhibitions in galleries. Not the same feeling, not the same gratification. I don't feel the work has the same effect'. There are many street artists and writers who have never exhibited in galleries, having always preferred to remain in the street.[92] In the early days in New York some writers did not accept this shift, either. Phase 2 and Kase 2 are amongst those who believed that the transition from subway trains to canvases was awkward and unacceptable as the art would have become an object produced only for money.[93] There was also a belief amongst many early writers that those who did make such transition were denying their own history to jump into something different and easier, thus denying 'their birthright'.[94] As noted by writer Sal 161, and reported in Andrea Nelli's university dissertation *Graffiti a New York*: 'It's true: when you do it on canvas you don't run the risk of someone writing over it; but I can't handle seeing my identity hung up on a wall! It's useless: it's better on the train's metal place'.[95]

Also, when Futura 2000 and Zephyr established a relationship with art collector Samuel Esses, several writers did not approve. Writer Bil Rock is reported noting, 'To be honest, I was pissed off with Futura, and the whole injection into the gallery scene was looking sour to me. We were about to get totally hoodwinked by art pimps'.[96] This point was also made by Cey Adams during our interview in New Jersey. Not only did he note that some writers of the 1980s did not approve painting on canvases, he also added that those who accepted doing that and kept on writing on trains were derided by 'pure' writers and had their train pieces destroyed as a sign of disapproval. Embracing the institutional art world was thus perceived by several writers as a betrayal of the soul of the graffiti subculture.

Allan Schwartzman, author of the 1985 photographic book *Street Art*, also delves into what he calls a 'thorny issue'. While he recognises that these 'reformed vandals' have entered the 'contemporary art world's upper strata' and that this should not be considered to be 'sell out' behaviour, he also notes that such evolution had the effect of downgrading their works. He indeed points out that 'in the art world's eventual embrace of graffiti the majority of former writers are now making commercially motivated paintings that are little more than "souvenirs" of what they once did for free on the subways'.[97]

92 One of them is Blu. See also a video by the London graffiti crew Burning Candy at www.youtube.com/watch?v=K--S_GoctnM (uploaded on YouTube in 2009). The video shows one of the crew members, LL Brainwashed, saying that graffiti and street art are often anti-establishment and the fact that several artists show in galleries, and accept a compromise with the traditional art world, is contradictory.

93 See also Miller, above fn. 38, 158.

94 Miller, above fn. 38, 170.

95 Andrea Nelli, Graffiti a New York (Wholetrain Press 2012) 26

96 Chalfant and Jenkins, above fn. 75, 32.

97 Allan Schwartzman, Street Art (Bantam Doubleday 1985) 102–103.

## MERCHANDISING

Several street artists and writers do exploit their art via merchandising. It is a way to raise money, for example, to fund their projects or to just put food on the table and support families. Some of them have started exploiting their pieces as NFTs so as to rely on an additional revenue stream. Chilean London-based artist Osch actually showed me NFT contracts he signed. One of them provided that one of his murals would be tokenized by a gallery into an NFT, with a maximum of 100,000 units – and the units would then be sold for US$1 per unit via the gallery sales channels. That contract also stated that NFT owners would have the option of participating in limited exploitation rights using the NFT artwork on various merchandising items such as prints, mugs, pillows, and other items to be decided by the artist and the gallery.

The sale of merchandise emerged during various interviews I conducted, for example, the one with Ben Eine. He said, 'I've a wife and kids, this is my job. As much as it would be nice to go around the world and painting for nothing, at the end of the day this is the way I earn my money. And one of the ways I do this is lending myself, merchandising my work, making T-shirts or cups just to make something out of my work'. On the same page are the artists Andre Trenier ('I've like a clothing company that does clothing T-shirts and different things and I've registered trademarks. I basically licence my artwork to my clothing company'), Damien Mitchell ('I've done merchandising and T-shirts for free, to promote exhibitions'), Royal King Bee ('Yes [i do] bags, posters, prints and toys'), and Anjl ('I have done a couple of things but nothing major, hats and a couple of things like that, but I haven't done a whole great deal of it, but I think that merchandising could be a good idea').[98] Also a few writers I spoke with have no problem producing goods bearing their graffiti. Mastro is one of them. He told me: 'in 2003 I started putting graffiti on hats and selling my customised hand-style hats to anyone that wanted to purchase them'.

Another New York artist, Greg Lamarche, expanded on his merchandising experience, showing that he has no problem working for a luxury company:

> I've done one project where we did kind of a 'capsule production'. It's like a bunch of different objects – T-shirts, pillows, and so on. This project is still going on and I'm comfortable with it in the sense that I've never tried to brand myself, so that's why I've never come out with my brand and I kind of just work for other people and then I do my own thing. So, this project is a very interesting test. Obviously, it was on a very large scale, it was for Bloomingdale's [a luxury department store chain]. Sure, there were some bumps across the way because

[98] Even Taki 183, one of the first New York teenagers who started writing his name and street number in the late 1960s all over New York, seemed to be interested, at least in principle, in merchandising. As reported in Roger Gastman's book *Wall Writers* (above fn. 32, 66), when asked, 'Could you see writing as a career?', Taki replied, 'Actually I was hoping one of the magic marker companies would ask me to endorse their marker, like Joe Namath [a former American football player]'.

> I didn't oversee the production of stuff, but for the most part everything was of quality and we were able to have a respectable amount of say in what happened and what went there.

Giacomo 'Run' Bufarini's interview is also interesting, as it describes the career path a street artist may experience. He said to me while painting a mural in the South London area of Peckham:

> I designed a little cup, but it was just a limited edition. Then I did T-shirts, it was just to promote a charity. Also six months ago a New York agent contacted me, he proposed me a thing, kind of promoting flights in Melbourne, London, and Mexico City. They asked me the picture of my mural so that they could use it to promote their business, 4k [4,000 euros] to keep the picture, 4k to use it. They did it and sent me an additional 4k: total madness, but positive. Everything can happen. I mean, if I think that me and Blu used to paint in squatters and derelict places, that's quite a different thing.

Some artists who have done merchandising have also manifested their interest in contractualising the relationship. Bill Blast, for example, told me: 'I once did something for a company in Chicago. I did a bunch of drawings and they were going to use portions of it. The pieces were painted on paper. So, they were doing merchandise with the images of the drawing and there was a royalty fee for the x amount of pieces they sold. Everything was contractual'.

Knowledge and awareness of contractual aspects of copyright, and the degree of control it gives, is also shown (again) by Greg Lamarche, who noted during our conversation, 'I remain the owner of copyright – basically the whole idea of the campaign is to kind of advertise the collaboration and that we "are working with you". In a project I hand-drew a lot of stuff and designed a lot of letter-based stuff. They paid for exclusivity and also limited usage. I was happy with the project the way they did it'. Similarly, Rubin said to me: 'I've collaborated with fashion brands (Nike, Converse, Heineken), and my murals ended up on some clothes. I had some requests from glasses and [watch] manufacturers. But I want to keep control on the use of my stuff, to be specified in the contract. I don't want it to be used in any other way years later'. Morley is on the same page. He commented, 'I've made agreements to license out my work, but I retain ownership of the copyright'.

I also heard artists confirming their acceptance of merchandising, but with some strings attached, for example, related to the quality of the products and the message conveyed. Clet Abraham noted in our interview: 'I'm thinking about merchandising. I'm collaborating with Smart [a German carmaker]. As long as it's quality and serious work, I don't see any problem. Also, if there's any chance to send messages through the merchandising[, it] is ok'. Likewise, Alice Pasquini said during our conversation that 'as far as T-shirts are concerned, I've never made them. I'd do that [merchandising] if there is a plan or strategy which interests me'. Similar concepts were expressed by Greg La Marche: ('[t]hey have to proof everything through me'),

Morley ('I've very clear boundaries'), and Rubin ('I do research and ask myself if it feels right for me. I try to be pretty selective in what I do').

Not all artists I spoke with showed interest in merchandising, though. Roadsworth is one of them. He said, '[W]ell, I did T-shirts once, but I've never licensed my images to anyone for that purpose. I've had people approaching me about that stuff, but I didn't want to do as it wasn't interesting for me'. Likewise, Depsone noted in our interview: 'I did it [merchandising] just one time, but it was with a very small company that had just started out. I sold them designs and with the designs they made T-shirts. It was a paper design – they wanted it done on paper'. Several others showed a clear dislike of this phenomenon. Jef Aerosol, for example, pointed out that 'since I started 35 years ago, so many brands have got in touch with me for that purpose. I always refuse. I don't do merchandising. I accepted a couple of times quite long ago and regretted [it]. You won't find sneakers, T-shirts, mugs, or baseball caps with my images in stores. I've plans with a guitar maker, but that's really a collaboration on something that for me can't be considered merchandising. We'll work together with two artists to make four hand pieces'. Similar answers were given by Stephen Palladino ('I said no to merchandising, I may eventually accept it, but to be honest I don't like it. It's not cool. It would kill my art') Daleast ('[N]o, I want to keep it as art. No branding please. Maybe in the future'), Fake ('[N]o, I wouldn't do it, because it's not good for my credibility as an artist. I've turned down offers in the past'), and New York writer Hoacs ('it is not for me').

## SIMILARITIES WITH ADVERTISING

There are also stark similarities between these artistic subcultures and the advertising world. Indeed, writers often behave in the same way as advertisers do – the tag, the throw-up, and piece being like brands affixed on the city.[99] Their mentality is similar to that of an advertising executive who wishes to place the company logo where it will gain maximum attention.[100] Both advertisers and writers must engage viewers (members of the general public in one case and other writers in the other) while delivering a specific message, often against the will of the passer-by.[101] As has been interestingly noted, 'All advertising asks is for the viewer to remember a name; graffiti does the same thing but emphasizes the embellishment and removes the product'.[102]

The comparison between these artistic movements and advertising is particularly evident when it comes to tagging. There is a certain analogy between writers'

[99] Iljadica, above fn. 16, 245 (noting that '[i]n the subculture the name functions akin to a brand').
[100] Lewisohn, above fn. 10, 45.
[101] Jamison Davies, Art Crimes? Theoretical Perspectives in Copyright Protection for Illegally-Created Graffiti Art (2013) *Me. L. Rev.* 27, 39. See also Blanché, above fn. 39, 13 (pointing out that '[f]or graffiti and also advertising it is often important that it is on a clearly visible spot').
[102] Lee Bofkin, Concrete Canvas: How Street Art is Changing the Way Our Cities Look (Octopus 2014) 12.

tagging and brands' penetration in our society. This point is stressed in the graffiti literature, and also emerged from my interviews. A tag painted on a wall or train car is basically not so different from a brand's logo placed on a high street's billboard. Both constitute a tool to communicate aesthetically and reach out artistically to audiences and help increase the tag's and brand's awareness, with both writers and advertisers fighting to catch the attention of other writers and people. It has been argued that 'graffiti appropriates and subverts this empty promise of individuality, and at the same time mirrors advertising's mode of simultaneous distribution, scattering across the city its tags which mark the stubborn ghost of individuality and intention in the mass culture, the ironic re-statement of the artist as "brand name"'.[103] Tags are indeed ubiquitous and repeat themselves continuously on urban surfaces, as members of the general public can also realise, even without 'understanding' them. In other words, taggers are like advertisers as they purchase space with their boldness and style rather than with money.[104] But while they appropriate public spaces like advertisers, they do not sell anything – they just leave their own name.[105]

The same goes for many street artists, who create images or street poetry instead of focusing on a name.[106] They often place their artworks in highly visible spots, making them instantly recognisable. Take the artworks created and repeatedly placed in urban environments by artists such as Toaster and Invader.[107] Another example is the infamous *Andre the Giant Has a Posse* sticker campaign of the 1990s that was masterminded and conducted by Shepard Fairey – a sort of conversion of a street art campaign into advertising.[108] Also, certain street artworks are stylistically created in a way which makes them look like advertising messages, which is the case of former US writer and now muralist and studio artist Stephen Powers (aka ESPO), who often uses a figurative style similar to the one used in advertising.[109] After all,

[103] Susan Stewart, 'Ceci Tuera Cela: Graffiti as Crime and Art', in John Fekete (ed.), *Life after Postmodernism: Essays on Value and Culture* (Macmillan 1987) 174–175.

[104] Richard Lachman, Graffiti as Career and Ideology (1988) 2/94 *The American Journal of Sociology*, 237 (also noting that that ads are rarely targeted by writers, as the latter admire advertising artistry and see a consonance between the ads' appropriation of space and their own artistic practices).

[105] Martha Cooper, Tag Town: The Origins of Writing (Dokument 2009) 7. See also Carlo McCormick, *Trespass: A History of Uncommissioned Urban Art Hardcover* (Taschen 2015), 130 (pointing out that '[a]t its most basic level, the tag mimics the ideographic compression, repetition and saturation that we would expect of corporate logos and marketing campaigns. As a matter of practicality an artist's tag must be fluent, fluid, flexible enough to be put up anywhere, quickly, under any conditions, and maintain that most primary of marketing directives: instant recognition').

[106] Lewisohn, above fn. 10, 111. See also Blanché, above fn. 39, 10 (noting that '[t]he reference and interaction with advertising is now often a hallmark of Street Art. Many Street Artists are coming from advertising or were inspired by advertising works').

[107] Ibidem.

[108] Damien Droney, 'The Business of "Getting Up": Street Art and Marketing in Los Angeles' (2010) 2(23) *Visual Anthropology*, 105; Blanché, above fn. 39, 56.

[109] See also Rafael Schacter, *The World Atlas of Street Art and Graffiti* (Aurum 2013) 19.

much street art is also a form of self-promotion,[110] Banksy being a good example. The famous Bristol artist appropriates strategies from the world of public relations, marketing, and advertising. He paradoxically uses such an approach to question and ridicule those very same strategies.[111]

The similarities between art placed in urban environments and the world of advertising have been evident from the very beginning of graffiti in the 1970s. As has been noted, what writers started doing in the New York subway system was transforming 'a traditionally clandestine activity into something akin to commercial advertising'.[112] Being continuously exposed to and bombarded with commercial signs within the city and in general in everyday life had just this effect. The writers of that era confirm this point. In Roger Gastman's book *Wall Writers*, Jag is reported as saying that 'we started advertising who we were. Like Coca-Cola, you say who you are – make a lot of advertisements and people will try you. That was the whole thing'.[113] SJK 171 echoes him: 'I would see Coca-Cola all over the place and I would say I want my name to be all over like Coca-Cola'.[114] Futura 2000 has a similar opinion, as per Nancy Macdonald in her book, where he is reported as saying that the tag is 'kind of like a logo in advertising, and it was the logos of those names I was initially inspired by'.[115]

The same similarities have been highlighted by several of my interviewees, including Skeme ('the tag is the writer's brand'), Cey Adams ('the tag was like a brand'), and Bates ('these days you need to protect your name which in a way is a brand'). I received similar comments from writers outside the US as well. While visiting the graffiti-friendly area of Puente Aranda in Bogotá together with Drop, the Colombian writer told me: 'I think my work sometimes looks like logos, as it has the same style all the time'. And Transı, a London writer I interviewed at a London Bridge café, said to me: 'my tag is original, it's my signature, a vehicle to get my name around. My street signature and brand'.[116]

Other interesting accounts of this comparison were given by US artist Gaia and London artist Pure Evil. The former noted in our interview: 'there is nothing anti-establishment in American street art, all of us are guerrilla branding, we're like advertisers, we promote our artistic creations. We repeatedly reproduce images that can be tied to something which can be purchased, basically art objects like canvases and sculptures'. And during our conversation, Pure Evil expanded on the hypocrisy which pervades certain sectors of these communities. He said:

[110] Ibidem, 48
[111] Ibidem, 210.
[112] Stewart, above fn. 54, 19.
[113] Gastman, above fn. 32, 72.
[114] Ibidem, 126.
[115] Nancy Macdonald, *The Graffiti Subculture: Youth, Masculinity and Identity in London and New York* (Palgrave MacMillan 2001), 69.
[116] The very same Al Diaz, who as mentioned created and popularised the SAMO© tag with Jean-Michel Basquiat in the late 1970s and early 1980s in New York, focused on this comparison during our conversation.

> [T]he truth is, we're all brands. Pure Evil is a brand, Stik is a brand. [...] So, although we're supposed to be urban street poets, we're also slightly capitalist, you know, sort of mini-corporations. We've to protect our brand from being you know, being taken over. I used to say 'I'm a socialist', but now I know, I'm a capitalist. [...] Also, now I see people who have probably just arrived in London, who want to go out there and get their name out and they're completely branding themselves. They create an image and they put it out with their website address and their details, you know.

Moreover, it is not uncommon for street artists and writers, especially those with consolidated experience, to take jobs such as doing commissioned hand-paint advertisements onto walls. These are artworks created in the context of corporate sponsorship,[117] and their actual execution is often 'made via the subcontracting of a separate company, specialising in advertising and promotion'.[118] There are dedicated companies which offer these services. One of these is Colossal Media, described as 'the global leader of hand painted outdoor advertising', which was once also used by Banksy in New York in 2008.[119] Companies in certain industries such as fashion, music, and food sometimes rely on this technique,[120] and they do so exactly to take advantage of the street cred and to try to catch the attention of passers-by. Their aim is 'to generate what is called a "soft sell" effect in which people "forgive" the ad (and hopefully buy the product) since they enjoy the look of the image on the wall'.[121]

Thus, we have seen that artists within these communities sometimes create art on demand, to promote commercial products and services, which brings us to another relevant point, that is, the effect of street and graffiti art on advertising itself. Graffiti has indeed had a significant impact on contemporary graphics, in particular the design and lettering style which is nowadays used in various commercial settings. As just mentioned, the proliferation of hand-painted advertising messages and imagery on urban surfaces has its roots in street and graffiti art.[122] Moreover, corporations and even small businesses increasingly use mural- and graffiti-inspired fonts and lettering styles, which has been labelled the 'guerrilla marketing' phenomenon[123]

[117] Young, above fn. 87, 99.

[118] Heitor Alvelos, 'The Desert of Imagination in the City of Signs: Cultural Implications of Sponsored Transgression and Branded Graffiti', in Jeff Ferrell, Keith Hayward, Wayne Morrison, and Mike Presdee (eds.), *Cultural Criminology Unleashed* (Routledge and Cavendish 2004) 183.

[119] Will Ellsworth-Jones, *Banksy: The Man behind the Wall*, 2nd rev. ed. (Frances Lincoln 2021) 171 (also noting that '[f]ive years later Banksy said he 'made a mistake in doing this. I totally overlooked how important it was to do it myself. Graffiti is an art form where the gesture is at least as important as the result, if not more so').

[120] Even chocolate bars and air-fresheners have been advertised using these techniques: see Lewisohn, above fn. 10, 112.

[121] Young, above fn. 87, 100.

[122] See Martha Cooper's comment in Claw Money, *Bombshell: The Life and Crimes of Claw Money* (Powerhouse Book 2010).

[123] The expression 'guerrilla marketing' is also used by Lewisohn, above fn. 10, 112; Kramer, above fn. 35, 35.

and which 'demonstrates how corporate interests have appropriated the fundamental techniques of street art'.[124] This appropriation of subcultural and countercultural references by mainstream forces[125] aims to instill an aura of 'coolness' and 'street credibility'[126] in the product or service which is offered for sale (in Chapter 3 I referred to such exploitation when covering legal cases started by street artists and writers against corporations which had profited from their art).[127] Heitor Alvelos has been one of the first scholars to highlight this phenomenon. He curiously gives the example of the flame logo used by the DJs collective and music band Massive Attack, which appears on the cover of their first two CDs and was also stencilled on walls in England,[128] arguably for promotional purposes.[129] Other music bands and artists have relied on this technique, including Daft Punk, Tricky, Wu-Tang Clan, Mariah Carey, Eminem, Gorillaz, and Justin Bieber. The music and fashion industries have also assimilated wheatpaste art techniques to promote concerts and products.[130]

Not only are the street and graffiti art styles and techniques imitated, so are the locations where the pieces are placed. Advertisers see and analyse where artworks are located in urban spaces and then appropriate these spots and place targeted ads in such locations.[131] Rooftops, trams, and train cars are sometimes filled with ads, such announcements being placed and positioned in the very same way graffiti pieces are.[132] During our conversation Zephyr satisfied my curiosity by showing me a photo of a subway train on which a commercial advertisement had been painted in a pure old graffiti style. Is this the completion of a circle? One may note that writers grow up surrounded by advertising and thus tend to incorporate ad images in their pieces. These pieces are then noted and analysed by advertisers, who appropriate them by placing the graffiti-inspired commercial ad on the very same surface chosen by writers and may even recruit the latter to exactly do that job.[133]

[124] Kramer, above fn. 35, 35.

[125] Heitor Alvelos, The Desert of Imagination in the City of Signs: Cultural Implications of Sponsored Transgression and Branded Graffiti in Jeff Ferrell, Keith Hayward, Wayne Morrison and Mike Presder (eds.) Cultural Criminology Unleashed (Routledge – Cavendish 2004) 185.

[126] As noted by Greg Lamarche in our conversation, corporations which exploit graffiti try to 'capitalize on *Cool Street*'.

[127] In certain areas of the world, for example, in Mexico and other Central and South American countries, artistic (and less artistic) murals are also used as a form of advertising. Here the purpose of instilling 'street cred' into the products or services which are promoted is less prominent, if not nonexistent. See also Magda Danysz, From Style Writing to Art: A Street Anthology (Drago Publishing 2011) 303.

[128] Alvelos, above fn. 125, 183–185.

[129] It is interesting to remember that the same flame logo has also been used by Banksy in some of his artworks, including murals, which suggests that the Massive Attack may be close to the famous artist. This seems also be confirmed by the fact that the (current and former) members of the band are all from Bristol, Banksy's hometown.

[130] Johannes Stahl, *Street Art* (HF Ulmann 2009) 277.

[131] Ross, Lennon, and Kramer, above fn. 42, 6.

[132] Stahl, above fn. 130, 278.

[133] Miller, above fn. 38, 178.

## CAREER PERSPECTIVES

Street artists and writers often end up embarking upon commercial careers in sectors of society different from the urban environment they come from. Such career trajectories have been described and analysed in the literature. First and foremost, the seminal book *Graffiti Lives* by Gregory Snyder teaches us how young writers enter the subculture ('get in'), strive and compete to gain popularity and success within that community ('get up'), and then as they grow older find job opportunities in one of the many fields of the creative industry ('get out').[134] Craig Castleman's early 1980s pioneer study also mentions this trajectory. He notes that 'writers frequently express a desire to go on to careers as cartoonists or animators. They take a greater interest in techniques of illustration, photography, calligraphy, printing, and painting'.[135] More recently, Ronald Kramer has pointed out that in the past three decades an increasing number of writers have not only painted legally and thus operated within the boundaries of the law, but have entered mainstream society, taking jobs as graphic designers, tattoo artists, and the like.[136] In other words, many of today's writers live conventional lives and subscribe to 'normal' values, trying to find a place within society.[137] Many of them have families, work responsibilities, mortgages, and careers and often display respect for private property and an acceptance for society's legal codes, even those which sometimes punish graffiti.[138] Peter Bengtsen made a similar point, and extended it to street artists. He noted that many of them presently see their art as a tool to build a commercial career, rather than as a goal in itself.[139] Having said that, as mentioned at the beginning of this chapter, it is inevitable that the interest in copyright will be further strengthened as practitioners of these forms of art progress in their careers.

Examples of artists who follow this career path abound. Futura 2000, now a successful studio artist and graphic designer, is one. He noted in an interview with Ivor Miller that there is a maturing process, that the life of an artist inevitably evolves, and that both street artists and writers may eventually abandon the art form totally or try to incorporate their work into something else.[140] My own ethnographic research confirms this point. New York writer Serk during our conversation in Brooklyn commented, '[A]t that point [when I started writing] I had no financial motivations. Later in the career I saw a potential for my artistic ability to be transformed into a

[134] Gregory Snyder, *Graffiti Lives: Beyond the Tag in New York's Urban Underground* (NYU Press 2009).

[135] Castleman, above fn. 69, 70.

[136] Kramer, above fn. 35, 236.

[137] Kramer, above fn. 35, 4. This also emerged in an interview I had with Bronx muralist Andre Trenier. He commented, 'I'm a reformed tagger. Like alcoholics, they wake up every day and say that they are not going to drink. I wake up every day and say, "I am not going to write my name" on people's property'.

[138] Kramer, above fn. 35, 128.

[139] Bengtsen, above fn. 14, 69.

[140] Lewisohn, above fn. 10, 67.

commercial opportunity, in [a] field like typography, layout, visual communication, etcetera. It took at least 10 years'. Former writers Dejer, Cey Adams, and Rubin expressed similar opinions during our encounters. While Dejer noted that 'graffiti opened me the door for an artistic path',[141] Cey Adams argued that 'there's a big difference between professional writers (they return email, they answer phone calls) and graffiti amateurs. Young writers are more amateur, older ones enter the professional world. You can't be an appreciated artist and not to choose professionalism'. And Rubin opined, 'I was so young when I started painting in the streets, nine years old. I did it because I wanted to be seen. A kind of egoistic motivation. I grew up in a pretty depressing area in Gothenburg [Sweden], grey concrete around me. I wanted to leave a sign in the concrete. But now it's also a job. It's still fun, and I also do some no-profit jobs like public schools. I want to help the community and beautify the neighbourhood, inspire kids. I never planned to make a career in art, when I started doing graffiti, but it happened'.

What should also be noted is that street and graffiti artists' careers are often built on the aura of illegality which surrounds these artistic movements. In other words, the fact that artists have placed artworks in the street illegally may help them later develop a successful career.[142] This is confirmed by artists and writers themselves. Lady Pink, cited by Henry Chalfant and Sacha Jenkins in their book *Training Days: The Subway Artists Then and Now*, notes, 'Graffiti was merely an education [...] that prepared us for all kinds of situations'.[143] Moreover, in the cult documentary *Style Wars*, Futura 2000 can be heard saying that 'if it wasn't for those initial important years [years of illegal graffiti bombing], I don't think we'd get where we are today'. Some of my own interviews also reveal this trajectory. Former New York writer KR commented:

> I used to do tags, throw-ups, and blockbusters (massive throw-ups, usually in blocky letters), mostly without permission. I never thought about copyright. I was young. I had no sense of commercial application. I wasn't writing graffiti for possible commercial ventures and many of my fellow writers were not thinking about it either. Things have changed a lot now. I've met young writers who say they plan on working in the street illegally to make a name for themselves and eventually do commercial work in the future. A new generation sees graffiti as a potential opportunity and career path.

What Roadsworth noted in our interview is also interesting: 'I wasn't known outside Montreal until I actually got arrested. This was a few years ago and there was a documentary about my story too. I got a lot of free publicity about my experience as well, so that was good. This was more than ten years ago though. [...] in the end it

[141] An opposite opinion was expressed by Oker. During our conversation he pointed out: 'I'm trying to get into the art world, but I'm afraid it could close more doors than it would open'.
[142] Bofkin, above fn. 102, 262.
[143] Chalfant and Sacha Jenkins, above fn. 75, 100–101.

ended up being a good experience that helped me grow with the publicity I got. It's strange that getting arrested actually sort of launched another phase of my career'.

Indeed, it is within such an illegal sphere that many street artists and writers find their audience, earning their profile, fame, respect, and recognition – all 'positive' attributes which can be infused in the commercial products which graffiti or street artists may end up creating or endorsing at a later stage of their career.[144] It is around that illegal 'feel' that marketing campaigns, especially in industries such as fashion, are sometimes devised, which makes products more appealing to certain demographics and psychographics.[145]

Finally, we can see how certain street artists and writers show different personalities throughout their career – one that manifests itself in the early years of their career and is very much rooted in the illegal and subversive DNA of these forms of art, and another that develops at a later stage and accepts the conventional rules of the commercial mainstream, including copyright. This is a sort of 'double personality', which in some cases may persist even after the initial years of practice. This is the case of Canadian writer DSTRBO, interviewed by art education scholar Janice Rhan: 'I can do as much commercial stuff as I want and as long as I am going out at night painting, I'm still keeping it real. […] So it already has become mainstream. But it's still very real. But it's very much out of the mainstream at the same time'.[146] DSTRBO's words show that the two different personalities can coexist within the same writer and do not contradict each other. Even some New York graffiti pioneers have lived this 'double life'. As narrated in Charlie Ahearn's book *Wild Style: The Sampler*, at night Lee Quiñones 'would steal off to bomb the trains and the next day he would appear at White Colums Gallery'.[147] A similar scenario was depicted by Zephyr during our conversation. He said:

> I wanted to be a commercial artists and graphic artist even before age 13 and 14. So, I was exposed and very enamoured to this kind of graphic, I wanted to do posters and book covers even as a child. This is what I was working towards. Graffiti was more something you did that was naughty and antisocial, and you did it on the weekends. It was like if you were playing music on the weekend with your band, but during the week you're a lawyer. Real art, graphic art, was what I was going to do. And I was going to go to art school and be a famous graphic artist, whereas graffiti was the thing I did on the weekend, and it was not smart to tell people.

[144] See also Bengtsen, above fn. 14, 126 (pointing out that 'the street artwork can therefore also be construed as a means to promote […] commercial work').

[145] Macdonald, above fn. 115, 74; Ross Lennon, and Kramer, above fn. 42, 6.

[146] Rhan, above fn. 11, 43.

[147] Charlie Ahearn, Wild Style: The Sampler (Powerhouse Book 2007) 91. On the issue of double personality see also the interviews by Rabiega and Burger, above fn. 12, 48.

# 6

# Sharing, *Biting*, and Social Norms

Another characterising element of street art and graffiti is their 'sharing' and 'appropriation' nature. Practitioners of these art forms borrow styles, concepts, and details not only from popular culture and the everyday world, including advertising,[1] but also from fellow colleagues. This happens frequently.[2] Also, street artists and writers often accept the idea of their creations being used by peers as a source of inspiration, accepting that their works and style might be borrowed by others within the community to create their own pieces. In other words, being able to imitate and learn from each other is crucial to enhancing the creative process.[3] What many also accept, and even appreciate and encourage, is the sharing of pictures and videos incorporating their art on social media (especially if their authorship is acknowledged). Spreading images of their pieces not only increases visibility and recognition inside and outside their circles, but also helps document these artistic movements and develop them further.

This chapter will make the point that this feature does not make street art and graffiti incompatible with copyight regimes. Indeed, while such a characteristic is recurrent, this does not necessarily entail that blatant copying, particularly where there is no acknowledgement of the earlier source by the imitating artist, is also accepted. Quite the contrary. Many writers and street artists express dissappointment at this phenomenon, known as *biting*. And they often react relying not on copyright but on well-tested and functioning social norms (this also happens after other unpleasant events occur, namely when another writer or artist intentionally paints over or somewhat damages the piece). Social norms are certainly important, but copyright also has an increasingly relevant (and complementary) role in regulating specific aspects of these artistic communities, especially when the imitator purports to take economic advantage of the street artwork or anyway uses it for aims which the *bitten* artist finds unacceptable.

1 During our conversation, Australian artist Crisp noted, 'I myself use Star Wars and other bits from popular culture, advertisement, and symbols of corporation, to convey messages'.

2 As noted by London writer Noir in our interview: 'this [appropriaton] is part of the scene and happens continuously'.

3 Marta Iljadica, *Copyright Beyond Law: Regulating Creativity in the Graffiti Subculture* (Bloomsbury 2016) 206.

## SHARING AND APPROPRIATION ETHOS

Writers frequently borrow. They do it by taking and recontextualising imagery rooted in popular culture and the advertisement world (as we have seen in Chapter 1, writers often incorporate figurative elements into their lettering-based murals). They are often inspired by cartoon characters, album cover art, movies, posters, TV commercials, billboards, and brands which surround their lives and cities.[4] As has been noted, '[W]riters do not create from nothing. Like other artists, they are influenced by the historical conditions in which they live and by their life experiences'.[5]

Graffiti practitioners also learn the art of graffiti lettering from each other, for example, by sharing and examining their sketchbooks (called 'blackbooks' by writers) and photographs of pieces, throw-ups, and tags.[6] My own fieldwork has confirmed this point. New York writer David Chino pointed out during our conversation: '[w]e all draw inspiration from other artists. There is no one under the sun who hasn't incorporated an element from another artist. My inspiration came from me seeing signatures in the street. The new school's inspiration comes from many things, including the internet'. Another New York writer, Mastro, reiterated this point during our encounter: '[y]ou look at stuff such as *Subway Art* [the photographic book by Martha Cooper and Henry Chalfant] and that was our inspiration. So, you look at that and emulate what you've seen like arrows, cuts, connectors, colour and schemes. Someone did the first piece with silver and black and then everyone else does silver and black without realizing that someone before them came up with this colour combo'. *Subway Art* is also mentioned by former US writer Stephen Powers (aka ESPO) in his own book, when remembering that he spent lots of time copying pieces out of that book.[7] Many other writers around the world have done exactly the same.

The same goes for street art, with practitioners often borrowing styles and details from each other as well as from popular culture and other artistic movements. Take Bristol artist and former writer Inkie, known for connecting Art Nouveau styles with an urban touch; US artist Shepard Fairey, who draws on socialist realism, Russian constructivism, and Soviet-style propaganda to emphasise the excesses of American society; or London artist Stik who in some works has taken inspiration from portrait painters of the eighteenth century. Memorial artists also use previous images, for instance, from mass-produced holy cards and religious calendars, which they then incorporate and adapt in their mural.[8]

Banksy is another artist who often appropriates and reinterprets pre-existing images and logos, especially from the advertising and consumerist world, with a

4 Anna Waclawek, Graffiti and Street Art (Thames & Hudson World of Art 2011) 47; Joe Austin, Taking the Train: How Graffiti Art Became an Urban Crisis in New York City (Columbia University Press 2002) 228.

5 Austin, above fn. 4, 62.

6 Karla Murray, *Broken Windows: Graffiti NYC* (Gingko Press 2009) 124.

7 Stephen Powers, *The Art of Getting Over: Graffiti at the Millennium* (St. Martin's Press 1999) 38.

8 Martha Cooper, Joseph Sciorra, *R.I.P.: New York Spraycan Memorials* (Thames & Hudson 1994) 25.

view to criticising its excesses and contradictions. He also takes inspiration from colleagues. It is well known that Banksy has widely drawn upon the style and ideas of French artist Blek le Rat,[9] one of the first artists pioneering the stencil technique in urban settings.[10] For example, the repeated use of rats in his art has clearly been borrowed by the Bristolian artist. I was aware of this when my interviewee, London writer Noir, asked, 'Do you think Banksy was the first person to use stencils or draw rats on walls?' Of course, I knew that – also because Banksy himself explicitly admitted it. He once pointed out that '[e]very time I think I've painted something slightly original, I find out that Blek Le Rat has done it as well, only twenty years earlier'.[11] It should also be noted that rats are a recurring theme in street art. As mentioned in Chapter 1,[12] they were used by New York artist Christy Rupp in 1979, when the Big Apple was hit by a three-week waste workers' strike, which caused accumulation of trash in the streets. What Rupp did is to take a sanitation ad depicting a rat from a subway car, had it printed on posters, and wheatpasted them on New York walls. During our interview at a café in Manhattan, Rupp confirmed that she took the ad from a subway car, created the posters, and attached two thousand of them close to trash sites. She clarified that she wanted to raise awareness about sanitation issues and stress that the city is part of the ecosystem.

It is thus clear that these forms of art are often based on 'shared resources of imagery',[13] with artists describing 'their initial activities as inspired by the work of others and a desire to create something comparable'.[14] Magda Danysz notes that 'documenting, transmitting, sharing, learning and debating are key components to the Movement. In order to improve, one has to see what others do. For all of them, way before the Internet age, sharing images of the work has also been a priority'.[15] Danysz moreover reports the opinion of New York street art duo Faile, who propose an interesting comparison with DJ sampling: '[o]ur process of creating work involves synthesizing images to create visually visceral experiences, very similar to the way a DJ samples beats to create an audible experience'.[16]

9 In his turn, Blek le Rat took inspiration from the French artist Ernest Pignon-Ernest (mentioned in Chapter 1), who since 1966 had placed art in the street, wheatpasting his monochromatic works. See Johannes Stahl, Street Art (HF Ulmann 2009) 107.

10 Banksy's stencils have also been influenced by the graffiti scene of the early 1980s in his hometown Bristol, which included talented artists such as Nick Walker. Steve Wright, "*Home Sweet Home - Banksy's Bristol*" (2008, Tangent Books) 5. Stencil art was also practiced within the British punk movement of the late 1970s and early 1980s, mainly by guerrilla artist Gee Vaucher for the anarchist band Crass. See Felix Braun, *Children of the Can: Bristol Graffiti and Street Art* (Tangent Books 2012) 8.

11 Garry Hunter, *Street Art: From around the World* (Arcturus Publishing 2012) 16.

12 See above fn. 3.

13 Jeff Ferrell, *Crimes of Style: Urban Graffiti and the Politics of Criminality* (Northeastern University Press 1996) 159.

14 Alison Young, *Street Art, Public City: Law, Crime and the Urban Imagination* (Routledge 2013) 25.

15 Magda Danysz, From *Style Writing to Art* (Drago Publishing 2011) 12.

16 Danysz, above fn. 15, 360.

This sharing ethos has always characterised the graffiti movement from its early days in New York. As noted by old-school New York writer Iz the Wiz in an interview with Joe Austin: 'we all went through it, and we all borrowed bits and bobs from each other in sort of an unwritten, unified manner'.[17] Likewise, in the book *Training Days* by Henry Chalfant and Sacha Jenkins, former US writer and artist Jon One is reported saying, 'I used to imitate tags from older writers such as Futura [and] Zephyr'.[18] One of the most shared details in the history of graffiti is probably the 'Smoker' haloed stick figure, taken from the British TV show of the 1960s *The Saint*, that was first painted and drawn by New York writer Stay High 149 in the early 1970s. It has become one of the most characteristic symbols used in tags.[19] It has been incorporated by many writers and street artists, including New York artist Cost (in his paste-ups) and Keo. When interviewing the latter in Brooklyn, he showed me with pride and respect his arm tattoo depicting the Saint's halo, and expanded on how influential Stay High 149 has been on his own writing style and art.

Blackbooks were particularly important at that time, as they were widely shared by writers so as to give them the opportunity to get inspired by, as well as borrow and learn from, others. In the book *Art in the Streets* by Jeffrey Deitch, Roger Gastman, and Aaron Rose, Lee Quiñones is reported as saying, 'The blackbooks were a form of inspiration. It was a visual discussion in those books – you looked at other drawings and tags, and you were like, wow, I can add that, and subtract that. It was just beautiful'.[20] Magazines incorporating pictures of pieces, throw-ups, and tags also had an impact on the sharing and further development of graffiti art. The first was started by Phase 2 and editor and graffiti advocate David Schmidlapp in 1983: the *IGT* (*International Graffiti Times*). Later, ESPO's *On the Go* magazine in the 1990s was also influential. Joe Austin's research gives an interesting account of the role played by magazines in the evolution of this form of art. He narrates that in 1990 a Manhattan writer had produced *Styles for Miles* (*SFM*), a magazine which was primarily a teaching tool, as it included outline drawings by experienced writers that were meant to be copied, drawn, and borrowed by other writers.[21]

## DOES TOLERATING APPROPRIATION AND SHARING PRACTICES CONTRADICT COPYRIGHT PRINCIPLES?

As we have just seen, many artists and writers accept this sharing ethos. Blek le Rat has even been thankful to Banksy for appropriating certain elements of his art. He was

[17] Joe Austin, *Taking the Train: How Graffiti Art Became an Urban Crisis in New York City* (Columbia University Press 2002) 61.

[18] Henry Chalfant and Sacha Jenkins, *Training Days: The Subway Artists Then and Now* (Thames & Hudson 2014) 59.

[19] Martha Cooper, *Tag Town: The Origins of Writing* (Dokument 2009) 53.

[20] Jeffrey Deitch, Roger Gastman, and Aaron Rose, *Art in the Streets* (Rizzoli 2011) 45.

[21] Joe Austin, 'From the City Walls to "Clean Trains", Graffiti in New York City, 1969–1990, in Jeffrey Ian Ross (ed.), *Routledge Handbook of Graffiti and Street Art* (Routledge 2016) 257.

reported as saying, 'People say he copies me, but I don't think so. I'm the old man, he's the new kid, and if I'm an inspiration to an artist that good, I love it. People want to know me now […] I have a major book deal with the biggest publisher in the world. I have waited thirty years for this. It's only today that my street art has become big news, and that's thanks to people saying Banksy is inspired by me'.[22] I had a chance to meet Blek le Rat. This happened in the Q&A session after the premiere for the documentary movie *Saving Banksy* at Bristol's Arnolfini Gallery in April 2017, which I attended. I provocatively asked him whether he feels frustrated about an artist who has borrowed so much from him becoming a superstar in the international art market. He replied to my question by saying, 'I'm proud to have inspired Banksy'. Whether or not his answer was somewhat compelled by the fact that he was in Banksy's hometown, where the latter is understandably loved by almost everybody, will remain for me a mystery.

That writers and street artists accept appropriation of their art, be it just styles or more detailed elements, on the basis that their pieces inspire colleagues, is a theme which has emerged in my ehtnographic research as well. London writer Transı told me that 'someone in an Arabic country wrote my tag with a different technique. He contacted me thanking for inspiring him. It wasn't a trouble for me, you've to look at that in a positive way. Another writer sent me a message from Indonesia, telling me again I'd inspired him and got him into graffiti'. Similarly, City Kitty recollected during our interview that another artist once started creating works so similar to his that people began to confuse them. He added that 'if you create artworks long enough, you are bound to influence other artists and to be influenced by other artists. It's a compliment and can create some healthy competition'.

Compliments, flattery, homage, and honour have been recurrent themes in my conversations. New York artists Bill Blast and Zimer are amongst them. Bill Blast noted, 'My form of reaction [to appropriation]? It happens! People will draw up a piece and they want to do something like you've done it. It's learning. I take it as flattery. Others learn from you and achieve something that you've achieved. It's like them saying, "Wow I like your style"'. And Zimer commented that 'imitation is the highest form of flattery. I've had novice artists send me their attempts at emulating my style or the result of my inspiration on them. When I see these pictures, I become very happy because I know I made a positive difference to people's lives'. Likewise, Roadsworth pointed out during our interview: 'sometimes I see works made by people I don't know, but it looks very similar to mine: it doesn't bother me, I consider it as a form of flattery to me. Imitation is the sincerest form of flattery. I think it depends on a case-by-case basis, but people have contacted me and asked if they can copy something I did and use it and I say yes, because they asked me'. The same goes for Gabriel Corti (who said he would most likely be annoyed by someone exactly copying him but he would at the same time be flattered), Pablo Power ('imitation is the greatest form of flattery and so some people would say, "Oh yeah you are promoting me"'), Claw Money ('at the end,

[22] Will Ellsworth-Jones, *Banksy: The Man Behind the Wall* (Aurum Press 2012) 65.

I'd take biting as a compliment, as a sort of homage'), Laser 3.14 ('[I]t's a big honour if other artists incorporate my art in their work. There was this guy who tagged who started using my same style. We met once and he was very nice. He asked me once if it bothered me, and if so he'd stop. I told him that I really didn't mind and really liked what he was doing'), Copyright ('as a homage that's fine'), Pablo Delgado ('if another artist is inspired by my idea or image, I'd take it as a compliment'), and Good Guy Boris ('for me it's a big compliment when people copy my stuff, because people see the value of my work and are trying to repeat it, so it's a great compliment for me').[23]

Artists are particularly happy about appropriation of their art when the appropriator duly acknowledges the source. New York writer Lee 163, active since the early 1970s, was reported as saying, 'They did bite my style, but Lee II did compliment it. So, I'll give him credit for that'.[24] Also, during our conversation US artist Gabriele Corti confirmed that he would recognise who has inspired him and acknowledge such influence: 'personally, I like to follow certain artist who do a good job with their letterings and colour pallets. What I like to do is taking inspiration from certain parts of these people's lettering. I'd never take their whole style and use it as my own. I'd only take a swirl or the way he did a curve or something and build from that completely. Sometimes I like to use other people's colour schemes because I struggle with colour, but I'd give them a shout out on the wall definitely'. Thus, artists may also acknowledge the source of inspiration in their own artwork, by incorporating a notice that the piece is based on an earlier work. This shows respect towards the artist whose work is used as a reference or anyway inspires the downstream creation. This is what New York artist Resa Piece confirmed during our encounter. She said, '[I]t's important to credit people – you know, even if I got inspiration from another artist to do a piece, I think that it's important to credit that artist and be like: "listen, I got inspiration from that artist and that's why my art looks like this". It's out of respect to the other artist. [...] I'm sure other artists do the same. I think that in street and graffiti art there's always some level of integrity'.[25]

One may note that the fact that street artists and writers often tolerate the appropriation of their works should suggest that copyright cannot fit into these creative subcultures. This has also emerged in the interview I had with US writer Cept. He pointed out that 'in graffiti, writers borrow from other people, if you have copyright, the evolution would be slowed down'.

Yet, this line of argument is not convincing. The history of art has already known artistic movements based on borrowing and appropriation. One of them is pop art, which

[23] Not all homages are appreciated, though, especially if the imitator makes money out of it. This is what Depsone told me: 'Doing homages for profit? I think that's completely unacceptable no matter what. There is no excuse if you're making money and saying that it's a tribute'.

[24] Stampa alternativa, Style: Writing from the Underground (Nuovi Equilibri 1998) 34–35.

[25] Resa Piece added that 'there is one of my favorite collage artists named Brandon, he has this character that I really liked. So I painted that character exactly like he had painted it. But I asked for permission and reached out to him on Instagram. I got permission from the artist before using his artwork and he said, "Okay", so it was not a problem'.

has challenged the traditional concept of fine art by incorporating elements from the news and advertising world, where material is often taken from its original context and transposed into a different one. Graffiti has the same 'cut and paste culture' as pop art.[26] After all, it was pop artist Andy Wharol who famously (and provocatively) noted that 'art is what you can get away with it', not to speak of the appropriation art movement, which is exactly based on the use and arrangement of pre-existing objects or images, the readymades of Marchel Duchamp being the most notable example. In general, there is a relatively widespread belief amongst art historians and critics that borrowing and sharing have been structural features of various forms of visual art for a long time. As has been noted, 'Artists have traditionally developed their skills and practice by copying'.[27]

Appropriating artists have even won cases where they had been accused of copyright infringement. In *Blanch v. Koons* (2006), for example, a US court found that Jeff Koons' appropriation of elements of a photograph from a fashion editorial in his collage piece *Niagara* was transformative fair use.[28] Also, in another US case, *Cariou v. Prince* (2013), it was found that Richard Prince's alteration of certain of Patrick Cariou's photographs of Jamaican Rastafarians and their incorporation into his series of paintings and collages named *Canal Zone* was again fair use because it was transformative enough.[29] While appropriating artists have also lost copyright cases on other occasions, sharing and borrowing certainly is not perceived as completely unacceptable within several artistic communities. As has been correctly noted, 'Prince, and others like him, have normalised the use of fabrication, outsourcing, artist teams, hosts of collaborators, and, of course, the prevalence of "copying" in contemporary art. [...] Prince has so successfully mainstreamed appropriation art'.[30]

What about the widespread practice of sharing digital pictures of graffiti and street artworks on social networks, which is accepted and even encouraged by artists and writers themselves?[31] Again, this does not mean that copyright is unfit to regulate these forms of art. It could here be argued that writers and artists grant an implied license to the people and organisations that take and share pictures of their works.[32] They have an interest in doing so, as dissemination of their art through these

[26] Nicole A. Grant, Outlawed Art: Finding a Home for Graffiti in Copyright Law (2012) 6, https://ssrn.com/abstract=2030514

[27] Jonathan Barrett, 'Copying Artistic Works: Copyright, Aesthetic, and Artistic Practice', in Jani McCutcheon and Fiona McGaughey (eds.), *Research Handbook on Art and Law* (Elgar 2020) 61.

[28] *Blanch v. Koons*, 467 F.3d 244 (2d Cir. 2006).

[29] *Cariou v. Prince*, 714 F.3d 694 (2d Cir. 2013).

[30] Barrett, above fn. 27, 88.

[31] This is not always the case, though. The 5*Pointz* mural point in New York, for example, showed a disclaimer reading 'no photo shoots, no video shoots'. Also, the very founder and curator of 5*Pointz*, Meres One, commented during our conversation: 'I refused many offers to shoot video at 5*Pointz*. I mean, it was for us. I didn't want to change 5*Pointz*'s nature'.

[32] The fact that many street artists and writers accept others sharing photographs of their works does not mean that they completely disregard a certain 'permission culture'. This was a point raised by London writer Transı during our interview. He told me: 'I like people asking if they can take a photo of my stuff during painting'.

platforms increases their visibility and may also have the effect of creating business opportunities, including commissions or merchandising. After all, as emerged in Jessica Silbey's research, sharing is the most popular form of distribution in other fields of human creativity and ingenuity, and can maximise the diffusion of works and products at low or no cost and potentially increase creators' revenues.[33]

Street art and graffiti are therefore not so different from other visual art movements and in general other creative sectors – and can be accommodated within existing copyright regimes in the very same way more traditional movements are. And once it is accepted that this intellectual property right is capable of regulating these subcultural art forms, street artists and writers need to stick to its rules, whether they like it or not. For example, they may lose the copyright infringement cases they bring against alleged infringers. This happened in 2011 in *Seltzer v. Green Day, Inc.*,[34] where the artist took legal action against the pop band Green Day because the latter had incorporated in a video backdrop (used at live concerts) an adapted version of Seltzer's poster *Scream Icon* placed on a Los Angeles wall. The California federal district and circuit judges rejected the artist's claims because the use of the artwork was found to be fair, as it was transformative and not overly commercial.

Practitioners of these forms of art may also be condemned for copyright infringement. This occurred in *Morris v. Thierry Guetta*, where the judge ruled that seven of Guetta's works (including a mural) based on photographer Dennis Morris' iconic 1977 picture of Sid Vicious, deceased musician of the punk band the Sex Pistols, was not protected by fair use becasue it was not transformative.[35] Another relevant case was started in 2011 by photographer Glen Friedman against (again) Guetta. The Central District of California granted summary judgment in favour of Friedman, finding that Guetta's work (in this case, not a street artwork, but a canvas) was substantially similar to Friedman's famous photograph of the rap group RUN DMC, and that Guetta's use of the photograph could not be considered fair use.[36] A similar fate would have probably awaited Shepard Fairey if he had not reached a settlement agreement with the Associated Press. The latter had sued the former, arguing that his use of Associated Press imagery depicting Barack Obama (that resulted in the iconic poster *Hope*, which came to represent Obama's presidential campaign) was not fair use and did constitute copyright infringement.

## DISTINGUISHING *BITING* FROM INSPIRATION

But where do we draw the line between (acceptable) inspiration and (intolerable) biting? This is a difficult question. The line distinguishing them is blurred, as is also recognised by Martha Cooper in her book *Tag Town* ('there is a fine line between

[33] Jessica Silbey, *The Eureka Myth: Creators, Innovators and Everyday Intellectual Property* (2014 Stanford University Press) 252, 257.

[34] *Seltzer v. Green Day, Inc.*, 725 F.3d 1170, 1173–74 (9th Cir. 2013).

[35] *Dennis Morris v. Thierry Guetta et al.*, No. LA CV12–00684.

[36] *Friedman v. Guetta*, No. CV 10–00014 DDP (C.D. Cal. May 27, 2011).

inspirations and plagiarism')[37] and my interviewees Skeme ('there is a fine line between inspiration and copying'), Damien Mitchell ('there is a fine line between *biting* and getting inspiration'), Andre Trenier ('there is a thin line between borrowing and *biting*'), Kristy ('the line is not clear-cut'), and Murrz ('I guess it depends on the motive at this point. I've a friend – he has a very distinct character. Somebody copied it like almost exactly and it literally looked almost exactly the same. There was maybe a different brush stroke but it seemed clear that it was copied. But then the artist who did it was like, "I did not even know who this guy was. I swear I didn't copy it". But look, if you put it side to side, it's almost exactly the same').

This is not even limited to street art and graffiti – in the whole visual art world the question of how to separate blatant imitation from simple inspiration is a thorny one. As pointed out by Joel Artista during our conversation, 'I think in art in general, you know, there is nothing that's completely new; no one just really creates something completely all alone. You're always getting inspiration from other people, from other things, and you borrow and that's part of the art. There's always that kind of line between what's stealing and what's borrowing and what's being inspired by, you know, but all art is at least influenced by other things'.

Other artists I spoke with have tried to give me some clues on how to distinguish *biting* from inspiration. Canadian artist Roadsworth told me: 'I've seen things that may be similar to my work – it's hard to prove it. It's hard to be 100 per cent original because there's so much inspiration to draw from now and I look at images all the time, so when I draw, I subconsciously may take inspiration from those pictures'. Greg Lamarche also highlighted how taking from other artists is sometimes inevitable. He pointed out in the interview that 'it is not *biting* anymore, it's called "interpreting". In my days you learned how to write your name, bubble letters, straight letters, then you learned how to do more wild style pieces. It's probably difficult to avoid an overlap in things that influence people. I know my peers and we're interested in the same things. We grew up and saw the same place as well as the same kind of things. And so we're all kind of pulling tricks out of the same hat'.

Some of my interviewees also stressed the fact that artworks and pieces which turn out to be similar may in fact be created independently by different artists. In these circumstances accusations of *biting* are inaccurate. Daleast noted that 'there are so many creations out there that it's sometimes difficult not to do something which has been done by someone else. Sometimes it happens without bad faith'. The same goes for Kristy ('[T]here's always the possibility that two creative minds come up with the same idea in different places in different times. And I've seen it. There have been times where I've sketched and then later seen a painting sketched by another artist that is so similar to what I've sketched'), Paul Richard ('often similarities in art are a coincidence'), Crisp ('[I]t's difficult to be original these days. For example, one time I was doing stickers with animals with gas masks to make a statement about

[37] Cooper, above fn. 19, 53.

pollution and another artist in Colombia accused me of copying him because he was doing the same. I didn't know him. But I think people have angles and styles which are different. I don't agree with artists copying, but it's ok if it's influence. You can't monopolise an idea'), and Andy Council ('I developed a style, but I can't claim ownership over it').

There is also a widespread belief that writers who borrow but also add something from their own repertoire cannot be considered *biters*.[38] Writers who take from others but also put in their work something personal abound. During our conversation Easy explained to me how he developed his tag: 'my tag takes something of my cousin's tag. He's not a real graffiti writer. Like you see the "e" and the "a" connecting to each other – that's from my cousin. It doesn't look like that, but it's very similar. But the rest, I've done it myself. It's just the "e" and "a" which I took – my cousin wrote SEAC. He probably wrote [it] one or two years so that's where that evolved'. Italian writer Fra 32 echoed these words. He commented, '[Y]ou need to add something of yours. You need to re-interpret'. David Chino also recognises the need to add something personal. He told me: 'we all borrow, but the real idea is to make your own idea. That's the challenge. You can borrow from somebody, but you need to give your touch on it'. Likewise, Skeme pointed out during our conversation:

> In the beginning all style masters borrowed things from each other. This wasn't *biting* because they were all masters of a similar skill level and they all contributed to the style depository. Since they all contributed, it was not *biting* because they were taking as well as giving back. It becomes biting when you are not a masterful individual, you are not creative and original and when your platform imitates my platform. When you are not elevating on what I'm doing it's also *biting*, because you're basically resting on the work that I accumulated, and that's *biting*. But we're all influenced, and influence is when you see something and attempt to imitate it – but we never did them, we only tried to study the mechanics of letters.

Street artists I talked to confirmed this very point. While Anjl told me: 'maybe I've been influenced from others, but at the end of the day it is coming from my creative energy as it flows', Italian artist Alice Pasquini said, 'I've a style, I use peculiar colours, lights, and shadows. I've a poetic touch and defined features linked to my style. Even if I use different tools, that's always my style. If you add something of

[38] See also Iljadica, above fn. 3, 180 (noting that most of the writers she interviewed 'demonstrated a concern with adding something new in the sense that it was the writer's own contribution to graffiti creativity as a whole'). For accounts of how creativity in the graffiti subculture is often cumulative see Nancy Macdonald, The Graffiti Subculture: Youth, Masculinity and Identity in London and New York (Palgrave MacMillan 2009) 82–83 (reporting the opinion of London writer Drax, whom she interviewed: '[e]veryone steals ideas from other places, little dots and stars and designs and stuff and a lot of people just rip off complete styles, but the combination will usually be, like, unique to somebody'); see also Ivor L. Miller, Aerosol Kingdom: Subway Painters of New York City (2012) University Press of Mississippi, 29 (noting that '[w]hen a new piece rode by on the rails, other writers would study it, incorporating the styles or images they liked the best into their own work, and a fresh style would be born soon after in the train yard. In this way the complex layers of the creative process continued to intertwine').

yours, that's an inspiration. You copy someone else when you don't have your own style, and you don't add anything substantial'.[39] Analogous opinions were expressed by Gabriel Corti (noting that he likes to study other artists and take inspiration from other letters, but that he would never use the whole letter exactly, limiting himself to use small parts and incorporating them in his work), Resa Piece ('[A] lot of street and graffiti artists do use like reference photos from the internet or something. So like all art is derivative, you know. When I paint something I use like a reference from Google images. But I always change it and the image to my style. If I copy something from the internet made by another artist and I make it look exactly like that, that would be not fair, you know'), and Ian Strange ('[I]t's more about the context behind copying my work. If they did something interesting with my work and copied it with their own inspirations, they might be able to take ownership of it and I wouldn't consider that copying as long as they take it in a different direction. But if someone takes someone's work and doesn't change it and adds no inspiration, that bothers me'). Similarly, New York illustrator and painter Murrz noted that 'all artists know "that" distinct feature of their work. So yes, we draw inspiration from other artists that inspire us or that we look up to, but at the end of the day we want to make something that is our own. It's like I want to make sure that what people see is Murzz work'. Likewise, Bill Blast noted: 'I think that in the earlier years people were learning from each other. For instance, if you saw a specific "S" people might be inspired by this and learn from it. Every street artist out there can say that he or she is inspired by person Z and X. That is how they learn and if you inspire people, that is a good thing. But if you do it identical, that's plagiarism'.

It should also be noted that writers often copy from their own mentors. This is obviously encouraged by the mentors themselves who teach their protégés according to their own styles, but it is then the latter's duty to evolve and grow a personal touch. Two New York writers and artists expanded on this point during our encounters. Greg Lamarche told me: 'you either had a mentor or you absorb what you see and try to develop it into your own style. I didn't have a mentor, but there were a couple of people that went to my school and that lived in my area and I definitely learned a lot from them. Through watching them I was able to eventually create my own style'. Keo has a similar view. He said to me: 'do you know how many there are who are using my style? So many. I've some that I personally taught and mentored, and they have permission and will hopefully take what I taught them and put their own original spin and elevate it. But they're my students and supposed to have some of my style. There are others that I didn't take under the wings who just copy me'.

[39] See also Braun, above fn. 10, 128 (reporting the opinion of Eko, an artist based in the French city of Pau: 'you take ideas from stuff, and it's up to you how you mix it up before you put it out again, it's reworking stuff to make it look original'; Roger Gastman and Caleb Neelon, The History of American Graffiti (Harper Design 2011) 104 (highlighting New York writer T-Kid's comment around transforming works created by someone else: 'incorporate it into your own piece, flip it around, and make it your own').

Generally speaking, young writers are more inclined to appropriate from older peers, whether they have or don't have a mentor.[40] This was confirmed by former New York writer Dejer during our conversation in Long Island: 'it's common amongst young writers to copy famous pieces from well-known writers, to train themselves'. Mastro acknowledged this practice as well, although with a self-critical angle. He said to me: 'I did *biting* consciously when I was 13 years old, I was garbage, drawing the throw-ups I saw in my area – I was very childish'.

The ability of writers to contribute and innovate with their own creative touch often materialises at a later stage of their career. Lots of graffiti (and street art) is about taking and re-adapting until artists discover their own style.[41] In his book former US writer ESPO brilliantly explains how toys (unexperienced writers) must have freedom to borrow and appropriate from others:

> Although being a toy seems undesirable, you should enjoy it while you can. At this stage you can bite all you want with no remorse. [...] So steal that dope connection, rob that color scheme, and loot whole letterforms. Don't worry about giving any credit, we'll pat ourselves on the back and brag how we're influencing the next generation. However, style isn't a crutch or a stick. It is understanding why that connection you bit flows, or why that color scheme bumps. [...]. This creative growth will amaze the old and young alike. Pretty soon somebody will steal your secret sauce and the cycle will be renewed. [...] Graffiti is the language of the ignored. If your style is stolen, someone heard you speaking. You got what you wanted from the very beginning, some attention, you big baby.[42]

While Espo glorifies *biting* made by young writers, he still believes that the trajectory a writer must follow should aim at building up in the long run a personalised style. He indeed further notes that '[s]tyle is the process to an appealing end. Once you got it down to a science, you can reinvent letterforms to suit yourself'.[43]

## DISLIKING BLATANT *BITING*

The fact that many within the street art and graffiti communities accept sharing and borrowing practices does not mean that blatant copying is always condoned. While some may let it go,[44] others cannot accept it, especially within the graffiti subculture, where issues of *biting* may be taken seriously and copying

40 This also happens in the street art scene, and has emerged in my fieldwork. Indeed, Dutch artist Fake informed me that 'there are fan kids that like my work and they copy me', adding that he has 'no problem with that'.

41 Cedar Lewisohn, *Street Art: The Graffiti Revolution* (Tate Publishing 2009), 114.

42 Powers, above fn. 7, 155.

43 Powers, above fn. 7, 155.

44 This is the case of New York artist Rubin, who noted during our conversation that 'biting happens all the time, both blatant copies and inspired things. I just let it go. I usually try to be classy – I'd much rather spend my time and energy in something more constructive'.

someone's else works, including tags, may even be seen as forgery and therefore unacceptable.[45]

Within these creative subcultures there is a great sense of honor and respect, and originality is still crucial (especially when it comes to experienced practitioners). Many writers of the 1970s and 1980s in New York also paid particular attention to being original and avoiding copying from others. Some of them wanted to distinguish themselves from each other if they had picked up similar or identical names. This is the case of Henry 161, who included in his tag a three-pointed crown on the upper left-hand corner and the number 1 on the upper right-hand corner because there was another writer called Henry 161, who had to include a number 2 by his name to distinguish himself.[46] Another New York writer, West One, has been quite vocal about his disapproval of *biting*. He has been reported as saying, 'I remember distinctly. I mean I remember it like yesterday, in 1985 beefing with this kid on 125th Street. This kid was trying to take like my whole style and particularly he had taken my "ES". And he was out there, and I was like, "Yo, you can't do that. Come up with your own shit". And there was no violence involved but it was like, "Yo, don't do that. You can't do that. That doesn't happen"'.[47] It is not just graffiti writers who were worried about *biting*. Even a young Jean-Michel Basquiat – who was not a writer focused on lettering, but used to spray-paint messages on walls in lower Manhattan – expressed anger at other people copying his and Al Diaz's SAMO tag.[48] Al Diaz himself confirmed during our conversation in Brooklyn that there were some fake SAMOs around, pictures of which have also been exhibited at MoMA.

The dislike of *biting* has clearly emerged in my research. Gabriel Corti commented during our encounter that he would be flattered if someone were to study his work and do similar pieces, but he would not approve if someone were to blatantly copy his art. A stronger opinion was expressed by former writer Good Guy Boris during our interview in Athens: 'there are writers and artists that have copied their entire careers off other people but at the end of the day, if you're a *biter*, you are known as *biter*. When you're copying other people's techniques, people will call you the second, like Banksy number two. You are always the something of something when you're a *biter*. These artists take other people's inspiration and turn them askew'. Likewise, New York writer and street artist Depsone told me during our conversation: 'I don't think that there's any acceptance in that [*biting*]. It's very hated and people get angry very quickly'. US artist Elle is on the same page, commenting that you should 'make your own name, just find another name and do your own art'. Similarly, New York writer Skeme expanded on the reasons why

45 Waclawek, above fn. 4, 28; Cooper, above fn. 19, 11.
46 Roger Gastman, Wall Writers (Gingko Press 2016) 94.
47 Murray, above fn. 6, 167.
48 Glenn O'Brien TV party interview with Basquiat of April 1979, available on YouTube.

*biting* is bad within the subculture. He noted during our encounter in Harlem that 'in graffiti we are not supposed to copy or bite, we're supposed to be original and respect the work that other people have put there. There have been several people copying my name. I don't take it in any negative way. But I know that there are trillions of variations in the alphabet and words in the dictionary that you can combine to come up with your own name. So, I never understand why you feel it necessary to just copy my name'.[49]

The boom of social media in recent years has certainly made *biting* more widespread and frequent, with the sharing of pictures of graffiti and street artworks all over the world giving it significant momentum. The impact of the internet was also highlighted by New York writer Mastro during our conversation in Brooklyn. He said:

> [I]n the world of graffiti, a lot of people borrow. I don't like this concept and this is also why I don't like the internet. That's because it makes it easier for anyone to borrow your book from your library and return it a little dishevelled. So, you've sketched some exotic connections and then you see that someone in your network have literally taken what you've done and applied it in their way. That's apparently learning from someone style, but I really see it as *biting*. So, unfortunately what happens in the world of graffiti is a lot of people going 'no, no I saw what you did and then did something different, look, my stuff is different'. Everybody *bites*.[50]

With that being said, one may reiterate that copyright systems do not fit into the street and graffiti art narrative because even those artists and writers who are disappointed and angry at colleagues who copy them do not take legal action to stop that. In other words, while a sentiment of anger may remain, almost all practitioners of these art forms do not even think about taking a copyright legal action.

But is this really something which makes these artistic movements incompatible with the whole copyright system? I believe this is not the case. Street artists

[49] Despite this widespread feeling about *biting*, a few of my interviewees have shown no concerns when appropriating creative elements of other artworks. For example, a street artist (who wanted to remain anonymous) said to me: 'if I'm using an image [as a reference], I don't really give a shit about copyright and licensing the image'. And Gaia pointed out that he sometimes borrows from other sources, even though he added (perhaps paradoxically) that he does feel bothered 'when someone does not ask permission' and copies his art.

[50] The impact of the internet on *biting* was also stressed by New York muralist Andre Trenier in our encounter in the Bronx, but from a different perspective. Trenier noted that appropriation is now more tolerated than it was in the old days exactly because of the internet and the practice of sharing and disseminating photographs, which would make biting easier, is widespread and to a certain extent less unacceptable. He pointed out that 'what was considered *biting* in the '80s might have been a lot harsher than what is considered *biting* now. People took offence to even the slightest borrowing and the slightest borrowing could end up in a fight or a long-term beef. I think now it's a lot more accepted because there is less enforcement of the graffiti rules whereas before the internet and before the world wide web culture it was very local'.

and writers who do not sue *biters* simply waive their right to do so. And not only waivers are admitted under copyright law; they are also not uncommon in other fields of creativity. Fine artists, graphic designers, and other creators often do not enforce their copyright. As mentioned in Chapter 3, Jessica Silbey's research has empirically confirmed this, highlighting that copyright regimes are flexible and malleable. Specifically, she makes a point that – I believe – could also be made when it comes to street artists and writers: 'so what if IP [intellectual property] rights are flexibly applied? Sometimes they are asserted and sometimes they are not. [...] Underutilization of the full panoply of rights granted under our IP system is simply that. It is not waste; it is freedom'.[51]

## SOCIAL NORMS

The street art and (to a larger extent) graffiti subcultures do have a set of social norms which regulate certain aspects of the creative processes and beyond. Rules such as 'don't go over' and 'don't *bite*' are often observed within these communities. The former has been labelled by Skeme in our conversation as one of the 'Ten Commandments': it prohibits painting over someone else's work, for example, a tag, throw-up, and piece. The latter forbids copying works made by other writers (or artists).[52] Those who break these norms may face some form of reaction by those whose artwork has been attacked or copied, the form and intensity of such reaction depending on how angry and rancorous the 'victim' feels. Several of my interviewees have called this system of rules 'street justice' or the 'court of the streets'.[53]

In particular, breaking the 'don't go over' rule may encourage the attacked writer (or artist) to reciprocate by going over the work created by the attacker. The feud which erupted in London between Banksy and Robbo in 2009–2011, mentioned in Chapter 1, perfectly epitomises how this social norm works. In 1985 Robbo, one of the early writers in England, painted the colourful piece *Robbo Inc.* on a wall beside Regent's Canal in Camden, North London. It resisted the weather elements and wild tagging over more than two decades, until in 2009 Banksy covered most of it with a stencil of a workman pasting wallpaper. What ensued was a feud consisting of painting over each other's murals on the same spot, which can also be labelled as an example of conversation (or clash) between artists in the street. After Banksy's provocative move, Robbo reclaimed his piece from Banksy's intervention by partially

[51] Silbey, above fn. 33, 45, 122–124, 147 (further noting that artists and even businesspeople frequently tolerate copyright infringement, and that deliberate under-enforcement of intellectual property rights may be a common strategy to build up demand and customer base and therefore generate new revenues).

[52] In her book Marta Iljadica expands on these rules by drawing from her own ethnographic research: see above fn. 3, 247–254.

[53] See also Iljadica, above fn. 3, 250.

covering it so the workman seemed to be painting 'KING ROBBO'. A few days later Banksy struck back and painted the letters 'FUC' just before the word 'KING' – a very clear message. Reciprocal overpainting on the same wall went on, including a mural by Robbo consisting of the Top Cat character leaning on a gravestone bearing the words 'R.I.P. Banksy's career'. Banksy, in turn, did not hesitate to mock Robbo, and in a 2010 interview was reported as addressing his rival in this way: 'if you're the type who gets sentimental about people scribbling over your stuff, I suggest graffiti is probably not the right hobby for you'.[54]

Writers and artists I interviewed also expanded on the 'don't go over' rule. Former New York writer Dejer told me that 'beefs start because some writers cross over, go over. But it's better not to end up in beefs. If a writer goes over me, that's simple, I go over him. I also want information on who the writer is, his crew, and where he comes from. I want my spot back. I'd go over him lightly though, not completely so I make him understand that what he did was wrong, and I had to react'. Similarly, London artist Pure Evil told me: 'beef means that you've a problem with them, so you paint over them, they'll paint over you and then you've a little war going on. I really think it is adrenaline for both people and it's something – you know I had that kind of thing with other artists where they painted over me and I've painted over. It may not even be the fact that you decided to paint over them, maybe their piece had already been painted over, but you took that wall and then it goes back and forward'. A specific incident was narrated to me by Christopher Chambers, who in 1980 (as mentioned) founded the AVANT art collective. He told me during our conversation in a restaurant in Brooklyn: 'a member of our group put a poster on a Fab Five Freddy tag. I apologised to him for that. But then he redid the tag on the poster'.

Crossing out artworks may also be a form of retaliation against *biting*. Several of my interviewees confirmed that, including Dejer ('*biting* provokes beefs and reactions in the form of crossing over'), Mastro ('if someone took something I did and copied it exactly and only switched like one letter, I'm going to go to that wall and write my name all over that shit. I'm going to let them know that I diss their shit because *biting* is for suckers') and Elle ('there would be beef among those artists, and they would sort that out among themselves and cross each other out'). This form

[54] See Banksy's interview with Ossian Ward for *Time Out London* (31 March 2010). The feud came to an end after Robbo entered a coma following a fall in his house in April 2011, with Banksy finally paying tribute to his old rival by painting on the same wall a tribute mural. Robbo would sadly die in 2014 due to that domestic accident. Pure Evil also gave me his opinion on this feud during our encounter in his Shoreditch studio in East London. He said, 'Robbo had an image, Banksy painted over it and disrespected him and then it escalated. Robbo always saw it as disrespect, but he admitted his career took off after that because people know we wouldn't be talking about Robbo if Banksy hadn't painted over Robbo'. What this dispute teaches us is that crossing over may also trigger the creation of additional works, a sort of conversation and dialogue between artists in the street. This is exactly what US writer Cept meant when he said to me during the interview that 'beefs produce more artworks – how? A spiral of going over!'

of reaction against *biting* has been popular with writers from the very beginning of the movement in the 1970s in New York.[55]

Another way *bitten* writers and artists react against copying is to reach out to and complain with the *biter*. This was confirmed to me by Anjl ('it depends, if it's someone I haven't met before, I'd approach it in a different way, saying, "hey please acknowledge some of my work next time you decide to paint it, including this one", but if it's someone I know I'd approach him more casually'), Murrz ('I guess it depends on how close it looks like my work. If it's very close, then I would talk to them and say: "This kind of look exactly like my work"'), Ian Strange ('I think if it was someone I knew, I'd talk to them directly first and see if we can sort it out. If it was someone I don't know, I'd send them a direct email just saying asking why and to stop'), Lexi Bella ('I'd contact the artist before I put them on blast. It's important to talk to each other to help foster respect and strengthen the community'), Reskew ('I'd have to contemplate what the best action would be. My first reaction might be too emotional and not productive. I'd probably confront the person, as calmly as I can and see if they can acknowledge what they are doing is wrong, and perhaps make a fair deal'), and former writer Dejer (when I asked him how he would have reacted had he been found a canvas incorporating his tag, he replied, '[I]t would have been unacceptable. I'd have contacted the seller, and said not nice things'). Likewise, US writer and muralist Kasso commented during our interview:

> Nowadays, if that happens the best thing to do is just contacting the person. So, normally nowadays that just takes either an email or a phone call. It doesn't have to get violent, you know? If it's another colleague who *bites*, you treat those situations a little more sensitive than what you'd do if it was a corporate company. You'd reach out to that person directly. Because the beautiful thing about the graffiti and street art scene is that it's vast, it's global, but it's still very tight knit. It's still that six degrees of separation. It's not difficult for me to get a hold of anyone that is doing something like that. It's normally a matter of a google search or finding out the right website and reaching out to that person directly.

Contacting *biters* may be productive and give tangible results. This was the experience of New York writer Easy. During our conversation in Brooklyn he said:

> I've seen this on Instagram. I found there were ten different people that wrote their name just like me. Ten different people from different countries. And they know who I am. I mean they can't write it like me, but they do it very close. And I contacted each and every one of them, instantly. I asked, 'You realize this is my name?' And you know, they were like, 'Wow glad to meet you'. That's what they said. That's not good. Because if they want to prosper in this game, I don't think you should try

[55] It has been noted that another way to resolve disputes over painting the same name in the early days of the graffiti movement in New York consisted of the older writer 'selling' the tag to the younger colleague for $5 in order to retain a sense of property. See Jack Stewart, Graffiti Kings: New York City Mass Transit Art of the 1970s (Abrams 2009) 28.

> to *bite* somebody. Because you won't be creating any type of legacy for your own. That's what I try to explain to them. I try to give them something to think about. They may be like yes maybe I should get my own name and I can paint my own path and get my own legacy, you know? Some of them said, 'Hey, I love this tag and I'm going to keep it'. I had someone who told me that: 'I'm just going to keep it'. I did get a little aggressive. I said, 'You better change your tag', and when I got like that, the guy changed his tag instantly. He said, 'Hey I'm sorry, sorry I did this'.

Spreading information about the *biting*, especially on social media platforms, is also a form of reaction writers and street artists rely on. This is a sort of negative gossip[56] which aims at publicly shaming the writer or artist who copies. This is what several of my interviewees confirmed with me, including Elle ('it happened to me. [...] I spread it online, on Instagram'), Lamkat ('I might post a photo on my Instagram with a comment'), Paul Richard ('[S]hame and bad publicity can also deter people from reproducing my art without permission. [...] if an artist copies me, the social media and the art audience will notice. That audience puts pressure on the offending party'), Depsone ('I'd confront them personally at first and if they don't stop, I'd use social media. Maybe that looks bad but at the same time it brings light on it and everyone can see and think, "Wait this is his work, I see now"'), Noir ('enough people are on social media to "call" someone out if it's a blatant copy. If you've created something that is too close to the mark you'll soon know about it, that's for sure'), and Claw Money ('[E]verybody *bites* me – I'm used to it. If it happens, I'd do nothing special, perhaps I'd just write a post about it on Instagram, nothing else. Should I say, "I punch you into your fucking face? Get the fuck out of here?" No way!').

Logan Hicks and Morley mentioned a similar approach. The former clarified that his reaction would depend upon the status of the *biter*, and that he would privately contact a *biter* who is just beginning his career ('I might be annoyed, but I would reach out and let them know that they need to find their own style and that they should move away from copying mine'). But 'if it's an established artist', he noted, 'I'd certainly reach out as well as try to bring attention to it through social media to set the precedent that others should not follow the same path'.[57] Morley also pointed out that he would use the internet if contacting directly the *biter* turns out to be useless. Specifically, he noted, 'I'd first reach out to them and try to start a conversation. I'd avoid creating a conflict especially one involving the public if I can, but if they don't respond sometimes you have to let your fans know and they can overwhelm the person with comments [on the internet], as a last resort'. Another artist, Damien

[56] This term is used by Iljadica, above fn. 3, 248.

[57] As mentioned in Chapter 4, Logan Hicks would also shame online whoever removes and decontextualises one of his murals. Yet, as far as the imitation of his art is concerned, Hicks clarified that 'my style is complex, and layered. It's not easy to copy. People can copy the subject matter but not necessarily the style. So I try to remember that every second that I waste complaining that someone did something that looks like my work, I could be actually making new work and staying ahead of those who would prefer to copy'.

Mitchell, would also rely on this form of reaction, being moved to do so because of the risk of being associated with art of low quality. He told me during our encounter in Brooklyn: 'if it happens, I'd contact this person and check if it's unintentional. I'd try to find out why this person has copied me. If I find out that it's been intentional, I'd write about it on social media, also to create a distinction between me and the *biter*, especially if the *biter* does poor stuff'.[58]

Violence or threatening to resort to violence is not an option anymore when it comes to reacting against imitation within the graffiti subculture. It used to be so in the early days in New York, when taking 'someone's name certainly caused a fight, the writer's alternative to a copyright infringement suit', as noted by Austin.[59] Castleman also reminds us about Bama, a New York writer from the 1970s whose style was often copied, commenting that 'a lot of writers would get angry if their style was *bitten*. Get angry and go over there and yell, scream, punch. "You took my style, man; what's wrong with you!" "But I just saw you doing it". "I don't care what the fuck you saw, you don't ever steal my style, man: what's wrong with you!"'[60] The writers and artists I interviewed during my fieldwork confirmed this point. Former writer and now street and studio artist Chris Stain noted that 'it's not acceptable to copy. It's the most basic rule of graffiti and street art. The artist who copies should be dealt with directly. I've seen everything from verbal to physical confrontations [referring to the 1980s era]'. Similarly, Kasso told me that 'in the early days, if you would see that person [the *biter*] on the street then, you know, it could get physical'. And Keo has even been clearer in his recollection of what used to happen in the past when *biting* occurred. He commented that 'if a colleague was blatantly copying me, in the old days we'd have to fight. And he'd have to give me his spray-paint to pay. So, you will get your ass whooped and you'll have to pay. But in the old days, I liked the trouble and violence and I ran with a crew. So, if somebody was *biting* our style, we would look for him with baseball bats'.

We have thus seen how social norms work in the graffiti (and street art) communities, and that practitioners of these art forms often rely on them. Not all are interested in following these rules, though. When I asked New York artist City Kitty whether he would react in case of *biting*, for example, by shaming the artist on social media, he answered that 'a negative public reaction wouldn't help anyone. Art is an important part of the world and I wouldn't want to hinder someone from creating. This is not to say I wouldn't be hurt if someone would mix up our work'. Similar opinions were expressed by Serk and Bill Blast during our conversations in New York. The former told me: 'if it [*biting*] happens at this point in life, I'd do nothing.

[58] Negative gossip following *biting* may also be channelled by the community at large. As my interviewee London writer Crane DPC pointed out, 'if they [the *biters*] get found out, they will usually get ridiculed by others. People will call them out for it'. Similarly, Greg Lamarche noted during our encounter that 'if people see someone *biting*, then you are going to get called down, especially now with all the social media. So you are not going to get away with that'.

[59] Austin, above fn. 21, 55.

[60] Craig Castleman, Getting Up: Subway Graffiti in New York (MIT Press 1984) 24.

I'd shake my head deeply disappointed but do nothing. Back on the day, I'd go over the work, I'd find his phone number and contact the writer'. And the latter commented, 'No, I don't get down like that and I don't waste my time. It happens that people go into these battles. I'm way passed over that. I don't go down that road. I find my path, you find yours. I stick to my directions'.

## COMPLEMENTARITY BETWEEN SOCIAL NORMS AND COPYRIGHT

As highlighted, social norms function well, and are capable of regulating certain behaviours within these creative communities, especially where copyright-related legal rules are not useful. The Banksy versus Robbo feud is a case in point. The latter evidently was not interested in a legal action against the former for originally going over his 1985 piece. Obviously, he did not file a complaint with the High Court in London claiming a violation of the moral right of integrity![61]

The lack of interest in legal actions following *biting* is also reflected in some of my interviews. When I asked US writer Cept what he would do if someone were to copy him, he answered, 'I'd go over, call him out on the wall by writing "don't *bite*". No legal action, of course'. Similarly, New York artist Kristy told me: 'I'd say something to the guy personally, but I wouldn't take legal action'. Such lack of interest in a copyright suit is particularly evident when the appropriator does not copy to take an economic advantage, or anyway is not able to accommodate requests for compensation. This is what Lady Pink noted. She told me:

> if it's a colleague [who copies], there are all kinds of measures you can take. It depends on how successful they are. If they're poor as dirt, it doesn't make sense taking them to court; what am I going to get out of it? You can't squeeze blood from a stone. You know? Dirt poor. These folks don't have any money, you can't track down people on the internet. In real life you have to spend, what? A gazillion dollars on a detective to find someone from the internet that robbed your work and is profiting 10 dollars from it. It isn't worth it. It isn't worth stressing out about, much less hunting these people down. They don't have any money. But if they're very successful and have some kind of money, then I'd go after it.

US artist Elle has been even clearer in this regard, again highlighting the boundaries between legal rules and social norms. She noted during our conversation at a Brooklyn café: 'I don't see a graffiti artist taking legal action against another graffiti artist, especially because there is no financial gain in it. If he was doing it on the street, he is not making money out of it in the first place. You're going to make a mess for yourself if you try to bring the law inside, it's like being a rat. I think that the street would regulate that more than a graffiti artist being like "I am going to go

[61] See also D. Schwender, 'Does Copyright Law Protect Graffiti and Street Art?' in Ross, above fn. 21, 460.

and sue the other graffiti artist because he copied my art"'. This is a clear statement by Elle. Yet, it does not mean that she is not interested in copyright at all. As mentioned in Chapter 3, she would consider suing if the person using her art is making significant profits.

There is undoubtedly more interest in bringing legal action against those who appropriate if they try to obtain economic advantage.[62] In these circumstances social norms are not useful and copyright law is capable of effectively serving street artists and writers, if they wish to press ahead with their allegations.[63] This typically happens when corporations exploit the artworks (and we have seen throughout this book several cases where street artists and writers have enforced copyright to stop such appropriations), but it may also occur when other fellow artists and writers try to use their pieces for economic gains.[64] The latter scenario occurred when a legal case was brought (and won) in 2011 by Italian writers KayOne and Tawa against another artist who also offered for sale at a low price eighty works that slavishly reproduced KayOne's (studio) pieces. KayOne and Tawa obtained a preliminary injunction from the Court of Milan, prohibiting the defendant from exploiting their art.[65] A few of my interviewees also mentioned such scenarios. Stephen Palladino, for example, said to me that 'there are artists making money copying other artists – these are careers based on someone else's creativity. Now more than ever, the possibility of making money push people to copy and commercialise'. And Keo confirmed he would send a cease-and-desist letter if another writer or artist starts selling T-shirts and hats incorporating his art.

Copyright could therefore be useful in these circumstances. Also, how could artists who want to manage and license out images of their murals make sure that these

[62] Such scenarios often enrage artists and writers whose art is imitated. In our conversation Morley revealed, 'I've had fans do "fan art" versions of my stuff and since they're usually just kids I let it slide, but if they start to profit from it, it becomes a problem for me'. The same goes for Zimer, who said to me: 'I've always considered my public art to be for the public. I encourage them to do with it as they please, but once someone commercialises those paintings, there is a major problem. They must have consent from the artist and hopefully pay them too. Yet, there are many artists that simply cannot be bought off. So, whether those artworks are public or not, they still must be protected through copyright or some other systems'.

[63] Grant, above fn. 26, 40.

[64] Artists also react without formally starting a legal action, but merely complaining about the copying – with such complaints evidently (and often impliedly) being based on copyright protection. For example, Dutch artist Fake told me that 'some guys started copying my street pieces and other artists' murals and start[ed] selling canvases. I emailed them and told them to stop and contacted auction houses to stop selling, and they stopped. No need to go to court'. Similarly, Akse commented in our interview: 'I see a lot of my artwork on Alami, people contact me to tell me they see prints of my artwork in markets or shops. On some occasions I've contacted people to stop selling my artwork and so far they have respected my request'.

[65] *Marco Mantovani, Igor Seghizzi and Stradearts S.r.l. v. Nicola Leonetti*, Court of Milan, decision of 2 November 2011. It should, however, be reminded that the works that had been imitated were canvases, not street artworks (as was confirmed in an email sent by KayOne to me in November 2018). I also referred to this case in Chapter 4, above fn. 3.

deals protect their interests? In such cases the community's norms may not be of great help – copyright-focused contracts are instead needed to clarify uses that are permitted and those that are prohibited. As I have mentioned in Chapter 3, London artist Stik exactly does that, that is, he authorises entities such as the British NHS to use his artworks to promote social causes he believes in, and has them respect the Stik Rules of Usage. Stik revealed during our conversation that he gave NHS employees a licence to use the *Sleeping Baby* image and also the right to reproduce it on leaflets, flyers, and banners. Without a copyright law infrastructure, he would not have been able to do so. Also, artists who want to try to preserve their pieces, for example, by preventing their destruction, or anyway ask for damages if the artwork is destroyed illegally, cannot not rely on social norms. They would need to enforce their moral right of integrity instead, in the very same way the *5Pointz* artists (successfully) did.

It therefore seems that legal rules and social norms are complementary here. As we have just seen, there are situations where the law cannot be an option, and other scenarios where social norms do their job perfectly instead. Where the latter norms cannot be effective,[66] copyright laws are there to fill the gap,[67] should artists and writers so wish. Indeed, lawyers – and in particular copyright lawyers – can be of help to writers and street artists. One of them is Jeff Gluck, a California attorney who assisted practitioners of these art forms in several US legal proceedings mentioned in this volume. Gluck also recently launched the Call My Lawyer campaign, which aims to spread awareness of the issue of corporate appropriation of urban art and provide solutions to this problem for those affected. Not only has Gluck produced and disseminated shirts bearing the Call My Lawyer slogan including his law firm's telephone number (which are then worn by artists in action) – he has also partnered with Montana (a famous manufacturer of spray-paint cans for writers) to produce aerosol cans bearing the same slogan.

The importance of copyright lawyers within the graffiti and street art world has also emerged in my interview with Colombian writer Drop. He told me during our conversation in Puente Aranda in Bogotá: 'I think lawyers are super important because sometimes people are rude and disrespectful and try to copy things and not give you any credit for it. I don't think street justice like going and painting over their work and stuff is going to get you anywhere here. What you want is some sort

[66] For arguments making the point that social norms are effective instead, see Al Roundtree, Graffiti Artists "Get Up" in Intellectual Property's Negative Space (2013) 31 *Cardozo Arts & Entertainment Law Journal*, 974, and Jamison Davies, Art Crimes? Theoretical Perspectives on Copyright Protection for Illegally-Created Graffiti Art (2012) 65 *Me. L. Rev.* 27.

[67] As highlighted above, this may happen where there are economic considerations at stake. Yet, in a few interviews I conducted I learnt that artists have relied on social norms when opposing the economic exploitation of their art. This was the case of Damien Mitchell, who told me: 'a guy was selling canvases and prints with my graffiti and street artworks. And I tried to steal them from him. He said, "What are you doing?" I replied, "Look, if you steal my works, you expect I steal this stuff right?" Then he stopped doing that').

of ownership over your own work and I think lawyers are the best thing for that'. This excerpt of the interview is interesting because it shows that copyright may be taken into account by writers also where non-economic considerations are at stake, for example, if mere issues of lack of (authorship) acknowledgment arise.[68] Another part of Drop's interview is also interesting as it reveals that a few writers he knows are also lawyers. Specifically, he noted that 'the funny thing is that there are some lawyers over here who are also graffiti writers!' This comment did not completely surprise me, though. I was already aware of another writer and street artist, the Italian Domenico Melillo (who started writing his name Frode in Milan in 1993), who is also a penal lawyer who regularly assists and defends writers embroiled in criminal proceedings for alleged property defacing. I recently met Domenico in the context of a research project on urban art managed by the Italian National Observatory in Urban Creativity in cooperation with the Italian Ministry of Culture.

Having said that, social norms and copyright rules are not only complementary – they can also be mutually supportive.[69] The *H&M v. Revok* case, mentioned in Chapters 3 and 5, epitomises this mutual support. When Revok complained about the fashion retailer H&M using his mural for promotional purposes, and after the company took him to court to get cleared of any wrongdoing, there was a robust reaction by the street art community praising Revok's reaction against what was considered a blatant corporate appropriation. Calls on social media platforms to boycott H&M products and actual paint attacks on the retailer's stores in several countries also occurred. Such a backlash may have had the indirect effect of strengthening Revok's case in the proceedings, as seems to be confirmed by the fact that the case was later abandoned by H&M following a settlement.

68 Other artists I interviewed expressed interest in copyright when the appropriator does not pursue an economic advantage. For example, US muralist Maria Rodriguez commented that '[if another artist copies me without commercial purpose] I'd probably state it on social networks – however, it is better to get a lawyer to write a letter to demonstrate how serious you are'. And Resa Piece pointed out that 'if it's a fellow artist who copies me, I'd be like "Why the fuck didn't you ask me first? What are you doing, asshole?" I'd be mean. Yeah, I think I'd take some legal action. It's not about the economics of it, but about the integrity and respect you know. That's what I think'.

69 For an opposite opinion, see Iljadica, above fn. 3, 287 (suggesting that the set of social norms within the graffiti subculture is an alternative to copyright). Indeed, legal rules and social norms might also be invoked cumulatively, so as to strengthen the case for the artist or writer. This is the case of New York artist Paul Richard. He told me during our encounter that if it is a company which copies him, 'in addition to a legal letter, I could send out a press release'.

# Epilogue

Hello readers! I hope you've enjoyed reading this book. What you have here in your hand (or even on your screen) is a monograph that represents a critical point in the history of graffiti. This is not only a book, but the culmination of years of advocacy and a symbol of progress. Graffiti writers have been writing for over fifty years, and with the publication of this book, we can say that the culture has successfully reached middle age. With artists no longer required to handle disputes on their own, this book represents a new phase not only in graffiti and street art, but also in terms of expanding the protection of artists' rights under the law.

What started as a thought experiment among certain intellectual property lawyers is now a reality. Graffiti writers and street artists – even those whose work is done illegally – have equal protection under the law from having their art appropriated by outside corporations and individuals for unauthorized economic gain. As crazy as this sounds, there have already been court cases around these issues and even rulings in favour of artists who place their work in public space. Numerous companies like H&M and McDonalds have been accused of misappropriating street and graffiti art. Indeed, as these forms of art have become more accepted, they have also become increasingly vulnerable to corporate exploitation.

In addition to the graffiti writers and street artists who have been helped by this cutting-edge legal argument, I myself was an early recipient of this intellectual bounty.

As part of the pre-production materials for my first book, *Graffiti Lives* (New York University Press, 2009), my publisher produced a little chap book to generate interest among their marketers. They had mocked up a crisp little design with a KASE2 piece smack dab in the middle. They were very proud of themselves, but I was shocked. First off, I wasn't consulted on the cover of my book, and also because KASE2 was a legend and had recently passed away, I argued that at best this was in poor taste.

I expressed this vociferously to my publisher, and they were blasé about it. They inferred I was naïve. Everyone loves the piece, they said, and the cover has already gone into production, they said, nothing can be done, they said, trust us, they said, this is the best cover, we know these things, blah, blah.

But I knew I was fucked. No matter how well researched my book was, if I came out with an unauthorized use of a writer's work who I respected like crazy, and who had recently died way too young, the graffiti community would see it for what it was – exploitation. I knew that if we used this photo, New York City writers would be coming for me – and those dudes don't come soft.

At this point I had to turn up the heat. I remembered that I had recently read an article in the *NY Times* that TATS CRU, a legendary Bronx crew that had transitioned into professional muralists, had discovered that some dentist had published a book of photographs with the University of Mississippi Press, titled *Tattooed Walls*. This dentist had 'columbussed' graffiti and went about his path of discovery, photographing the hard-edged artwork in hardscrabble urban settings. The colonizer/author/dentist claimed that the art was public and that he couldn't get in touch with any of the artists. And TATS CRU – and specifically LADY PINK – were pissed.

I sent the *NY Times* article by David Gonzalez (4 June 2007) to my publisher and let them know that if they didn't change the cover photo, they could be vulnerable to legal action, especially since KASE's estate was very protective of their loved one's legacy. And the University of Mississippi Press had already 'removed the book from its catalog, a month after its release.' It also helped that Jane Ginsburg, a Columbia University law professor of intellectual property, was quoted in the article as saying that 'creative works are automatically protected, regardless of where they are displayed.' Woo hoo.

Well, as you can imagine the publisher quickly changed their tune (thanks TATS CRU) and I thought, great, now I can choose the cover, but they went even further. The blasé attitude now became one of extreme caution. Within a week, my publisher presented me with a consent form, and my job was to contact all the writers to get permission to use the photos of their work, and as a treat, New York University Press agreed that each writer who said yes would receive a free copy of the book. Not only was it the right thing to do (thanks New York University), it was also good marketing, and good timing. So I put myself to work reaching out to the likes of LADY PINK, KET, and others. I mention PINK because I was intimidated to reach out to her, but she was super nice and even mentioned that this was what she had hoped dentist dude had done. Whew.

This was the background for the day in October 2016 that Enrico walked into my office at Baruch College in New York City and started explaining the 5POINTZ case to me. Not only was his argument convincing, focusing on the nuances of VARA (the Visual Artists Rights Act) and making it easy to understand like he does in this book, but I knew, like Enrico did, that this meant we were on the verge of an historic development. With this book, Enrico has codified this moment, and this is no small thing. Enrico, who loved graffiti as a kid in his home town of Pisa, Italy, grew up, studied the law, and wrote an incredibly ground-breaking work that argues in defense of the right of artists, *even when that art is done illegally*. But not only has he advocated a legal argument, he's also now every writer's lawyer.

So what we have here in this book is an exhaustive, impeccably researched, well-sourced survey of writers' opinions and attitudes from around the world, including from Bogotá to New York City, to London and Athens, Milan, Madrid, Los Angeles and Melbourne. But make no mistake – this book is the result of not only research but advocacy. For almost a decade Enrico has interviewed and counselled a multitude of graffiti writers and street artists, and that advocacy not only has resulted in a book, but has increased the connections between members of a subculture that is both demonized and valorised, and he has helped to articulate their rights. What we have here is a testament to the power of an idea, and this book represents the current state of play. If my publisher was willing to change its tune over an article, think what this book will do the next time a junior ad executive suggests to their boss that maybe stealing from graffiti and street artists is a bad idea that comes with consequences. This isn't selling out – it's getting older and wiser.

So yeah, this graffiti we all love is now middle-aged, and as you get older, it's not cool or even healthy to invite transgressors to 'throw hands' as some younger and even some older writers are wont to do. But you can't challenge a corporation to a fistfight. Even though some of them could use a good ass-whooping, today's writers and street artists have options when it comes to dealing with the theft of their intellectual property. Today's writers and street artists owe a great debt to the long line of courageous pioneers that came before them. These writers in cities around the world persisted in creating an art movement that has continued to impress and inspire. But today's artist, in an ironic twist of history, and with the help of people like Enrico Bonadio, can now articulate and defend their rights as artists and people, and thus continue to make art and to profit in their own way.

Not only is that winning in a pure sense, but it is also a testament to the growth and power of this global movement – and also this book's author. Enrico has spread his gospel over the whole of the subculture, and the movement is better for it. This book breaks new ground not only with the collection of interviews and the broad range of ideas and opinions; it is also symbolic of a moment. Graffiti writers and street artists indeed have rights, and were it not for guys like Enrico (and a handful of others) they'd probably still be struggling to find a voice. The success of this well-thought-out legal argument also makes clear that graffiti and street art (to a degree) make up the most important and interesting art movement to take place over the last half century. And now we have the legal protections to prove it. Come get these hands, or better yet, 'call my lawyer'.

**Gregory Snyder**
**Professor of Sociology at Baruch College, City University of New York**

For EU product safety concerns, contact us at Calle de José Abascal, 56–1°, 28003 Madrid, Spain or eugpsr@cambridge.org.

www.ingramcontent.com/pod-product-compliance
Lightning Source LLC
LaVergne TN
LVHW022219200926
848481LV00006B/2031

"Bonadio has done very thorough research on graffiti and street art cultures and has included interviews, opinions and comments from some of its key players. The case studies and examples are unquestionably relevant, and useful for navigating a very real obstacle that creators of public art are faced with today."
Al Diaz, author of *SAMO©...SINCE 1978*

"Enrico Bonadio is an accomplished scholar of street art, graffiti and the law. In this book he provides a comprehensive well-researched overview of copyright laws as perceived by the practitioners of these forms of art, highlighting the ramifications experienced across creative fields and the many issues facing the legal (and non-legal) protections afforded to street art and graffiti."
Jeff Gluck, Gluck Law Firm P.C., focusing on representing street artists and graffiti writers and enforcing their intellectual property rights

"Enrico Bonadio is the one who better knows and understands the world of graffiti and street art, and their intersection with copyright regimes. In this new book, he takes a step further and offers us a direct and authentic perspective of this complex and ever evolving artistic reality – and he does so through the opinions of its protagonists. Bonadio's study is essential for a better understanding of the graffiti and street art phenomenon and to steer a much-needed legal analysis."
Elena Vicente Domingo – Professor of Law at the University of Burgos (Spain)

ENRICO BONADIO is Reader at City, University of London. He teaches, lectures and advises in the field of intellectual property (IP) law. He is editor of *The Cambridge Handbook of Copyright in Street Art and Graffiti* (2019) and *Non-Conventional Copyright – Do New and Atypical Works Deserve Protection?* (2018). Enrico is also a street and graffiti art aficionado.

Cover image: Cover art and photograph by MUSCOOL

CAMBRIDGE UNIVERSITY PRESS

ISBN 978-1-009-19863-9

Designed by EMC Design Ltd